Sedan 1870

Sedan 1870

The Eclipse of France

Douglas Fermer

Pen & Sword
MILITARY

For Leoni

First published in Great Britain in 2008
and reprinted in this format in 2015 by
Pen & Sword Military
an imprint of
Pen & Sword Books Ltd
47 Church Street
Barnsley
South Yorkshire
S70 2AS

ISBN 978-1-47382-889-6

Typeset in 11/13 Ehrhardt by Concept, Huddersfield, West Yorkshire
Printed and bound in Great Britain by CPI Group (UK) Ltd, Croydon, CR0 4YY

Pen & Sword Books Ltd incorporates the imprints of Pen & Sword Archaeology, Atlas,
Aviation, Battleground, Discovery, Family History, History, Maritime, Military, Naval,
Politics, Railways, Select, Social History, Transport, True Crime, and Claymore Press,
Frontline Books, Leo Cooper, Praetorian Press, Remember When, Seaforth Publishing and
Wharncliffe.

For a complete list of Pen & Sword titles please contact
PEN & SWORD BOOKS LIMITED
47 Church Street, Barnsley, South Yorkshire, S70 2AS, England
E-mail: enquiries@pen-and-sword.co.uk
Website: www.pen-and-sword.co.uk

Contents

List of Maps

List of Illustrations

Negotiations for capitulation at the Mayor's house in Donchery on the night of the battle. Painting by Anton von Werner, 1885. From left to right: French; Captain d'Orcet (with bandaged head), Chief of Staff General Faure (seated with back to viewer), General Castelnau, General de Wimpffen (standing with hand on table): German; General Podbielski (seated behind table), Moltke (standing at table), and Bismarck. German staff officers: Captain Winterfeld, Count Nostitz (with notebook), Major Krause, Lt. Col. Bronsart von Schellendorff, Lt. Col. Verdy du Vernois, Major Blume and Major de Claer.

Napoleon III, escorted by Bismarck, goes to meet King Wilhelm on 2 September. Painting by Wilhelm Camphausen, 1876.

French Prisoners of War.

Picture sources: Nos. 1–5, 7–11 and 25–29 from J. F. Maurice, *The Franco-German War* (1900); Nos. 13, 14, 16 and 24 from L. Rousset, *Histoire Générale de la Guerre Franco-Allemande* (illustrated edition, 1912); No. 15 from J. Claretie, *Histoire de la Révolution de 1870–71* (1872); Nos. 17–23 from E. Véron, *La Troisième Invasion* (1876–7); Nos. 6, 12 and 30 from A. Le Faure, *Histoire de la Guerre Franco-Allemande 1870–71* (1875). Photography by Tony Weller.

Preface

The Franco-Prussian War was a turning point in the history of nineteenth-century Europe, and the Battle of Sedan, fought on Thursday, 1 September 1870, was the pivotal event of that war. A generation of Germans celebrated 2 September, the day of the formal French surrender, as 'Sedan Day', which, even more than the acclamation of King Wilhelm I of Prussia as the German Emperor at Versailles in January 1871, symbolized the birth of their nation, forged in steel and tempered in the blood of the common enemy. For the Germans it was a dazzling victory, fought out in a suitably spectacular natural setting overlooking the Meuse valley on a halcyon September day. Anton von Werner's painting of a bareheaded Count Reille, aide-de-camp to the French Emperor Napoleon III, bowing before the King of Prussia as he delivered Napoleon's note of submission on the evening of the battle, became one of the most celebrated images of the founding legend of the German Second Reich. It was one moment of high drama on a day that saw many.

Yet the German triumphal dream was a French nightmare. 'I never imagined the catastrophe would be so terrible,'[1] confessed Napoleon III, and to suffer a Sedan remains a byword in French for catastrophic failure in any endeavour. A whole army was surrounded, bombarded into submission and captured. Sedan was a more complete and humiliating defeat than Waterloo, ending the reign of an Emperor who had ruled France for two decades and who had once seemed the most powerful man in Europe. If his fall had elements of tragedy, many Frenchmen found it hard to comprehend or forgive the disaster he had brought upon their country. In trying to revive the imagined glories of his uncle Napoleon I, he had ended by presiding over the end of France's claims to be the foremost military power of the Continent and had opened the country to all the sufferings of invasion. When news of the defeat and his surrender reached Paris it sparked a revolution that deposed his dynasty. His enemies would celebrate that revolution which ushered in a Republic that, in the event, outlived the German Empire. Yet it was Sedan that made the Republic possible, and therefore had as great an impact on the political future of France as it did upon that of Germany; even if it was hardly an event that any Frenchman would wish to remember.

Thus the story of Sedan is that of the fall of one empire and the rise of another. It was on one side a milestone in the achievement of German unity, and on the other the culmination of a series of French errors that brought national calamity and the exile of the Bonapartes. It is a story of mutual fear and insecurity that tempted both governments to seek a solution to domestic tensions by a war against the other; as well as the military story of how that war was fought and how Sedan came about. Above all, of course, it is the story of the men who fought and, if they were lucky, survived; but if they were unlucky were wounded, perished from sickness in captivity, or died violent, often agonizing deaths, not knowing whether the battle they fought in was won or lost.

This account of that climactic clash between two great continental rivals has no pretension other than to offer a narrative introduction to events. Its justification may be that, although in the English-speaking world there is still a great appetite for books on the First and Second World Wars, there is apparently far less curiosity about a war that founded the modern German state, dominated European consciousness for a generation, and in some senses lay at the root of what happened in 1914. Of course, the origins of the Great War reach well beyond the Franco-German quarrel, but equally its outbreak is incomprehensible without reference to Sedan and its legacy. For no Balkan or colonial quarrel could have ignited a general European and world war had it not been for the rivalries of highly militarized alliances, central to which were political and military tensions between France and Germany resulting from the conflict of 1870. Besides, whether as a case study, a human drama, a terrible warning, or simply an exploration of the past on its own terms, the story of that violent, fateful summer of 1870 is one that should invite retelling and reflection for as long as Europeans are concerned with their past.

Douglas Fermer
2007

Acknowledgements

My principal debt is to Rupert Harding, Commissioning Editor of Pen & Sword Books, who suggested that a new survey of the Sedan campaign, of manageable length, might be of interest to readers for whom the Franco-Prussian War remains a relatively unfamiliar subject. It is also a pleasure to record my thanks to the librarians of King's College, London, the Institute of Historical Research, the British Library, and the Wellcome Library; and to those of Croydon Central Library for obtaining photocopies of rare items. I am immensely grateful to Tony Weller for photography and to Nick Stansfeld for checking some of my translations from German sources, and for several fascinating discussions of them. I owe a special debt to John Cook for the skill and patience with which he has drawn the maps from my sketches, and to his son Matthew Cook for processing them digitally. My happy experience has been that, when it comes to producing maps, one simply cannot have too many Cooks. Susan Milligan cast an expert editorial eye over the text. Finally, the bibliography is but a pale hint of the immeasurable debt any researcher in this field owes to the distinguished company of German, French, British and American scholars, living and dead, who have explored it before him. Though the standards set by the giants of the subject – Rousset, Palat ('Pierre Lehautcourt'), La Gorce, Picard and Howard – are humbling, they are in equal measure inspiring. Needless to say, however, any errors of fact or interpretation are mine alone.

D. F.

Chapter 1

Hereditary Enemies?

The Pendulum of Conquest

It was a catastrophic defeat. Fear of the growing power of the old enemy beyond the Rhine had come to a head over a diplomatic insult. Urged on by patriotic crowds demonstrating in the capital, an overconfident government had gone to war over a point of honour. Yet the country was without firm allies, its generals were hidebound and, for all his wife's bellicosity, the head of state had inherited no spark of his illustrious forebear's military ability. The army that had amazed Europe half a century ago was living on its past reputation and proved no match for a modern enemy intelligently commanded. Pursuing a hesitant strategy, it had been outmanoeuvred then crushed after a brief campaign culminating in a day of battle. Now the state lay at the mercy of the conqueror, and the ruling dynasty fled the capital.

Such was the plight of the Kingdom of Prussia in October 1806, following her defeat by Napoleon I at the Battle of Jena. The French Emperor entered Berlin in triumph, visited the tomb of Frederick the Great and symbolically confiscated the sword of the king who had routed a French army in 1757. French occupation brought partial dismemberment of the state and imposition of a crushing war indemnity. These humiliations, and the ruin of her trade by enforced obedience to Napoleon's continental blockade of Great Britain, were long remembered in Prussia. Widespread economic misery was compounded by conscription, forced labour, requisitioning and predations committed by French troops and deserters. Stories of shootings and hangings by French soldiers entered Prussian folklore. Eventually, after Napoleon had overreached himself and ruined his Grand Army in Russia in 1812, Prussia threw off her forced allegiance to him and made common cause with the Russians. In March 1813 King Friedrich Wilhelm III summoned his subjects to arms against the French. The stakes were high, for had Napoleon regained the upper hand in the fighting in Germany that year he would have eliminated the Prussian state. Only by combining forces did Russia, Prussia and Austria finally bring Napoleon to bay and defeat him in a huge battle at Leipzig in October 1813. The allied invasion of France followed and, despite defeats at the hands of the resourceful French Emperor, numbers and determination eventually prevailed.

In March 1814 allied armies entered Paris. Napoleon abdicated and went into exile on Elba.

When Napoleon returned and tried to re-establish himself in 1815, Prussian forces under Field Marshal Blücher in cooperation with Wellington ensured the Anglo–German victory of 18 June; called Waterloo in Britain but, fittingly, La Belle Alliance in Germany. Returning to Paris in vengeful mood, Blücher was only narrowly dissuaded from destroying those prominent monuments to Napoleon's military glory, the Pont de Iéna and the Vendôme column. Impoverished Prussia proved the most implacable and exacting of the Allies: her requisitions on the French population were extremely harsh. Only reluctantly did she yield to pressure from the other Allies to moderate her demands for war reparations, agreeing in 1817 to the reduction of the occupying forces, then to an early end to the agreed five-year occupation period. The last allied troops left France in November 1818.

The Peace Settlement of 1815

After a quarter-century of exhausting wars against France, the victorious Allies met at Vienna and redrew the map of Europe. Prussia, the strongest German state north of the River Main, but the least of the five Great Powers, was compensated for losing many of her Polish territories to Russia with lands that included the west bank of the Rhine, so giving her a frontier with France. The other Allies thus made her the bulwark against any renewed French aggression. France was stripped of all her gains since 1790, some strategic parcels of land on her north-eastern frontier, and Nice and Savoy to the south-east. Prussia now held the German-speaking Rhineland, which the French had regarded as within their 'natural frontiers'. However, Prussian demands that France should also cede German-speaking Alsace and Lorraine on her eastern frontier were ruled out by Britain and Russia, who were unwilling to jeopardize the restored Bourbon monarchy in France by excessive demands.

Prussia's newly acquired wealthy west German provinces were very different from the poor, flat, sandy acres of old Prussia east of the River Elbe, farmed by her Protestant squires and their peasants. Integration presented problems. Yet from Prussia's beginnings her ruling Hohenzollern dynasty, styled kings only since 1701, had governed a varying agglomeration of territories with no natural frontiers. More awkward was the separation of her eastern and western provinces by the lands of other princes. Prussia had survived and grown, but had become a kingdom split in two.

'Germany' remained a geographical expression describing a patchwork of independent states ruled by kings, electors and dukes. A divided Germany suited the Great Powers, for each feared any other dominating central Europe.

The French had reorganized Germany in their own interests, reducing some 360 petty states and free cities to three dozen. The Allies at Vienna redrew some boundaries but, for all their conservatism, did not attempt the impossible task of restoring the old order. To ensure stability in the German states they created a federal body, the German Confederation, presided over by the Habsburg Emperor of Austria, ruler of the most powerful central European state. All member states of the Confederation sent representatives to an assembly (called the Federal Diet) at Frankfurt-am-Main. In practice decisions in the Diet depended on the agreement of its two most powerful members, old rivals Austria and Prussia, while attempts to strengthen its powers always foundered on the reluctance of the smaller states to surrender any of their cherished sovereignty. Those who had hoped for some more effective form of German union were disappointed.

Nevertheless, the Vienna settlement and the determination of the victors to maintain it gave Europe nearly four decades of peace. Only when their cooperation broke down in the 1850s did it become possible for a new generation of rulers to bury the 1815 settlement and redraw the map of Europe in pursuit of their territorial ambitions. Those ambitions included unquenched French aspirations and Prussian hopes of consolidating her territories. They would feed upon the growth of nationalism among Italians and Germans.

The Ferment of Nationalism
In conquering Europe, French armies had seen themselves as carrying their revolutionary ideas of liberty and equality with them; but, to their indignation, the peoples they exploited as inferiors resented occupation, and began in varying degrees to assert their identities.

For most Germans, 'patriotism' meant loyalty to their state and prince. Yet a sense of German identity was rooted in Lutheran tradition and had been fostered by the writings of particular historians, journalists and philosophers. Fichte's *Addresses to the German Nation*, delivered at the Berlin Academy during the occupation, had limited immediate impact, but demonstrated that French occupation was the major stimulus to German nationalism. If nationalism preached community of interest between people sharing the same language, culture and history, in practice it was virtually defined by hatred of the French and resentment of their domination.

From 1811 the nationalist writer Friedrich Jahn organized gymnastic societies which combined enthusiasm for strenuous drill in physical exercise with that for creation of a German national state. Ernst Moritz Arndt, poet and advocate of German nationalism, preached that the French were the 'hereditary enemy'. After the end of what they styled the 'War of Liberation', student associations sought to perpetuate enthusiasm for a German nation. Yet the restored German rulers acted to suppress the radical ideas of the nationalists, which threatened to bring social upheaval and to topple their thrones. In the reactionary post-war years the student associations and gymnastic societies were banned. Police action, surveillance and censorship curbed nationalist agitation.

When revolution broke out afresh in Europe in 1830 it was unrest in France, not Germany, that threatened international peace. In July Parisians overthrew the reactionary Bourbon Charles X and replaced him with the 'Citizen King', Louis-Philippe of the House of Orléans. The German Confederation took alarm as revolution began spreading across its frontiers. Simultaneously, the Belgians rose up to throw off the rule of the King of the Netherlands, declared their independence and called upon France for assistance. Demonstrators in Paris clamoured for the French troops to march to the Belgians' aid, demanding the annexation of Belgium and the left bank of the Rhine into the bargain. The King of the Netherlands in his turn called on the allied powers for help. When Prussia promptly mobilized 80,000 men, Louis-Philippe warned that if they set foot in Belgium, 'it's war'. The confrontation was defused by a conference in London, at which the Great Powers agreed to recognize Belgian independence and guaranteed the neutrality of the new state. By restraint and compromise, a European war was avoided.

A new war scare flared up in 1840, not over European boundary disputes but about French ambitions in Egypt, which were thwarted by the other four powers. The French ministry, headed by Adolphe Thiers, reacted with ostentatious military preparations. A storm of bellicose indignation was unleashed in the Paris press. A revolutionary war to break the domination of the absolutist powers, to overthrow the 1815 settlement and retake the Rhine frontier was openly advocated to chants of the Marseillaise, with its bloodthirsty sentiments towards foreigners. French nationalism and nostalgia for *la gloire* increasingly expressed themselves through the cult of Napoleon among a generation of young men who felt stifled under the monarchy and had no recollection of the conscription, heavy taxes and endless bloodshed that had wearied France of Napoleon's rule. Thiers, an eminent historian, exploited the legend for the benefit of the bourgeois monarchy, and was arranging to have the great man's remains returned from St Helena for ceremonial entombment at Les Invalides.

Yet by threatening war to reassert French prestige, Thiers stirred a hornets' nest across the Rhine, where reaction was resolute. The Federal Diet approved a Prussian proposal to arm German fortresses and muster troops. Prussia and Austria agreed to come to each other's aid if attacked by France, and popular feeling reached fever pitch. The crisis popularized poems and songs expressing German sentiments: Becker's 'Rheinlied' ('They shall not have the free

German Rhine'), Schneckenburger's poem 'Die Wacht am Rhein' (later set to music by Carl Wilhelm) and Hoffmann von Fallersleben's 'Deutschland über alles'. Arndt called for the invasion of France and the annexation of Alsace and Lorraine, and his theme was echoed in the German press.

Unlike in 1870, the powers drew back from the brink. Louis-Philippe removed Thiers, but the revelation of the depths of Franco-German antagonism had been startling. Another legacy of the crisis was the ring of fortifications that Thiers started constructing around Paris to defend the French capital in the event of a new invasion.

After the 1840 crisis German nationalism became more deeply rooted, even as new roads, canals, railways and the electric telegraph broke down barriers of time and space between German communities. The growth of the press diffused nationalism beyond its narrow academic and middle-class base and broadened political participation. Prussia lifted the ban on gymnastic societies in 1842. Like choral societies and shooting clubs, they flourished, promoting nationalism throughout the German states at festivals which provided a platform for Liberal politicians to urge the benefits of a united state that could throw off the political and economic constraints imposed by the fragmentation of the German-speaking lands. For, despite political repression, economic cooperation between German states was becoming a reality. Since 1818 Prussia had worked to abolish restrictive tariff barriers in her own interest. Her initiatives, and others in the south, resulted in the creation of a German Customs Union in 1834, forming a low-tariff trade area under Prussian domination which added more member states over the next two decades. Closer economic integration boosted Liberal and nationalist hopes that internal political barriers might also come down. In 1848 the advocates of greater German unity were presented with an arena for their ambitions.

Napoleon III Takes Power

That year revolutions ignited by economic distress swept Europe. Paris, that powder keg of revolutionary passions, erupted in February. King Louis-Philippe, despised for his cautious and inglorious foreign policy, abdicated and fled to England. The Second Republic was proclaimed by Paris radicals, but France became embroiled in internal troubles. Such was the need felt in the country for a man of order that the presidential election held on 10 December produced a result undreamt of by the revolutionaries of February when they introduced universal male suffrage: a Bonaparte was restored to power in France.

Louis-Napoleon Bonaparte was elected President of France by 5.5 million votes: far ahead of his nearest rival. Born in 1808, he was the nephew of the great

Emperor, on whose knee he had been dandled as a child and whose legend he revered. After Waterloo Louis had lived in exile in Switzerland with his mother Hortense Beauharnais, and spoke French with a German accent. During disturbances in Italy in 1831 he had sided with the revolutionaries against the Austrian regime there. After both his elder brother and his cousin, 'Napoleon II', died in 1831–2, Louis assumed the role of Bonapartist pretender to the French throne. His pamphlets, notably *Napoleonic Ideas* (1839), promoted the myth Napoleon had woven around himself in exile on St Helena: of Napoleon the Liberal, Napoleon the friend of nationalities working for a united Europe, who had been thwarted by the reactionary monarchies. However, his first attempts to exploit his uncle's legend against King Louis-Philippe ended in farce. An attempted military rising at Strasbourg in 1836 was a debacle and earned him a sentence of exile. A second attempt, a landing at Boulogne in 1840 with a boatload of volunteers and mercenaries who had joined him in London, was quickly overpowered by royal troops. This time Louis was imprisoned in the damp northern fortress of Ham. He escaped disguised as a workman in 1846 and fled to London where, supplied with money by his rich friends and English mistress, he was well placed to take advantage of events unfolding in 1848.

In the presidential campaign his supporters adeptly promoted the power of the Bonaparte name, using images that appealed to classes who had never before had the vote. Not for the last time, bourgeois professional politicians underestimated the powers of this unimpressive figure, whose tendency to stoutness, drooping eyelids, and hesitant, heavily accented delivery belied his political skills and determination. As Prince-President, he swore to defend the Republic and toured the country, promoting himself as the only man who could defend both liberty and order and reconcile internal divisions that lately had made France seem ungovernable. Continuing radical disturbances rallied conservatives to him as a man of order. Catholics approved of a new education law favouring religious schools, and of the despatch of an expeditionary force to protect the Pope from revolutionaries at Rome. Louis-Napoleon's championship of universal male suffrage against the bourgeois politicians of the National Assembly who tried to restrict it made him appear a defender of democracy.

His appeal to many groups, combined with shrewd appointments of supporters to key posts, put him in a strong position to extend his presidency, which was due to end in 1852. The National Assembly, however, blocked his attempt to achieve this legally. Louis, with careful planning by his inner circle and the support of reliable generals and his police chief, staged a coup d'état on the night of 2 December 1851, the anniversary of his uncle's victory at

Austerlitz. The Assembly was locked out; its leading politicians were arrested and imprisoned.

'Operation Rubicon' did not go as smoothly as planned, however. On 3 December a Deputy of the National Assembly, Dr Baudin, was killed on a Paris barricade. Next day over a thousand protestors manned barricades in the city. Troops opened fire and killed dozens of them and bystanders too. In the provinces over 26,000 people were arrested, half of whom were deported, banished or imprisoned. Throughout the nineteen years of his rule, the 'crime of 2 December' blighted Louis-Napoleon's attempts to win over a hard core of opponents to accept the legitimacy of his regime. Nevertheless, the great majority of French voters supported him when he sought popular endorsement of his coup. He had brought something new to European politics; a dictatorship resting on popular approval, but supported by strict censorship, police surveillance and electoral manipulation. Pressing his advantage, in November 1852 he sought approval for restoration of the Empire and got it by 8 million votes to 250,000, with 2 million abstentions. With effect from 2 December 1852 he declared himself Napoleon III, Emperor of the French, and shortly promulgated a constitution that preserved the forms but not the substance of parliamentary government.

To calm fears at home and abroad that the return of the Empire meant war, he declared at Bordeaux in October 1852 that 'The Empire means peace', and that his focus would be on internal improvements like building roads, railways, dockyards and canals. He was careful to cultivate his uncle's old nemesis, Great Britain. Despite his peaceful professions, he cultivated the army, recreated an elite Imperial Guard, and frequently appeared in military uniform, in deliberate contrast to the black-coated dullness of Louis-Philippe's court. Like all French governments since Waterloo, he nurtured hopes of burying the 1815 treaties. Unlike the Bourbon monarchs, but like the republicans of 1848, he sympathized with the cause of nationalities in Europe. He might be expected to act in their favour where opportunities arose.

Broken Dreams of German Unity

Meanwhile, the Liberal and nationalist politicians who had ridden the wave of revolution across the German states in 1848 had seemed tantalizingly close to creating a new German nation. After bloody riots in Berlin in March, King Friedrich Wilhelm IV of Prussia sought to conciliate the crowds by wearing the black, red and gold German nationalist colours and declaring, 'Henceforth, Prussia is merged into Germany.' A German Parliament met at Frankfurt in May and drew up a federal constitution for the German states based on universal manhood suffrage.

Hopes that this impressive constitution might be peacefully accepted by the existing states were disappointed. By late 1848 the Prussian government had recovered its nerve: the Liberal ministry was dismissed and the army re-entered Berlin. When the Frankfurt Parliament respectfully offered Friedrich Wilhelm the title of German Emperor in April 1849, he refused it. To him, the acceptance of a crown 'from the gutter' with a Liberal constitution was anathema. Within weeks a further wave of popular uprisings across Germany demanding the Frankfurt constitution was brutally suppressed by Prussian troops commanded by the king's brother, Prince Wilhelm. By July, Prussian firing squads in Berlin, Saxony and Baden had extinguished revolution throughout Germany.

The defunct Frankfurt Parliament had been frustrated partly because it had no armed forces of its own to enforce its will. Yet its deliberations had shown that German nationalism was no more peaceable than any other variety. The Frankfurt Parliament declared war on Denmark in 1848 when it attempted to incorporate the mixed-race Duchy of Schleswig, which was not even part of the Confederation. Prussia was initially willing to mount an invasion on the German Parliament's behalf, but had to call an armistice when Russia, Britain and France brought diplomatic pressure to bear. Impotent in the face of Great Power solidarity, the furious Frankfurt Parliament had to accept that Prussia was no longer prepared to fight its German nationalist war.

The Frankfurt debates also addressed the basis on which 'Germany' might be unified. Was it to be a 'Greater Germany', incorporating all the Confederation plus some Germans currently beyond its borders? Or a 'Little Germany' excluding the Habsburg lands? The 'Greater Germany' solution included Austria and looked to her for leadership, and was favoured by the pre-dominantly Catholic southern states. The 'Little Germany' solution looked to Prussian leadership and was favoured by representatives of the predominantly Protestant northern states. It was this view that prevailed by a narrow majority and led to the abortive offer of a German imperial crown to the King of Prussia.

Austria, shaken by revolution throughout her multi-national empire, was temporarily in no position to reassert her leadership in Germany. In 1848 her armies were busy suppressing revolts by her Czech and Italian subject nationalities, before retaking Vienna from the revolutionaries by storm in October. The Hungarian revolt was crushed with the help of the Russian army in 1849. The multi-national nature of her empire made Austria unwilling to countenance the creation of a German nation-state. Nor would she tolerate Prussian pretensions to lead one.

For, even after his refusal of the imperial crown offered by the German Parliament, Friedrich Wilhelm nurtured hopes of creating a German Union by agreement with his fellow princes, but one with an authoritarian constitution like the one he promulgated in Prussia. He had some success in building a league while Austria remained weakened by insurrection, but in 1850 she returned to the German arena to thwart his ambitions. The cooperation of three decades after 1815 had given way to naked rivalry between Austria and Prussia. So likely did war between them appear in 1850 that President Louis-Napoleon of France secretly offered Prussia an alliance, at the price of ceding France the Bavarian Palatinate in the event of victory: but no Prussian government with aspirations to lead and defend the German national cause could afford to buy French support at such a price.

Armed confrontation between Austria and Prussia came in October 1850 over whether Prussia or Austria had the right to intervene in the troubled small state of Hesse-Cassel, through which ran the road connecting Prussia's eastern and western provinces. Austria led the Diet in a vote to field a large army to enforce its power. Both sides used the nascent German railway network, begun in 1834, to concentrate their troops: Austria and her allies relatively smoothly, Prussia ineptly and with much confusion. Skirmishing between the two forces had begun when Friedrich Wilhelm backed away from conflict, swayed partly by the Czar's intimation of Russian intervention in Austria's favour. Hesse-Cassel was occupied by Confederation troops. At Olmütz in Moravia in November, Prussia agreed to the dissolution of her 'Erfurt Union', to demobilization, and to the re-establishment of the old Confederation, which resumed fully in 1851. Friedrich Wilhelm swung back to the policy favoured by Prussian conservatives of solidarity and reactionary cooperation with Austria.

Thus any hope of creating a unified Germany by agreement between the princes seemed as dead as that of one created by Liberal politicians. The groundswell of middle-class support for German unity in 1848 was no transient phenomenon, yet it proved powerless to achieve its goal. Only if the balance between the Great Powers that produced deadlock in 1850 were ever to shift significantly might the intractable 'German question' be reopened.

A Franco-German Crisis, 1859

A shift in Great Power relations came sooner than anyone foresaw, as a result of the Crimean War of 1854–6, in which Britain and France combined to defeat Russia's attack on the ailing Turkish Empire. The defeat her army suffered at allied hands at the long siege of Sebastopol exposed Russia's weaknesses and discouraged her from active intervention in European politics for two decades while she undertook internal and military reforms.

The war had another important consequence for European and German politics: it isolated Austria. Like Prussia, Austria had wished to stay neutral, but Russian forces at the mouth of the Danube intruded on her vital interests. Her long resistance to joining the western camp won her no friends; yet her eventual signature of an ultimatum to Russia weighed heavily in Russia's decision to accept peace terms. Russia regarded Austria's action as rank ingratitude for the military help she had received in 1849, and an intolerable betrayal by a fellow conservative power. In future Austria could expect no Russian help if she needed it; indeed, Russian court circles desired to see her punished. Prussia, which had not intervened against Russia and had a common interest in keeping the Poles suppressed, was on the contrary seen as Russia's only friend in Europe.

If Russia and Austria were losers, victorious France gained prestige. Napoleon III's army had acquitted itself well, albeit at the cost of 95,615 French lives.[1] It had made up the majority of allied land forces and had shown itself less incompetent than any other in the field; even if the latest communications technology, the electric telegraph, had proved a mixed blessing. One French commander-in-chief in the Crimea, Canrobert, had resigned in despair over orders wired direct from the Emperor in Paris. The 1856 peace conference was held in Paris, where Napoleon invited the delegates to banquet and waltz at the Tuileries Palace and savoured his moment as arbiter of Europe. His chances of founding a stable dynasty improved when the Empress Eugénie gave birth to a healthy male son, Louis, the Prince Imperial.

In 1858 Napoleon exploited his diplomatic and military advantages in the hope of 'doing something for Italy'. Having long desired to help the Liberal and national cause there, he secretly agreed with the Kingdom of Piedmont to drive the Austrians out of the parts of Italy they had occupied since 1815. Napoleon was mixing idealism with opportunism, for he had the chance to achieve military success, weaken reactionary Austria while she was isolated, create client states in northern Italy, and regain Nice and Savoy as the price of his support. Yet, as conflict became imminent, his resolve faltered, even once he was sure of Russia's neutrality. Napoleon was finally pulled over the brink only when, provoked by Piedmontese military preparations, Austria obligingly declared war in April 1859.

The Italian campaign showed how much warfare had changed since Waterloo. The French army was transported by railway and steamship, debouching over the Alps and to the port of Genoa in three weeks. At close hand there was much that was chaotic about French supply arrangements: Napoleon lamented privately to his War Minister that 'What grieves me about the organization of the army is that we seem always to be ... like children who have never made war ... Please understand that I am not reproaching you personally; rather the general system whereby in France we are never ready for war.'[2] Yet to outside observers it seemed that the French army was again proving itself the best in the world. With no interference from the sluggish Austrians it completed its concentration, outmanoeuvred the enemy and marched across the north Italian plain, winning bloody battles at Magenta and Solferino in June. If little tactical brilliance was on display, French troops showed the superior élan and willingness to get to close quarters that made them so formidable. Their senior commanders, driven by the instinct that getting close to the enemy was the path to honours and promotion, included men who would command armies in 1870. The courtly aristocrat Maurice MacMahon, already distinguished for his successful assault on the formidable defences of Sebastopol in the Crimea, won his marshal's baton and the title of Duke for his performance as a corps commander at Magenta.

Decorations, promotions, and victory parades in Milan and Paris were one side of French success in Italy, but another shocked European opinion. Solferino, a savage battle involving 300,000 men, produced 36,000 casualties by the time a thunderstorm of extraordinary violence put an end to fighting. With none of his uncle's ruthless indifference to high casualties, Napoleon III was sickened by what he saw and smelled on the battlefield next day. In a famous pamphlet, the Swiss traveller Henry Dunant described the horrors of the battlefield. The army medical services were overwhelmed. Dunant's lurid description rallied widespread support for the initiative of a group of Swiss philanthropists, who in 1863 founded the International Society for Aid to the Wounded, later known as the International Red Cross. The Society's efforts gave birth to the Geneva Convention of 1864, which laid down an international code for the humane treatment of wounded enemies and prisoners of war, and conferred neutral status on medical personnel. Prussia was among the first and most enthusiastic states to sign the Convention. France signed too at the Emperor's behest, despite the reservations of military men who had no wish to see hordes of civilian volunteers working in the battle zone.

This was for the future. In the wake of Solferino Napoleon decided to end the war. He and Emperor Franz Josef of Austria met and agreed peace terms at Villafranca on 11 July. It was not simply that Napoleon had little stomach for further battles. Typhus was spreading in his badly fed army, camped under the torrid Italian sun. He had conquered Lombardy for Piedmont, but if he wanted to force the Austrians out of Venetia he faced a long and difficult war for which there would be diminishing support in France. Revolutionary support for Italian unification in central Italy was getting out of hand, threatening the Papal territories around Rome and alarming French Catholics. Worryingly, too, Prussia was mobilizing her army.

In the German states, Napoleon's war in Italy was execrated as naked aggression against Austria. Fear that Napoleon's next goal would be the Rhine revived enthusiasm for and debate about German unity as nothing else could. Newspaper and pamphlet denunciation of French ambitions was as virulent as in the crisis of 1840, and much slower to subside. Yet popular sentiment did not produce cooperation between Prussia and Austria. As she had in the Crimean War, Prussia obstructed proposals for the German Confederation to mobilize forces to support Austria. Finally, in mid-June, Prussia mobilized six of her nine army corps, but as the price of her support sought command of Confederation forces on the Rhine front. The suggestion made sense while Austria was under attack in Italy, but her mistrust of Prussian ambitions in Germany was such that she refused to yield precedence on this point. For the Austrians too, Prussian mobilization provided an incentive to make peace rapidly.

Even without an ultimatum, Prussia's show of strength was sufficient to cause Napoleon alarm for his eastern frontier. He feared that the Prussians could put 400,000 men on the Rhine in a fortnight. This expectation was slightly exaggerated. Helmuth von Moltke, the studious and methodical Prussian Chief of General Staff, worried that in the present state of the German railway net-work – much of which was still single-tracked – it would take at least six weeks to move a quarter of a million men to the frontier. At all events, Napoleon concluded that he was in no position to fight the Prussians while continuing his campaign against Austria. Peace was concluded. The Prussians demobilized from 25 July, and the French eventually withdrew all their forces from Italy save for a garrison to protect the Papal territory of Rome, which Catholic opinion at home demanded. As his price for accepting the transfer of the central Italian states to Piedmont, Napoleon received Nice and Savoy following plebiscites in all the affected areas. The recovery of these two territories on France's south-eastern border was his first reversal of a loss France had suffered in 1815: a gain which boosted the popularity of his regime at home. The other powers, and particularly the German states, were greatly alarmed that it might not be his last. After his Italian adventure it was hardly surprising that Napoleon III was feared as the ruler most likely to disturb the peace of Europe.

Chapter 2

Prussia Conquers North Germany

Prussian Army Reform

The confrontation with France in 1859 added urgency to military reforms Prussia had initiated under her new ruler, Prince Wilhelm, who became regent in 1858 after his brother's stroke and was crowned king on Friedrich Wilhelm IV's death in 1861. Wilhelm I, an upright, impressively bewhiskered man in his sixties, was a professional soldier through and through. Although not brilliant intellectually, he was hard-working, experienced, pious, and very clear about what he wanted; a strong professional army directly under royal control. In his teens in 1814 Wilhelm had fought in the Prussian army against Napoleon I in France, winning the Iron Cross at the Battle of Arcis-sur-Aube. His advocacy of force against the 1848 revolutionaries earned him the nickname 'Prince Grapeshot', which he lived up to the following year. In 1850 he had argued against his brother's reluctance to face military confrontation with Austria, and was determined that Prussia should never again be as weak in the international arena as she had appeared at Olmütz.

Wilhelm demonstrated a capacity for military decision-making uncharacteristic of his brother. He was convinced of the suitability for general infantry use of the breech-loading rifle patented by Johann Nikolaus von Dreyse in 1838. The expensive 'needle gun' (so called for its novel bolt and firing-pin system) had been in production since 1841, and after extensive testing had been issued to selected regiments over the following years, as the rate of manufacture permitted. Wilhelm cut short the continuing debate about the extent to which rifled muzzle-loaders should be retained, ordering the needle gun to be issued to all remaining regiments. He had been similarly impressed by the cast-steel breech-loading cannon developed by Alfred Krupp, whose Essen factory lay in the western territories acquired by Prussia in 1815. Krupp had for years importuned the government with limited success for railway and armament contracts to bolster the viability of his business, but the Prince Regent's favour opened doors. In 1859 Wilhelm ordered 300 of Krupp's expensive but amazingly durable barrels five days after witnessing tests: triple the number recommended by the responsible army commission.

Wilhelm appointed his son's aide-de-camp, Moltke, Chief of General Staff; at this stage a considerably less important post than that of War Minister. Moltke had a long-standing interest in the technical challenges of adapting Prussia's expanding commercial railway network to military uses. He addressed weaknesses exposed by the mobilization of 1859, sending staff to study French railway mobilization for the Italian campaign, and planned how to transport hundreds of thousands of men in formed units rapidly to the western frontier. One of his staff represented Prussia on the Austrian-chaired commission set up by the Federal Diet in 1861 to study how German railways should be utilized in the event of an attack by France. The commission's recommendations stressed the need for double track, for all civilian traffic to be halted during mobilization, and for a central authority including both military and railway men to oversee the transportation operation. Its report formed the embryo of plans that were elaborated over the next decade. In Prussia in 1861 orders were given for Field Railway Detachments to be formed to deal with breakdowns. NCOs were trained in transporting their units by rail. Detailed regulations on how military trains should be loaded and moved were laid down and practised.

Such technical problems of armament and transportation could be settled by royal authority, but the biggest military reform provoked a political crisis. Wilhelm, abetted by his huge, beetle-browed War Minister, General Albrecht von Roon, wanted radical changes to the conscription laws to greatly enlarge his army. This was not unreasonable, given that Prussia's population had nearly doubled since 1820 when the existing quotas had been set, but Liberals in the Prussian Parliament – the *Landtag* – strongly objected to changes that would transform the army's character. Under the current system the territorial militia, the *Landwehr*, had a prominent role in the active army. This was intended to give civilians a stake in the country's defence. Wilhelm and Roon objected to this system on grounds of military efficiency. They mistrusted these imperfectly disciplined 'civilians in uniform', who included older, less fit men, often with families. They wanted to relegate the *Landwehr* to garrison duty and to replace it with a highly trained professional army which could be rapidly expanded in wartime by calling on reservists who had undergone the same level of training. Thus men would serve three years in the active army, five in the reserve and eleven in the *Landwehr* (as opposed to two and a half, two and fourteen years respectively under the existing system).

The reform met bitter opposition in the *Landtag* which, under even the emasculated constitution of 1850 which Wilhelm had sworn to observe, had to vote the necessary increases in expenditure. Beyond wrangles over money and periods of service, Liberals feared that the reforms would create a military machine in the service of reaction, dominated by an aristocratic officer class:

and indeed Wilhelm wanted an army of full-time regulars who would be unquestioningly obedient to the crown in the event of civil unrest.

For three years the impasse worsened. Wilhelm resented Parliament's attempt to dictate to him in military questions, and in 1861 he dedicated the flags of forty-nine new regiments over the tomb of Frederick the Great in Potsdam. When a furious *Landtag* rejected the next military budget Wilhelm dissolved it, but his opponents returned triumphant at the May 1862 elections. Roon was by now prepared to compromise on a two-year term of active service, but Wilhelm obstinately insisted that three years were essential to master the needle gun and to imbibe the necessary degree of professionalism and loyalty. He threatened to abdicate if he did not get his way. The Prussian monarchy seemed to be approaching a crisis. Hard-liners urged Wilhelm to disperse the *Landtag* by a military coup. Instead, he allowed Roon to persuade him to try the political skills of the Prussian Minister in Paris. Anxious lest the king change his mind, Roon forthwith telegraphed his friend, Otto von Bismarck: 'Danger in delay. Come quickly.'

Bismarck Comes to Power

Following an interview with the king on 22 September 1862, Bismarck was appointed Minister-President and Foreign Minister of Prussia. Tall, with a bald pate, hooded eyelids, a fearsome stare and heavy moustache, he liked to project himself as the archetypal Junker, or country nobleman. Born on his father's estate of Schönhausen in Brandenburg in 1815, he retained a lifelong taste for hunting and the rural life, a gargantuan appetite for food and drink, and distaste for the new Prussia of burgeoning industrial cities and smoke-belching factory chimneys. But he was anything but a typical backwoods squire. His maternal grandfather had been a high official at the Prussian court, and though Bismarck had spent his university days at Göttingen in duelling and drinking, he had a formidable and incisive intellect. Too wilful to make a good civil servant, yet restless and unhappy managing his estate, he entered political life in 1847. Throughout the revolutionary turmoil of 1848–9 he had been a stalwart royalist and champion of reaction. He had initially been an advocate of conservative cooperation with Austria, and had been rewarded with the post of Prussian Minister to the Federal Diet from 1851 until 1859, when he had been moved to the post of Minister to Russia at St Petersburg, then in May 1862 to Paris as Minister to France. Although he considered himself above all a loyal servant of the king, his independence of mind, unconventional behaviour, and ability to express provocative views in lucid, forceful German prose had branded him as a maverick.

Bismarck took office after promising the king that army reorganization could be carried through without subjecting the monarch to the will of the parliamentary majority. Yet his initial attempts to find a compromise that might split the opposition met with no more success than those of his predecessors. At a meeting with the lower house budget committee on 30 September, Bismarck vainly attempted to win over the Liberals by urging the importance of an enlarged Prussian army if the state were to provide leadership in Germany:

> Prussia's borders under the treaties of Vienna are not favourable to the healthy existence of the state. The great questions of the day will not be settled by speeches and majority decisions – that was the great mistake of 1848 and 1849 – but by iron and blood.[1]

The Liberal press denounced his words. He was widely mistrusted as a feudal anachronism whose tenure of power would be short. Were not the Liberals riding the wave of the future towards greater parliamentary power and German unity? Did not Queen Augusta, the Crown Prince and his English wife Princess Victoria detest Bismarck and the reaction he stood for? Bismarck changed tactics, demonstrating that his power rested on the favour of the king, to whom alone he was answerable and to whom he made himself indispensable. Unable to break the deadlock with Parliament, he bypassed it, declaring that a 'gap' existed in the constitution. The crown held all the machinery of state in its hands and simply collected the taxes it needed. Bismarck flouted legality and ruthlessly used every means of intimidation, censorship and undue influence the government could bring to bear against the Liberals, but he kept his promise to the king. Wilhelm got his enlarged army.

The army soon faced a test in a campaign against Denmark. The Duchies of Schleswig and Holstein had remained a bone of contention between Danes and Germans since the 1848 war. When in November 1863 the Danes sought to bind Schleswig by closer constitutional ties, nationalist sentiment ignited across Germany, and the Federal Diet clamoured to send troops.

Bismarck worked not to champion but to forestall the nationalists. His conversations and writings were peppered with contempt for German nationalism, which he considered a 'swindle'. 'I am a Prussian, not a German,' was his attitude, and he had claimed that Bavarians were as foreign to him as Spaniards.[2] For Bismarck, vigorous pursuit of Prussian interests was the only rational basis for the conduct of foreign policy; not Liberal, nationalist or indeed conservative ideology. He had visualized more clearly than fellow conservatives how Prussia might one day harness German nationalism to extend her power, but without being taken prisoner by it. To the disgust of the other states, Prussia and

Austria announced that they, not the Confederation, would take the lead against Denmark, and only on the basis of existing international treaties. Austria risked alienating the German states to ally with Prussia because her ministers thought it the best means of controlling Prussian ambitions, and the racial diversity of her empire made it dangerous for Austria to champion nationalism. An ultimatum to the Danes required them to evacuate Schleswig. When they refused, a joint force of 65,000 Austrian and Prussian troops entered it on 1 February 1864.

How would the Prussian army perform? Evidently it had improved since embarrassed French and British observers had watched its inept manoeuvres in 1861, when the French General Forey remarked that the Prussians risked compromising the profession of arms. Moving across the snow-swept duchies against a smaller opponent, Prussian infantry seemed solid rather than remarkable, showing neither the dash of Austrian troops nor their élan with the bayonet. Prussian troops and supplies rolled smoothly to the front by railway under Moltke's direction, but the advance of the Prussian contingent seemed cautious. Only after much urging by Bismarck was the king's nephew, Prince Friedrich Karl, persuaded to mount the assault which resulted in the storming of the redoubtable Danish fortifications at Düppel on 18 April.

The victory unleashed patriotic celebration in Prussia and, just in time, strengthened Bismarck's hand at the conference of the powers on the Danish question which convened in London, necessitating an armistice. International divisions favoured Prussia. French sympathy for the Poles during their 1863 rebellion had sharply cooled Napoleon III's relations with Russia. His call for a European Congress in November 1863, declaring that the 1815 treaties had 'ceased to exist', had been rebuffed by the other powers, who rightly suspected Napoleon's ambitions on the left bank of the Rhine. Britain, disillusioned by Napoleon's annexations in Italy and his building of an armoured fleet, had indignantly rejected the proposal. Russia, Britain and France were not disposed to cooperate to save the Danes, who had obstinately put themselves in breach of international treaties of which Bismarck posed as the defender. The London conference broke up in June 1864, leaving him a free hand.

When fighting resumed, the Danes were compelled to ask for terms in barely a fortnight. Observers scarcely had time to note what some brisk skirmishes revealed of the needle gun's potential in the hands of well trained and commanded units. For instance, at Lundby on 3 July 180 Danes armed with rifled muskets surprised 124 Prussians armed with needle guns. Within twenty minutes half the Danes were dead or wounded and the rest driven off. The Prussians suffered three wounded. General Bourbaki, who visited Prussian rifle ranges that year with King Wilhelm's permission, reported to Napoleon III on the remarkable accuracy and rapidity of fire of the needle gun. Other foreign observers were less impressed. Certainly the needle gun allowed the infantry-man to fire and reload from the prone position, so exposing himself less to enemy fire, and to fire more rapidly than an enemy armed with a muzzle-loader. But its effective range was inferior to the muzzle-loader and the firing pin had a tendency to break. Serious questions remained about whether the open tactics favoured by the Prussians to reduce casualties would allow officers to control their men adequately during attacks. Moreover, the very rapidity of fire could lead inexperienced men to burn their ammunition too quickly and wildly: no trivial problem when supplies were limited. The Austrian example of mass bayonet charges, based on French tactics in Italy, seemed to many experts better adapted for use by conscripts and more likely to give decisive results in any future conflict.

Bismarck Confronts Austria

Despite their alliance for the Danish war, Bismarck's attitude towards Austria had become abrasive since his days as Prussian representative to the Diet. Austrian arrogance had convinced him that 'The policy of Vienna means that Germany is just too small for us both; so long as an honourable arrangement concerning the influence of each cannot be concluded and carried out, we will both plough the same disputed acre.' He thought that 'in the not too distant future, we shall have to fight for our existence against Austria and ... it is not within our power to prevent that, since the course of events in Germany has no other solution.'[3] During both the Crimean and the Italian wars Bismarck had argued that Prussia should take advantage of Austria's difficulties. Instead of heading for the Rhine in 1859 he suggested that while Austria was fighting France Prussian troops should march south 'with boundary posts in their knapsacks' as far as the Protestant religion predominated.[4] Once in power, Bismarck frankly told the Austrian ambassador that he aimed to establish Prussian domination in northern Germany, hopefully with Austrian cooperation, but hinting strongly that other methods were not debarred if Austria opposed him.

By the peace treaty of October 1864, defeated Denmark yielded the duchies to the joint sovereignty of Austria and Prussia. Disputes between the two powers over their conquest led within two years to a war in which the stake was nothing less than mastery in Germany. From the start Bismarck pursued annexation of the duchies to Prussia. The Austrians had no long-term interest in the duchies and were willing to consider a bargain whereby Prussia might annex them in return for compensation to Austria elsewhere. Despite her failing finances, enormous national debt and the growing demands of her non-

German subject nationalities, Austria sought to maintain her power both in Germany and Italy. Bismarck set out to challenge these pretensions in the manner of Aesop's lion, insisting on having half the donkey's meal, then repeatedly demanding half of what the donkey had left.

Yet the Austrians had no wish to give Bismarck any pretext for hostilities. In August 1865 they sent an emissary to Wilhelm while he was taking the waters at Bad Gastein, and a compromise was agreed. Prussia and Austria would retain joint sovereignty over the duchies, but Prussia would administer Schleswig and Austria Holstein. Prussia would also retain important rights in Holstein, including rights of transit and two concessions vital to German naval ambitions: control of the base at Kiel plus the right to build a canal from the Baltic to the North Sea. Notwithstanding that Bismarck had the best of this bargain, he was seeking new quarrels with Austria within weeks. Playing the bully, he mixed threats with protests of injured innocence. By 28 February 1866 the Prussian crown council was making plans for the probability of war. Only the Crown Prince protested at such a course.

In challenging Austria, Bismarck's hand was strengthened by the economic transformation that had taken place since the confrontation over Hesse-Cassel in 1850, when Prussia's army totalled 131,000 against Austria's armed forces of 434,000. Since 1850 Prussia's heavy industry, communications, commerce and banking had developed by leaps and bounds. By comparison, Austria's over-extended empire had grown more slowly by almost any measure. But production statistics alone could not ensure victory. Austria could field a formidable 400,000 men in 1866. Moltke urged the necessity of allying with Italy, whose army of 200,000, opening a southern front against Austria, should enable Prussia's 300,000 to meet the Austrians on equal terms on the northern front. The Italians were amenable, being eager to take Venetia from the Habsburgs as spoil from an Austro-Prussian contest. A secret military alliance, signed on 8 April, committed the Italians to join a war against Austria if Prussia began one within three months. This virtually set a deadline for the commencement of hostilities, and breached the constitution of the German Confederation which forbade alliances directed against member states.

Prussia had the advantage that Austria needed twice as long to mobilize and therefore would have to make the first move. Preliminary Austrian troop movements in March gave Bismarck a pretext for accusing Austria of aggression and enabled him to persuade Wilhelm to initiate similar moves. In April the Austrians proposed disarmament, and at the Prussian court opponents of a fratricidal war sought to counter the bellicose influence of Bismarck and Roon. Briefly it appeared that the doves might prevail, but on 20 April information reached Vienna of Italian troop concentrations on the Venetian border. Franz

Josef ordered mobilization in the south to begin next day. Italy followed suit. Urged on by his generals, the Austrian Emperor ordered mobilization in the north on 1 May. An indignant Wilhelm responded by ordering Prussian mobilization. War was now all but certain. While mobilization proceeded, both sides engaged in a contest to win over German opinion. On 10 June Prussia presented a plan to the Diet for a new German Union excluding Austria. Austria responded by calling for Confederate mobilization against Prussia, and the vote was carried on the 14th. Next day Prussia declared the Confederation dissolved and her representative walked out.

The smaller German states had long dreaded and sought to avoid this choice, fearing that their sovereignty and independence would be ground between the upper and nether millstones of Prussia and Austria. When it was forced, most, save for some small states and free cities which were dependent upon Prussia, ranged themselves with Austria against her feared rival. The war against Austria was widely deplored. In the last days of peace the prime minister of Bavaria appealed to Bismarck: 'Peace and war are in your hands. As a German, I pray you to examine your conscience one last time before saying the decisive word, the consequences of which are incalculable.'[5] But the die was cast. Prussia sent ultimatums to her neighbours, Saxony, Hanover and Hesse-Cassel, requiring them to disarm. When they refused, Prussian troops began moving at midnight of 15 June. The Austro-Prussian War had begun.

Napoleon III Watches the Rhine

In setting out to coerce Austria out of Germany, Bismarck knew that the diplomatic situation continued to favour Prussian ambitions. Neither Russia nor Britain was inclined to an active role in European politics. France, however, remained a key piece on his chessboard. Before making any final decision for war he had been at pains to ensure her neutrality. He had visited the Emperor at the storm-swept resort of Biarritz in south-west France in October 1865 to reassure him that no anti-French alliance had been made at Gastein; nor had Prussia guaranteed Austria's possession of Venetia, in which the Emperor made clear his close interest. Napoleon listened politely to Bismarck's suggestions that an enlarged Prussia would be no threat to France, significantly raising no objection. Although no definite commitments apparently were asked for or given on either side, the outcome encouraged Bismarck to reassure Wilhelm that France would not stand in Prussia's way.

Napoleon seemed to be in an excellent position as the quarrel between Austria and Prussia deepened. Military experts thought Austria the stronger party, but a long war was likely from which France might reap rewards. If he favoured any side, Napoleon seemed to lean towards Prussia, which was a force for change and might prove a useful protégé and even ally in northern Germany. A weakened Austria would enable France to gain influence in the South German states. It would also allow Napoleon to fulfil his promises made in 1859 by liberating restless Venetia from Austrian rule, thereby perhaps restoring his tarnished prestige and influence in Italy. Napoleon encouraged the Italians to ally with Prussia, so facilitating the war.

Would the Emperor ask any reward for his neutrality other than Venetia for the Italians? Napoleon dropped hints to the Prussian ambassador, mentioning the frontiers of 1814 and the Bavarian Palatinate, but declined to specify what he might demand. 'I cannot point to an item of compensation; I can only assure you of my benevolent neutrality: I shall come to an understanding with your king later,' he intimated in March 1866. In May he hinted to the ambassador that the Austrians were making overtures to him and that: 'The eyes of my country are turned towards the banks of the Rhine.'[6] He appeared to be playing a clever hand, keeping his options open to exploit the situation whatever the outcome of an Austro-Prussian War.

Although Napoleon's diplomacy was secret, enough was known to inform a powerful public attack. Adolphe Thiers, leader of the French Government in the 1840 crisis, had been imprisoned and exiled briefly by Louis-Napoleon after the coup d'état of 1851. He had returned to politics in 1863, being elected to the Legislature. On 3 May 1866 he gave a superb performance in the Chamber, pushing the boundaries of criticism permitted by the imperial regime. He pointed to the dangers of encouraging Prussia's aggressive designs and questioned the wisdom of France promoting a new German power and Italian unification. Thiers saw no advantage in revising the 1815 settlement of Germany. Stung by the attack and the stir it created, Napoleon declared at Auxerre three days later that he 'detested' the treaties of 1815.

The Emperor's speech alarmed business circles and the public. Was he about to embark on some new foreign adventure? There was a run on the stock exchange. Ever attentive to public opinion, which strongly favoured peace and neutrality, Napoleon called for a European Congress to settle current disputes. To Bismarck's relief, Austria would accept only on condition that no power should gain territory, effectively killing the proposal.

In the last days of peace, in June 1866, Napoleon nevertheless could be confident that his diplomacy would win Venetia for the Italians however the war turned out. In return for his pledge of neutrality, the Austrians undertook to surrender Venetia to him if they won. They also agreed verbally that, if they beat the Prussians, Napoleon could have Belgium, and the Rhineland would become a buffer state. Thus, as Prussian troops marched south, it seemed that Napoleon might gain handsomely from the war without shedding a drop of French blood. The Austrians, in desperation, had already offered him his price. Bismarck, meanwhile, was taking a double gamble, both on the military outcome of the war, and on the unspecified reward France might exact for neutrality.

A Battle in Bohemia

Prussia's offensive against Austria and her allies was executed with a speed and daring not seen since the days of Napoleon I. Moltke, the brain behind this strategy, champed with frustration during the political negotiations that followed the decision to mobilize, seeking to convince the king that with every passing week Prussia was losing her precious advantage in time. That advantage derived firstly from the Prussian system of stationing units in their home regions, so that they and their reservists reached their depots quickly upon mobilization; secondly from efficient use of the railway network to deploy forces close to the southern frontier in readiness for the advance. Moltke deployed his forces around an arc of 500 kilometres; partly because, to his irritation, he could not move them closer together until he was authorized to cross frontiers; partly because feeding masses of men was easier while they were dispersed; but also because a widely spread net created opportunities for confusing and enveloping the enemy. Moving his armies separately enabled them to move faster, and he boldly accepted the risks of leaving concentration until a trap could be closed.

Wilhelm would not be pushed into war prematurely to keep to his generals' timetables, but he did clarify the chain of command for the coming campaign. On 2 June he empowered Moltke to issue orders directly to field commanders – a mark of the value he had learned to place on his advice. Moltke, not the War Minister, would be the king's principal adviser on campaign. Although all orders came nominally from the king, Moltke as Chief of General Staff became de facto director of military operations.

As soon as hostilities began, the German states' forces had to be eliminated. They might have joined the Austrians, giving them a heavy numerical advantage, or have threatened Prussia's supply lines as her armies moved south. In practice, the state contingents were disunited, and some were amateurish compared to Prussian infantry. Within days Prussia occupied Saxony, Hanover and Hesse-Cassel. The 23,000-strong Saxon contingent managed to slip southwards to join the Austrians. The King of Hanover's small army at least gave an incautious brigade of Prussian *Landwehr* a bloody nose at Langensalza before being surrounded and forced to capitulate on 29 June. Bavarian forces were forced westwards. Prussia had effectively conquered Germany in a fortnight.

The three main Prussian armies, a quarter of a million men directed by Moltke by telegraph from Berlin, began crossing the borders of the Austrian Empire on 22 June. They moved concentrically, like a huge line of beaters, seeking to find the main Austrian force and to pin it in front while lapping round its flanks and rear. Within a week they secured the mountain passes into Bohemia, fighting actions that revealed the devastating fire power of the needle gun. Austrian troops launching massed bayonet charges suffered four times more casualties than the Prussians. Shocked and demoralized survivors saw comrades slaughtered by bullets fired by a largely unseen enemy.

Yet not everything ran like clockwork for the Prussians as their columns marched down into the Bohemian plain. The level of central planning and control that had been applied to moving men by rail was lacking for trans-porting supplies. As would happen to the French in 1870, rations piled up at railheads far distant from the units they were intended to feed. Rain-soaked Prussian infantrymen were forced to rely on requisitions from a hostile Czech population, and many went hungry. The two main Prussian forces, First Army commanded by Prince Friedrich Karl and Second Army commanded by his cousin the Crown Prince, remained widely separated. Moltke, now in the field accompanying the king, planned to bring these forces onto the battlefield simul-taneously only once the Austrian main force was found.

The polyglot Austrian army lacked firm and imaginative direction. Hungry and exhausted by long marches from every corner of the empire, it took position overlooking the Bistritz stream, north-west of the fortress of Königgrätz. Once Prussian scouts had located it late on 2 July, an officer on a fast horse was despatched through the dark to summon the Crown Prince to close in on the Austrian right flank while First Army attacked their left.

The climactic battle of the long rivalry between Austria and Prussia was fought on 3 July 1866. It was the largest in Europe since Leipzig, with 221,000 Prussians confronting 215,000 Austrians and Saxons, each army having about 770 guns. Fighting defensively, using earthworks and bringing well-handled artillery to bear, the Austrians severely bloodied First Army, keeping it at bay throughout a drizzly morning. On their left, the Saxon Corps, ably commanded by Crown Prince Albert, inflicted punishment on the Elbe Army, Moltke's third force. But at the northern apex of their line the Austrians squandered brigade after brigade in piecemeal bayonet charges into forests where the Prussians had penetrated. The needle gun filled these pulverized, smoke-filled acres with thousands of Austrian corpses. To reinforce this sector, the Austrians had unwisely denuded their right wing when the Prussian Second Army struck it in full force in early afternoon. Austrian units holding isolated villages found themselves cut off by swarms of spike-helmeted skirmishers moving through mist and sodden crops to right and left. Desperately but in vain the Austrians fought to hold back the tide in and around burning villages. Finally, their massed batteries succeeded in holding open a line of escape and the Prussians failed to close a ring around them. By evening, the badly beaten Austrian army was in flight south-eastwards, having lost over 44,000 men killed, wounded, missing or taken prisoner. The victorious Prussians suffered over 9,000 casualties.

The war lasted only another three weeks. Despite lengthening supply lines and the appearance of cholera in the army, King Wilhelm and his generals wanted a triumphal entry into Vienna and major annexations from the defeated enemy. Bismarck vehemently opposed such a course. The war for him had been a high risk for a high stake, yet it had been fought for a specific objective – the exclusion of Austria from Germany. That objective was attainable without seizing Habsburg territories which Prussia did not need. Such demands might drive Austria to seek allies alarmed by Prussian success. Following a tempestuous scene between Bismarck and the king, Wilhelm agreed to 'bite the sour apple' of a moderate peace with Austria.

The Austrians for their part wished to conclude a disastrous conflict before it imperilled the existence of their empire. They had salvaged honour on the southern front, having defeated the Italians at Custozza on 24 June and having sunk the pride of the Italian fleet off the island of Lissa in the Adriatic on 20 July. But even before the Battle of Königgrätz (or Sadowa as it became known outside Germany), they had approached the Emperor of the French to mediate on the southern front, agreeing to cede Venetia to him immediately. Napoleon's diplomatic intervention after the battle sharpened Bismarck's arguments for an early peace and shaped the final settlement of this 'Seven Weeks' War'.

Germany Reshaped

On 4 July 1866 Napoleon, suffering from chronic bladder stone, was preparing to leave Paris to take a cure at Vichy when news of the Battle of Sadowa arrived 'like a thunderclap' from the summer sky, confounding expectations.[7] As the extent of the Austrian disaster became known in Paris the shock was palpable. 'We felt', wrote one commentator, 'that something in the landscape of the old Europe had just crumbled.'[8] Next day the Council of Ministers, convened by the Emperor at his palace of Saint-Cloud, was divided on how to respond. The Empress Eugénie, the Foreign Minister and the War Minister were for massing forces on Prussia's frontier to restrain her and enforce arbitration, and initially Napoleon agreed. On the other side of the debate Interior Minister La Valette and the Emperor's spokesman in the Legislature, the tough Auvergnat lawyer Eugène Rouher, advised caution. To launch a war from a standing start would be unpopular with the overwhelmingly pacific French public. Did the Emperor wish to tie himself to the corpse of Austria, bastion of the 1815 settlement, against the forces of German and Italian nationalism which he had aspired to champion? How would this look once his promotion of the Prusso-Italian alliance became known? Since the Austrians had agreed to cede Venetia to him, and the King of Prussia seemed receptive to his telegrammed proposal of an armistice, was force necessary or justified? And if her bluff were called, could France be sure of victory, with her troops armed with muzzle-loaders and her best regiments in Algeria and Mexico? Napoleon pondered such arguments overnight and next day deferred mobilization, presenting himself instead as a benevolent mediator. An official announcement that France had secured Venetia for the Italians and implying that an armistice was imminent was greeted by illuminations in Paris and across the country as relieved crowds celebrated that France had kept out of the war while apparently maintaining her prestige as arbiter of Europe.

Bismarck later boasted that he had frightened Napoleon off intervention by threatening to unleash German national passions against French forces, but at the time he took care to accommodate Napoleon's views about the future shape of Germany. He was pleasantly surprised when the Emperor willingly accepted that Prussia should be dominant north of the Main, stipulating only that Saxony should retain its identity rather than be annexed outright. South of the Main, Napoleon insisted that Bavaria, Württemberg, Hesse-Darmstadt and Baden should maintain an independent existence. Austria, like the other defeated states, would pay Prussia a war indemnity, but would lose no territory except Venetia. Thus North Germany was united, giving partial satisfaction to German national aspirations. But the former German Confederation was actually divided into three, leaving the appearance that a balance of power was being maintained in Central Europe. The middle tranche – the South German states – might even prove a fertile field for French influence. Napoleon also asked that the Danes of Northern Schleswig should be allowed a free vote on whether they wished to join Denmark.

Bismarck incorporated these points in the peace preliminaries signed by Prussia and Austria at Nikolsburg on 26 July and formalized in the Treaty of Prague of 23 August. By its terms the Emperor of Austria ceded Schleswig and Holstein to Prussia, accepted the dissolution of the German Confederation and Austria's exclusion north of the River Main, and agreed to recognize whatever arrangements Prussia made there.

Bismarck proceeded to make those arrangements speedily and without regard for the principle of legitimacy. In addition to Schleswig-Holstein, the defeated

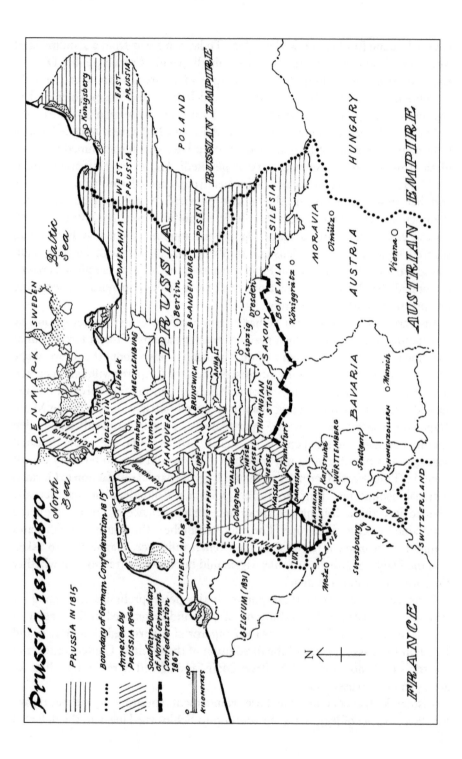

Prussia 1815-1870

PRUSSIA IN 1815

Boundary of German Confederation 1815

Annexed by PRUSSIA 1866

Southern Boundary of North German Confederation 1867

0   100
KILOMETRES

N

North Sea

Baltic Sea

DENMARK

SWEDEN

SCHLESWIG

HOLSTEIN

Lübeck

MECKLENBURG

Hamburg

Bremen

OLDENBURG

HANOVER

BRUNSWICK

LIPPE

WALDECK

HESSE

WESTPHALIA

Cologne

NASSAU

DARMSTADT

RHINELAND

NETHERLANDS

BELGIUM (1831)

LUX

METZ

LORRAINE

ALSACE

Strasbourg

FRANCE

SWITZERLAND

BADEN

Karlsruhe

BAVARIAN PALATINATE

WÜRTTEMBERG

Stuttgart

HOHENZOLLERN

BAVARIA

Munich

PRUSSIA

Königsberg

EAST PRUSSIA

WEST PRUSSIA

POMERANIA

Berlin

BRANDENBURG

POSEN

POLAND

RUSSIAN EMPIRE

ANHALT

Leipzig

Dresden

SAXONY

THURINGIAN STATES

CASSEL

HESSE

Frankfurt

SILESIA

BOHEMIA

Königgrätz

MORAVIA

Olmütz

AUSTRIA

Vienna

HUNGARY

AUSTRIAN EMPIRE

states of Hanover, Hesse-Cassel and Nassau were annexed and occupied. Their rulers were deposed and their fortunes confiscated: a violation of the monarchical principle shocking to Prussian conservatives and the Czar. From the Liberal city of Frankfurt-am-Main, refuge of his critics, Bismarck spitefully demanded such a huge indemnity that the city's mayor hanged himself.

However, most Germans north of the Main were jubilant at the transformation that had been wrought. Though at its outbreak the 'Cabinet war' of 1866 had been unpopular, many former critics now lionized Bismarck, who had cut the Gordian knot of the German question and had presented them with the object of their ambitions. Elections in Prussia saw substantial conservative gains at Liberal expense. Bismarck capitalized on success not by dispersing the *Landtag* and curtailing the constitution, as reactionaries hoped, but by offering Liberals an olive branch – albeit one designed to divide them. The Indemnity Bill legalized the government's collection of taxes since 1862, so acknowledging that the *Landtag*'s consent was necessary for budget bills.

Rather than seeing this as a Faustian bargain, most Liberals welcomed release from a political impasse that had sapped their support in the country. After all, the king was nearly 70: neither he nor Bismarck could last much longer before the Liberal-inclined Crown Prince succeeded to the throne. The Indemnity Bill, passed on 3 September 1866 by 230 votes to 75, ended the bitter constitutional conflict.

Thus the political map of 1815 had been redrawn in Prussia's favour by her startling and hard-fought victory. She had joined up the divided territories assigned her by the Congress of Vienna. Her population had grown at a stroke from 18 million to nearly 25 million and she had displaced Austria as the dominant German power. Her industrial and military might made her henceforth a Great Power to be reckoned with, and a formidable neighbour for France.

Chapter 3

Dark Clouds on the Horizon

The French Search for 'Compensation'

How France should react towards the newly enlarged Prussia was warmly debated in the government and the country in the months following Sadowa. War Minister Marshal Randon's bitter verdict that 'It is we who have been defeated at Sadowa'[1] expressed the views of many generals and of the Catholic right, notably the Empress. Sympathizing with Austria, they held that France should take a hard line with Prussia, demand territorial compensations, and revert to the centuries-old French security policy of keeping Germany divided. Among many Liberals and republicans, conversely, the defeat of the reactionary Habsburg Empire was welcome, and there was a conviction that if France were sincere in championing the principle of self-determination she must accept the new German power and seek to promote a Europe based on mutual cooperation and peace. Over the next four years each side was to blame the Emperor for favouring the other policy, but the greatest failing of his government was that it veered inconsistently from one policy to the other, only to demonstrate that 'between two stools the fool falls to the ground'.

In accepting German unity north of the Main, Napoleon had seemed a disinterested mediator, but public opinion soon swung strongly to the view that France should have made gains. 'People say we played the game badly,'[2] reported an official from Toulouse, and such opinions were voiced across the country. A minister advised Napoleon that, 'Everybody says that greatness is relative and that a country can be diminished while remaining the same when new forces increase around it.'[3] Yielding to such pressures, Napoleon belatedly submitted what Bismarck contemptuously dubbed his 'inn keeper's bill'. Just before the Peace of Nikolsburg was signed, France secretly asked for the restoration of the frontiers of 1814, the Bavarian Palatinate on the left bank of the Rhine, including the city of Mainz, and Luxembourg. In brazenly asking for such a generous slice of German-speaking territory, the French urged the great service their neutrality had supposedly rendered to Prussia.

Bismarck was no longer a supplicant, anxious for French neutrality, nor bound by any treaty with France. To surrender any German-speaking territory to her would put him in serious political danger at home. He refused the request, then demonstrated just how clever and ruthless a political operator he was by leaking details of the French demands to the Paris press, letting it be known for home consumption that war might result if the French persisted. The German press was outraged, and bayed for war rather than yield an inch of German territory.

Napoleon was publicly humiliated. He appeared before Europe to be repeating his Italian strategy of 1859–60, fomenting war in the name of national self-determination in the hope of territorial gain. He disowned the policy by sacrificing his Foreign Minister, but within a fortnight returned with a variation of the compensation strategy. At the urging of Rouher, French ambassador Vincent Benedetti was instructed to seek an alliance with Prussia. Under the terms proposed, France would not oppose a future union between North Germany and the South German states, but in return Prussia would facilitate the French acquisition of Luxembourg and would give France armed support should the Emperor 'be led by circumstances to have his troops enter Belgium or to conquer it'.

Benedetti drafted the treaty in his own hand in late August and left a copy with Bismarck, who kept it safe. Before the war of 1866 Bismarck had encouraged the French government to expect his support if it chose to expand 'wherever French is spoken', but he had no interest in allying with France to fight the British, as must inevitably happen if she seized Belgium. He became evasive, went sick, then let the matter drop. When the French tried to raise it again in connection with the North German settlement, he flew into a rage and accused them of meddling in German internal affairs.

Bismarck's publication of the earlier French demands for compensation had enabled him to start subverting the provisions of the Treaty of Prague relating to South Germany even before the document was signed. The revelation of French designs on their territory, combined with Bismarck's offer to reduce the war indemnities he had imposed on them, pushed the South German states in mid-August into secret offensive-defensive alliances with Prussia. By their terms the troops of these states would come under Prussian command if they were attacked, and would be trained to Prussian standards. It would take two or three years for southern troops to be fully trained and integrated with Prussian forces, but military union between North and South Germany had begun. Had Napoleon known this, he might have been even more 'alarmed at his Frankenstein', as a British diplomat put it.[4]

Having come away empty-handed from the reshaping of Europe, Napoleon put the best face he could on things for the benefit of the French public. A circular published on 17 September declared that France had gained by the final destruction of the treaties of 1815 and the break-up of the alliance of the other European Powers against her. Italy had been unified by French efforts, and the application of the national principle to Germany was to be welcomed, not feared. What was the rationalization of the number of smaller states but a continuation of the work of his uncle, Napoleon I? With ostensible reference to Northern Germany, but with a covert allusion to his designs on Belgium and Luxembourg, the circular questioned whether 'it should be a matter of regret that an irresistible force is driving peoples to join themselves together in large groupings, while causing minor states to disappear?'

In all, the circular argued, France was still a Great Power and had nothing to fear: 'The Emperor does not believe that the greatness of a country depends on the weakness of neighbouring peoples, and sees a true balance of power only in the satisfied aspirations of the nations of Europe.'[5] But if this reassuring picture was true and France secure, why did she need to 'perfect her military organization without delay'? The circular did little to allay a growing French sense of grievance, and a perception that their ruler had been duped by the Prussians. By autumn the possibility of war was being openly talked of, especially in the eastern regions of the country, even though they would have most to suffer.

The Luxembourg Affair

Throughout winter and spring Bismarck was preoccupied with securing the adoption of a constitution for the new North German Confederation. A parliament, or Reichstag, would be elected by universal male suffrage, but would have limited powers. It could question ministers, but not hold them accountable. The states would be represented in a Federal Council and keep their powers of local administration. This reassured them that they would retain their own identities, and was intended to signal to the watching South German states that particularism would be respected in the new Confederation. Nevertheless, as a Baden politician quipped, this was the alliance of the Prussian dog with its fleas.[6] Prussia had sufficient votes in the Federal Council to block any unwelcome law. Her king became President of the Confederation, with sole power to decide issues of war and peace, and commander of the army, whose soldiers would be bound to him by personal oath. The army would be even less answerable to Parliament than under the Prussian system, for Bismarck attempted to design out, in the government's favour, all the causes of conflict under the Prussian constitution. The size of the army, fixed at 1 per cent of the population at a standard rate of costs, and the Roon terms of military service were written into the constitution. Moreover, he aimed to put the regular military budget, over 90 per cent of government expenditure, beyond the Reichstag's reach: though eventually he accepted a limited right for it to review this 'iron budget' in four years' time.

Thus the new Confederation solidly entrenched the power of Prussia, its king and its army behind a democratic façade, and equally Bismarck's position as linchpin of the whole system. As Foreign Minister he continued to be responsible only to Wilhelm for conducting the policy of the new state, and himself took the role of Federal Chancellor. Yet, for all that the new system was designed to enhance his authority, Bismarck needed the Reichstag, which convened in February 1867, and ultimately yielded some safeguards of parliamentary immunity, limits on the royal power to prorogue, and the secret ballot to secure its support for the constitution. The dominant party in the Reichstag was the National Liberals, and Bismarck as a German statesman had to be more attentive to their nationalist views than he had been as a Prussian minister.

Bismarck increasingly affected military uniform, much to Moltke's indignation at his non-regulation style. As Bismarck well knew, in Prussian tradition spiked helmets and jackboots commanded more respect than black coats, but his martial air also smacked of the French style of uniformed autocracy legitimized by popular votes and a superficially democratic constitution. The Goncourt brothers remarked of this modern Caesarism: 'It is a curious thing, in these days of progress, revolution, the rights of the people, the reign of the masses and universal suffrage, that there have never been greater examples of the despotism and all powerful influence of a single will, namely our Emperor and Bismarck.'[7]

Actually Napoleon III was under pressure in early 1867 to concede greater political freedom and to make good on the hint given early in his reign that the political edifice might be crowned with liberty. His imperial regime was fifteen years old, and in a country as restive as France criticism and pressures for change were accumulating. Since the 1863 elections opposition in the Legislature had become better organized and vocal, and included not only the minority of republicans but some Orleanists and Bonapartists of Liberal persuasion. Napoleon sought to pre-empt his critics by announcing a package of Liberal measures, including the right to interpellate ministers and greater freedom of the press and of assembly. When he read out these plans at the opening of the Legislature in February he looked old and ill, delivering his speech from the throne in a lacklustre manner, and the paper he read from trembled.

The Legislature received him coolly, and was no more impressed with his reiterated claims that acceptance of the new German state had been the wisest and only possible course, since the public had wanted peace. In March

Thiers attacked the imperial government's conduct of foreign affairs as 'fatal, chimerical, puerile', condemning its championship of the principle of nationality and connivance at Prussian enlargement when it should have preserved a balance of power suiting French interests. Cruelly contrasting Bismarck's boldness with French hesitancy, he concluded, 'There isn't a single mistake left to make.' Rouher – the 'Vice-Emperor' as Émile Ollivier would dub him – defended himself by boasting of the decisive part France supposedly had played in halting the Prussians before Vienna and in ensuring the division of the old German Confederation into three.

Bismarck's response to Rouher's vainglorious assertions came within days, with his publication of the offensive-defensive treaties signed with the South German states the previous August. Intended as a warning to France, it came as a further blow to the optimistic claims of the Emperor and Rouher, and caused shock and consternation in Paris. For Bismarck, publication adroitly deflected criticism in the Reichstag that by agreeing to the Main frontier he had left the southern states vulnerable to foreign influences.

Loss of face at home made Napoleon more anxious for a foreign policy success, and he pressed forward with plans to purchase the Grand Duchy of Luxembourg from its sovereign, the King of the Netherlands. The French believed they had Bismarck's agreement, for in previous discussions about compensation he had raised no objection to the idea. In August 1866 he had spoken of Prussian willingness to make 'important sacrifices' for good relations with France, and of his wish to be obliging.[8] He had even indicated to Benedetti in December that, although the initiative must come from the French and they should act quickly, he would respond publicly with only a token protest.

Most Luxemburgers spoke a German dialect, though their government was conducted in French. The duchy had been part of the old German Confederation, still housed a large federal fortress manned by Prussian troops, and was a member of the German Customs Union. Yet, left to themselves, probably only a small fraction of the inhabitants would have voted for union with either France or Germany, and all were glad to have been left aside in the recent German upheavals.

The Dutch king, who had expensive tastes, was tempted by the financial offer the French made him for a duchy he had no wish to retain. By late March all seemed set fair. French agents moved into Luxembourg to stir up anti-Prussian feeling. The King of the Netherlands prepared to sell his rights as Grand Duke on the understanding that France and Prussia were in accord about the transaction but, to avoid complications with his powerful new neighbour, he prudently sought the approval of the King of Prussia. Word of the transaction was seeping out in any case, and it was hardly realistic of the French to imagine that it could be carried through in secrecy.

The Luxembourg affair triggered one of those periodic paroxysms of francophobia that stirred Germans as little else could. Bismarck complained privately to French representatives that his hands were tied now that the matter had become official, picturing himself as a captive of public opinion. Questioned in the Reichstag on 1 April about the truth of the Luxembourg story, and what measures he was taking to safeguard 'German' territory and protect the garrison, he replied in measured diplomatic terms. Behind the scenes, however, he was stoking the crisis in the press and doing all he could to block French plans, and probably had arranged the interpellation himself. Though previously he had admitted that Luxemburgers had no love for Prussia and that the duchy was of little consequence, he now spoke of Luxembourg as being a 'German' territory that must remain so; and of the fortress as a key to the defence of Germany that must continue to be occupied. Feverish work was set in hand to strengthen the fortifications. The King of the Netherlands was pointedly told that peace could not be guaranteed if he proceeded with the sale. Intimidated by these threats and by the furore in Germany, he withdrew from the transaction. France had been thwarted once more.

In Paris there was anger. Even the Emperor's customary calm was ruffled. A Hanoverian diplomat in the French capital noted that 'Among the masses, [the prospect of] war with Prussia was most popular; everywhere, in workers' bars as in bourgeois salons, in editorial offices and political cafés, people spoke of nothing else but the chances of the coming campaign: they spoke of the generals who would command the different units and discussed plans of campaign, calculating the time it would take the French armies to reach Berlin, for no one doubted success. In barracks, enthusiasm was at its peak, and victory was toasted in officers' messes.' Perhaps businessmen and industrialists did not share this bellicose enthusiasm, he admitted, 'but animosity against Prussia was such that they scarcely dared show feelings that would have been thought unpatriotic.'[9]

Equal and opposite sentiments were in evidence across the Rhine. Among them could be heard an undercurrent of German nationalist demands for Alsace, which had been part of France since the seventeenth century but where the majority of people still spoke German, and similarly for German-speaking eastern Lorraine, French since the eighteenth century. It was axiomatic in such circles that German-speakers under foreign rule must be 'oppressed'. An appeal for peace by leading citizens of Strasbourg with German names, pointing out that they had no desire to be other than French and to live in peace and amity, could hardly dent the fervour of that minority of German nationalists who yearned for political dominion wherever German was spoken, and who had their sights on that great city of eastern France, sitting within its massive fortifications just across the Rhine.

In speaking of a possible war to defend German honour over Luxembourg, Bismarck was exploiting national passions for all their worth. Not only did this further boost his credit with nationalist opinion; it conveniently eased passage of the North German constitution through the Reichstag. The timing could hardly have been better, and Bismarck sought to prolong the crisis until the constitution had been agreed. Nevertheless, although the military were keen for war, Bismarck privately thought the tiny duchy not worth such a wager. Besides, the excitement had not stimulated southern enthusiasm for union with the North to the extent he had hoped. Nor had his usual mixture of threats and lures directed at the other Great Powers succeeded in isolating France. He agreed to a Russian proposal for a conference, which was convened in London in May.

Napoleon too, though feeling that he had been led into a trap by Bismarck's duplicity, had no inclination for war over the issue, particularly while the country remained militarily ill prepared. His advisers counselled conciliation. His Foreign Minister, Lionel de Moustier, kept his nerve and worked to extricate France from her faux pas as best he could. He used restrained and conciliatory language, avoiding anything that might further raise the political temperature or serve as provocation. He let it be known that France wanted a peaceful solution, but pressed firmly for the evacuation of the Prussian fortress in Luxembourg. As the old German Confederation had ceased to exist, what was the legal justification for maintaining the Prussian garrison there? With the support of Austria, Britain and Russia this argument prevailed at the London conference. It was agreed that Luxembourg, still under the personal sovereignty of the Dutch king, would become a neutral state under the guarantee of the Great Powers. France would not take it, but neither would Prussia, which would demolish the fortress and withdraw her garrison.

So the crisis subsided, to general relief in France once spirits had cooled. In Germany the impression had been strengthened that her neighbour remained jealous of her nationhood and arrogantly inclined to meddle in German affairs and to covet 'German' territory. Withdrawal of the garrison rankled with nationalists and the military. The French government, on the other hand, felt itself cheated of even a small compensation for its 'benevolent neutrality' in July 1866 when, ironically, a bold demand for Luxembourg could have succeeded. The French had been caught out in an act of rapacity, and the sequel left them no illusions about the sincerity or worth of Bismarck's earlier assurances of friendship and goodwill.

This was underscored when they pressed him to act on his 1866 agreement to hold a plebiscite in northern Schleswig. Bismarck, knowing that nationalist opinion would never stand for returning any territory to Denmark, made conditions about German security. When the French pointed out that the Treaty of Prague made no such conditions, Bismarck informed them tartly that it had been an agreement between Austria and Prussia which did not concern them. He had not the slightest intention of honouring a clause which had been included at Napoleon III's request to protect the Schleswig Danes. (Germany formally renounced it in 1879.) The French backed down, but this succession of humiliations at Bismarck's hands left them ill disposed ever to suffer another. It strengthened the view of many right-wing Bonapartists that the dented prestige of the dynasty could not withstand another public rebuff from Prussia. After the Luxembourg crisis, war between the two powers began to be talked of with fatalism. As for the armies, no soldier on either side had any doubt as to who the next enemy would be.

Once the war scare over Luxembourg had passed, Paris gave itself over to the splendours of the Universal Exhibition, held in a vast oval structure temporarily erected on the Champ de Mars. Fifteen million visitors marvelled at this celebration of the achievements of industry and labour. Among varied examples of the arts of civilization stood specimens of modern artillery, including Krupp's giant steel guns in the Prussian section. Also to be seen was the latest field hospital equipment, demonstrating how medical advances would ease the plight of the wounded in war. 'Strange epoch', reflected one visitor, 'that with equal enthusiasm cultivates the science of killing and the science of healing!'[10]

For many tourists that summer, the worthy contents of the Exhibition were less appealing than the crowded pleasure gardens, bars, shops, theatres and concert halls where the music of Offenbach and the younger Strauss held sway – or than the lure of illicit pleasures. Whatever the attraction, they flocked to Paris for the event of the year. For Napoleon III it was a chance to welcome his fellow sovereigns and to take pride in a peaceful and popular French triumph. On 1 June Czar Alexander arrived, greeted by demonstrators shouting 'Long live Poland!' Four days later his uncle, King Wilhelm of Prussia, alighted in his turn at the Gare du Nord. Charming and courteous, Wilhelm meant to be complimentary when he exclaimed, 'What splendid things you've done since I was last here!' – a reference to his presence with the forces that had taken the French capital in 1814. There were no hostile demonstrations, and the crowds studied Bismarck with curiosity. He was the soul of bonhomie, and was hugely amused by the comedy of the moment, *The Grand Duchess of Gerolstein*, which poked fun at the militarism of a fictional small German court.

The highlight of the ceremonial was a military review at Longchamp on 6 June. In radiant sunshine, the assembled sovereigns watched the cream of the French army march past in immaculate and colourful uniforms; the infantry, including sappers, grenadiers, Zouaves, chasseurs-à-pied and gendarmes as well as the red-trousered line infantry; then the cavalry, including cuirassiers, lancers and dragoons, followed by four regiments of artillery with their brass cannon. All went perfectly until, as Napoleon rode back in an open carriage with the Czar in late afternoon, a student in the crowd shot at Alexander. Although one of Napoleon's equerries pushed his mount forward to intercept the shot, a pall was cast over events. In July the would-be assassin, a young Pole named Antoine Berezowski, was defended by republican lawyer Emmanuel Arago with the plea of 'extenuating circumstances', and the French court passed a sentence of hard labour rather than death. Alexander, who had been prepared to ask for clemency, was affronted, and the incident reopened the Franco-Russian rift over Poland.

Still worse news marred the Paris festivities at the beginning of July, just as the Emperor was about to present prizes at the Exhibition. The new transatlantic cable brought confirmation that the Austrian Archduke Maximilian, Napoleon's puppet emperor of Mexico, had been shot by Mexican forces which had recovered control of the country following the departure of the French. The execution was a tragic postscript to a humiliating French failure, immortalized by the republican artist Manet in a canvas that was refused admission to the 1869 Salon by the authorities. Described by Rouher at its outset as 'the great idea of the reign', the Mexican expedition had always been unpopular. From its sailing in 1861 to final withdrawal in 1867 under a virtual ultimatum from the United States, the French expeditionary force had lost at least 7,000 men in battle, fighting guerrillas or to disease, for no gain. Napoleon could only make a voyage of condolence to Salzburg in August to commiserate with Emperor Franz Josef on the loss of his younger brother. Courtesies were exchanged, but for some at the Austrian court Napoleon would always be the man who had taken Italy from them, who had encouraged the Prussians to attack them in Germany, and had sent a Habsburg prince to his death in Mexico. The centre of political power within the Habsburg Empire had anyway shifted eastwards as a consequence of defeat in Germany. The Hungarians now held equal power with the German half of the 'Dual Monarchy', and had no interest in an alliance with France that might involve them in a war of revenge against Prussia. The two emperors merely agreed that the status quo should be maintained.

Other news was discouraging for Napoleon. The harvest was bad, and in Algeria Governor General MacMahon had to cope with famine and cholera. On his return from Salzburg, addressing an audience at Lille, Napoleon contrasted the good fortune of the early years of his rule with the 'dark clouds' gathering on the horizon. That autumn workmen demolished the Exhibition venue, in what seemed like symbolism of the departed glories of his reign. At the same time the Kingdom of Italy which he had nurtured became a further source of embarrassment. Far from being grateful for the French gift of Venetia as a prize of the war of 1866, the Italian government resented not having won it by its own efforts. Having digested Venetia, its appetite to make the Papal city of Rome the capital of Italy was merely whetted. Conservative and clerical opinion in France made it impossible for Napoleon to yield in this matter to the nation he had seen as a protégé. In December 1866 he had withdrawn French troops from Rome, relying on volunteer forces to defend it. But it became clear that the Italian government could not be relied upon to keep its agreement to defend remaining Papal territory. In October a force of Italian radicals under national hero Garibaldi marched on Rome and began fighting Papal troops in its suburbs. Reluctantly and with his usual hesitations, Napoleon despatched a French expeditionary force which arrived just in time to repulse Garibaldi bloodily at Mentana on 3 November. A French garrison would have to stay to guard against further attempts. Napoleon, the would-be liberator of Italy and champion of the principle of nationality, appeared both to Italians and French radicals as the betrayer of that cause and the defender of clerical reaction. Worse, France had not a single ally in Europe.

French Army Reform

In the wake of Sadowa, on 30 August 1866, Napoleon signed a decree to re-arm his infantry with breech-loading rifles. The weapon adopted was the Chassepot, named after its inventor Alphonse Chassepot, who for a dozen years had been developing and improving it with encouragement from the Emperor and Marshal MacMahon but in the face of resistance from the War Ministry. Tests of the latest model showed it to be a fine weapon, with a range of 1,200 metres; twice that of the needle gun, to which it was superior in all respects. It could fire six or seven 11mm rounds per minute, and the ammunition was sufficiently light to enable the infantryman to carry ninety rounds with him. It could be fitted with a fearsome-looking sabre-bayonet. Production was put in hand in French arsenals and by contracts placed abroad, and by mid-1870 the army had over a million Chassepots. The weapon was tried out against tribesmen in Algeria, and most spectacularly against Garibaldi's men at Mentana. 'The Chassepot worked wonders,' wired General de Failly to Paris,[11] to the horror of Liberals everywhere, but the news seemed to give assurance that French infantry would be able to meet the Prussians on better than even terms.

Great hopes were placed too on a secret weapon, the *mitrailleuse*, a machine gun resembling a cannon with a barrel consisting of twenty-five rifled tubes. By inserting pre-loaded blocks, fired by a rotating hand crank, the 'coffee grinder' could fire 100 rounds per minute, albeit into a small area, and had an effective range of 1,500 metres. Napoleon had funded development himself up to its adoption in 1865, and five years later 215 were stored ready for use. Beyond a few trained teams, no one knew much about using the new weapon, and it had yet to be tried in battle; but taken together the new armaments would surely give great advantages to the tactical defence.

French weaponry might be a source of confidence, but when Napoleon opened the Legislature in February 1867 he urged that 'A nation's influence depends on the number of men it can put under arms.'[12] However, in pressing for a greatly enlarged army, the imperial government faced a dilemma. If it sounded alarmist about the threat from Prussia it would contradict its own claims to foreign policy success, and could raise tensions that might precipitate a war. Its political credit had sunk so low that its programme was vigorously opposed in the country on the basis of Napoleon's past record rather than on any dispassionate assessment of the danger to France.

The French army in the 1860s required a seven-year term of service. Men reaching the age of 21 were subject to conscription, but a lottery system gave them a reasonable chance of escaping the obligation to serve. If a conscript drew a 'good number' in the lottery, he was free of any further obligation. Even if he drew a 'bad number' and was drafted into the 'first contingent' of the army, budgetary limitations meant he was unlikely to serve his full term. For the Legislature jealously guarded its right to fix annually the size of the contingent required and the military budget. If the conscript was drafted into the 'second contingent' he might have to do only a few weeks' training in the reserve before being sent home, though he remained subject to recall in wartime. Or he might be in an exempt occupation, and even if he were not the system enacted in 1855 allowed those with money to buy themselves out of the army.

The funds raised from these payments went towards bounties that encouraged serving soldiers to re-enlist, and towards hiring replacements. In theory this provided a long-service force of seasoned professionals; in practice it reinforced a tendency for the army to be the home of 'old soldiers' in every sense of the term, supervised by ageing NCOs with some bad ingrained habits. The 15 per cent of soldiers who were hired replacements were viewed as a mercenary element that damaged morale and effectiveness. Promotion in the army was slow, initiative and study were frowned upon, and the stultifying routine of over-crowded barracks far from home, low pay, hard discipline and hard drinking scarcely encouraged educated and ambitious young men to enter the ranks if they could possibly avoid it. Budgetary restraints also kept the army below strength: 390,000 men in 1866, including non-combatants, compared to half a million at the time of the Crimean War.

Napoleon, long an advocate of universal military service, wanted to overhaul the system radically to increase the regular army to 800,000 men, and to form a new territorial army – the Garde Mobile – on the lines of the Prussian *Landwehr*, that France could call upon for home defence in wartime. As War Minister he replaced the ageing Randon, who was unconvinced of the case for change, with its ablest advocate, Marshal Niel, who tried to steer army reform through the Legislature during 1867.

The plan to extend military obligations met determined opposition from many quarters. Republicans saw it as a sinister plot to foment war by an untrustworthy authoritarian regime. Their faith in the efficacy of the *levée en masse* that had saved revolutionary France from invading Prussians and Austrians in 1792–3 remained deep-rooted. Jules Simon advocated the Swiss militia system on the premise that the breasts of patriots who kept a rifle over the hearth would, given a few weeks' training, be a more than sufficient bulwark against the conscript hordes of foreign despots. The Peace League, which had been born from the Luxembourg crisis, pleaded that in the mid-nineteenth century Europe should be moving towards a brotherhood of nations, and that there should be no place in a prosperous and progressive society for anachronistic militarism. Many bourgeois, though enamoured with histories of France's military glory, were aghast that they would no longer be able to buy their sons out of military service, and at the prospect of higher taxes. Peasants too resented the blood tax that would take them from the plough. On the right, conservative generals were comfortable with the existing system and indignant at the suggestion that a long-service professional army, toughened by combat in Algeria, Italy, Mexico and the Far East, could not see off double their numbers of enemy conscripts. They found their spokesman in Thiers, who extolled quality over quantity and ridiculed claims about the number of men Prussia could put in the field. This supreme confidence in French military excellence was widely shared, even by those convinced that a war with Prussia was on the horizon. Government supporters feared that universal conscription would be so unpopular that they would lose their seats at the next elections, and Rouher shared their assessment.

Although Niel's law was finally enacted in February 1868, concessions had eroded the government's original proposals. The Legislature's right to decide the size of the annual intake, the lottery, the two-tier contingent system and the right to buy oneself out of the regular army were retained. Conscripted men in the first contingent would serve a total of nine years, including four in the reserve. Men in the second contingent would go straight into the reserve and serve five months. In theory, the obligation to serve five years in the new Garde Mobile would catch all those who escaped service in the first contingent: those who had drawn a 'good number' in the lottery, those who hired replacements, those in the second contingent who had completed their time in the reserve, and some who had been exempted from army service. The value of the Garde Mobile was vitiated, however, by the restrictions placed on its training by a Legislature mistrustful of the regime's militarist designs. Instead of the twenty-five consecutive days of annual training sought by Niel, training was limited to a derisory fifteen days with no overnight stays in barracks.

In his 1869 message Napoleon assured the nation that the reform had been a great success. An official circular declared that the army was now so well prepared to meet all eventualities that France could be 'confident in her strength'.[13] These claims, and the figures published to support them, may have been intended to mislead the Germans, but they were a delusion. The Niel law resembled universal military obligation sufficiently to make the government deeply unpopular, but failed abjectly in its aim of doubling the number of trained men available for call-up in case of war. The Garde Mobile soon proved a farce. Attempts to muster it at Paris, Bordeaux and Toulouse led to serious disorders. After Niel's death in August 1869 his successor, Edmond Le Bœuf, did not repeat the experiment, and in July 1870 the Garde Mobile was formidable on paper only. Little provision had been made even to equip it. Partly Le Bœuf was governed by budgetary constraints, just as the government could obtain only a fraction of the funds requested for the programme of modernizing the eastern fortresses begun after Sadowa. But he also shared the scepticism of the upper echelons of the military, who had overweening confidence in the regular army and despised the very idea of a citizen militia. Indeed, they feared that arming and training one would put guns in the hands of revolutionaries who might overthrow the regime.

The unpopularity of conscription merged into a wider wave of discontent that seemed to herald the approaching end of the Second Empire. Relaxation of laws governing the press and public meetings in 1868 produced a proliferation of newspapers and a 'revolution of contempt' directed at the regime. Amid this rising tide of criticism and ridicule, the most stinging attacks appeared in *La Lanterne*, a pamphlet by the aristocratic vaudeville satirist Henri Rochefort. His mordant wit made it a runaway best-seller and a dozen editions were published before the government banned it. In November a young lawyer from Cahors, Léon Gambetta, made a slashing courtroom attack on the Empire while defending the revolutionary Charles Delescluze for organizing a sub-scription to erect a memorial to Baudin, the half-forgotten deputy who had been killed during the 1851 coup d'état. The charismatic, passionate and eloquent Gambetta emerged as foremost among a new generation of republicans impatient for change to whom the reputation of Napoleon III as the 'man of order' who had saved the country from anarchy after the 1848 revolution meant nothing.

In 1869 France seemed bound for revolution, and the government to have lost its grip. It was often a handicap to be identified as a government candidate in the elections that summer and the big cities voted heavily against the Empire. The elections were accompanied by riots in the cities, and by a wave of industrial unrest which saw striking miners shot down by troops. Although socialists and representatives of the extreme left did not do well in the elections, the results were an impressive showing for republicans. Opposition candidates polled 3.3 million votes against 4.4 million for government candidates. Gambetta was elected for the working-class Paris district of Belleville, standing on a radical platform that included a condemnation of standing armies as 'a cause of financial ruin' and 'a source of hatred between peoples'. However, he opted to represent a Marseilles constituency where he had also been elected, and at a by-election for Belleville in November Rochefort, returned from exile in Belgium, was elected in his place.

Although Napoleon continued to command the political centre ground, he slowly made concessions in the face of mounting opposition. He granted the Chamber additional powers. Rouher resigned, though he remained a confidential adviser and became President of the Senate. In December the Liberal Émile Ollivier, a former republican, was invited to form a ministry. This appeared to Napoleon to be the best way of saving his regime, though it created tensions among its loyal supporters. Those, including the Empress, Baron Jerome David (another nephew of Napoleon I) and Rouher, who believed that the imperial government needed more authoritarianism, not less, would await their opportunity to sabotage what they saw as the dangerous experiment of the 'Liberal Empire'.

Moltke is Ready

The victory of Sadowa made General von Moltke a celebrity, though an unlikely one. Intellectual, thin, clean-shaven, crisp and dry in speech and writing, he had the air more of an ascetic than a warrior. Although a gifted translator, he was so taciturn that the joke went that he could be silent in seven different languages. In 1867 he accompanied the king to the Paris Exhibition, was presented with the Grand Cross of the Legion of Honour, and had conversations with French marshals Niel and Canrobert. The social niceties over, he returned to his office in Berlin to devote his thought to the problems of waging war against France. As professional military men, both he and Niel privately believed that a war between France and the North German Confederation was inevitable. As Niel once put it, the two countries were not so much at peace as in a state of armistice.[14] It was Moltke's job, as it was Niel's, to ensure that his country was ready when the test came, and he went about his task diligently. As a conservative Prussian, he saw France as the principal source of the dangerous infections of democracy, radicalism and anarchy. As a German, he shared the nationalist belief that Germany could become secure only by neutralizing the French threat once and for all.

Following the war of 1866, the Prussian army became the core of the Army of the North German Confederation. Under War Minister Roon's direction, integration of the contingents of the annexed states into the Prussian military system proceeded without delay. As Prussian units were regionally based, other states' forces were readily accommodated into the order of battle while respecting state loyalties. Thus troops from Schleswig-Holstein became IX Corps of the Confederation Army, those of Hanover X Corps, those of Hesse, Nassau and Frankfurt XI Corps and the forces of Saxony XII Corps. In addition to the manpower provided by this regional expansion, the new army could call upon the enlarged pool of trained reserves produced by Roon's earlier reforms. While maintaining an active army of 312,000 men in 1867, the Confederation could call on 500,000 more fully trained reservists on mobilization, plus the *Landwehr* for home defence. Once the southern states' forces were included following the signing of military alliances, the numbers available swelled still further. By 1870 Germany would be able to mobilize over a million men.

The world had hardly seen such a large and well-disciplined force. Its backbone was the Prussian army, combat-hardened and commanded by experienced leaders, which had won the 1866 campaign. The post-war period allowed time to make promotions, weed out unsuitable commanders, and learn lessons of what could have been done better. The time was well used.

For instance, Prussian artillery had not performed as effectively as hoped against the Austrians for several reasons: faulty deployment, lack of coordination with other arms, technical failures, and want of tactical experience in handling a mixture of muzzle-loading smoothbores and the new breech-loading steel rifled cannons. All these deficiencies were addressed. At the king's insistence, Krupp's steel breech-loaders became standard, this time with Krupp's own more reliable breech blocks. From 1867 General von Hindersin required gunners to train hard at a practice range in Berlin until firing rapidly and accurately at distant targets became second nature. Batteries also practised rushing forward together in mass, even ahead of their infantry, to bring enemy infantry quickly under converging fire. Time and again, this would prove a devastating tactic. If the Battle of Waterloo proverbially was won on the playing fields of Eton, it is small exaggeration to say that Sedan was won on Germany's artillery ranges. The proficiency of German gunnery was to astound the French in 1870.

Less spectacular but equally important in conserving the lives of German troops were improvements to the medical service. The huge numbers of wounded after Sadowa had swamped the medical services. Disease and infection had spread rapidly in overcrowded field hospitals. In 1867 the best civilian and military doctors were called to Berlin, and their recommendations for reform were implemented over the next two years. The medical service was put in charge of a Surgeon General and army doctors were given enhanced authority and rank. Sanitary arrangements for the health of troops in the field were revised and their enforcement became part of the regular duties of troop commanders, who were also issued with pamphlets explaining their responsibilities under the 1864 Geneva Convention. Troops were issued with individual field-dressings to staunch bleeding. Medical units were created and all their personnel issued with Red Cross armbands. The units included stretcher-bearers trained in first aid who would be responsible for evacuating the wounded from the front to field hospitals. From there evacuation to base hospitals would be by rail using specially fitted out hospital trains. Once back in Germany, where the new Red Cross movement was taken very seriously, the wounded would be cared for with the help of civilian doctors assisted by volunteer nurses recruited and trained under the active patronage of Queen Augusta. Yet there would be no conflict of authorities in wartime, nor any room for civilian volunteers wandering about the combat zone under their own devices. The work of civilian doctors and nurses would be directed by a central military authority in Berlin. Like the artillery, the medical service was transformed between 1866 and 1870 by a systematic approach to overcoming the problems experienced in modern war.

This approach was epitomized by the General Staff itself under Moltke's direction. In 1866 the General Staff had established itself as the controlling brain of the army and had won confidence by its success. It recruited only the very best graduates from the Army War College, and had expanded to over one hundred officers, who were assigned either to specialist sections or to field commands. Its task was to ensure that the army in wartime operated like a well-oiled machine to a common plan. It worked effectively because it was well integrated with the command chain and avoided unnecessary centralization. Army corps were responsible for carrying out their part of the plan. The commander of every major unit had a chief of staff who was in effect Moltke's representative. Many senior commanders had themselves done staff duties, just as General Staff officers were required periodically to move to operational duties so that they understood the problems of field commanders. Germany's 15,000 officers were expected to show initiative in achieving objectives laid out in a general plan, and to understand their duty to support other units in pursuit of it. Moltke organized regular staff rides and war games to provide his officers with experience in solving command problems, together with related skills like map reading in the field. Intelligence on French forces and plans was continuously gathered and updated.

Between 1867 and 1870 Moltke continually revised plans for the rapid mobilization of German forces and their deployment on the French frontier. The expansion of the railway network, the increasing number of double-track lines, and continual refinements in planning enabled him to cut down the time needed for this operation from over four weeks in 1867 to just three weeks by 1870. Six main lines would carry North German troops to the western frontier, while three lines were available to the forces of the southern states. Every unit had detailed instructions and a precise timetable for moving from its depot to its destination and had practised embarkation. Arrangements were made for the provision of meals at fixed points along the route. However, efforts to improve arrangements for running supply trains behind the troops to avoid the problems of 1866 met with limited success, as events were to prove.

From 1868 Moltke's planning moved beyond how to cope with a possible French invasion of Germany to envisage an invasion of France. He would use three armies, plus one in reserve, to enter Lorraine and Alsace, where the French might be expected to gather their forces around the fortresses of Metz and Strasbourg respectively. Once across the frontier, he would seek to find and engage the French main force with his largest, centrally positioned force (Second Army) while bringing his right and left wings around to envelop the enemy. In this first phase he expected to be able to bring over 330,000 men into action against an estimated 250,000 French. He provided for the possibility of having to deploy an additional 100,000 men to face the Austrians in the south and the Danes in the north, as both might be expected to join in a war of revenge. These potential threats made it imperative to beat the French as quickly as possible. Such a war on several fronts had to be provided for, even though in early 1868 the Russians promised that in the event of a Franco-German war they would mobilize along their frontier with Austria to deter that power – Russia's rival in the Balkans – from intervening against Prussia. In either case, but particularly if France remained isolated, Moltke was confident that speed and mass were on his side, and that his strategic offensive could beat the French on their own ground. For all the care that went into his planning, flexibility was its essence. His memorandum to the General Staff of 6 May 1870 stated: 'The operations against France will consist simply in our advancing in as dense formation as possible for a few marches on French soil till we meet the French army and then fight a battle. The general direction of this advance is towards Paris, because in that direction we are most certain to hit the mark we are aiming at, the enemy's army.'[15]

France Lives on her Military Heritage

The French did not lack information about developments in Germany. Marshal Niel had spies there, and Moltke's staff rides along the frontier were kept under observation. From Strasbourg General Auguste Ducrot, commander of the 6th Military Division, kept up a stream of warnings about German military preparations and the activities of German spies in Alsace. Some of Ducrot's apprehensions were exaggerated and could be discounted and even ridiculed because of their intemperate tone. He was an advocate of a strike into southern Germany to restore French power, and was credulous of sources that encouraged him to believe that the French would be welcomed as liberators there. Ducrot's alarmist reports grew so irksome to the Emperor's advisors that they tried to move him to another command. Better balanced and informed reports came from Baron Stoffel, the French military attaché in Berlin, who kept his government abreast of troop numbers, improvements in artillery, the role of the General Staff, and the excellent training and spirit of the German army. He had experienced German hostility personally. While attending Prussian army manoeuvres at Stettin in September 1869 his carriage was pelted with stones amid shouts of 'French pig!' Stoffel warned that year that 'war is inevitable and at the mercy of an incident'[16] and contrasted Prussian foresight with French heedlessness and ignorance.

Yet Stoffel too was regarded as a Cassandra. The French high command remained confident. The Italian War of 1859 seemed to show that any problems on mobilization would be compensated for by the offensive spirit and their incomparable infantry. At the War Ministry there was fear of any radical reform which might disrupt tried and trusted routines. General Jules Trochu, whose contribution to the debate on army reform, *L'Armée française en 1867* offered many pertinent criticisms, became a pariah in official circles, and was identified with the political opposition.

The army certainly looked impressive on the parade ground. Every August since 1857 it had put on a show at Châlons Camp that drew enormous holiday crowds. The troops would march past the Emperor and recreate historic French victories in carefully choreographed exercises with a predetermined outcome. But behind the showy uniforms and the brass bands, how ready was the army to fight a war against an industrialized and highly organized European power?

After defeat in 1870 it became almost too easy to contrast German efficiency with French muddle, and to distract attention from bad command decisions by blaming organizational faults. Yet undeniably the French failure to plan and prepare systematically for mobilization dramatically reduced their chances of victory. Not that there were no war plans. In 1867 General Frossard, a military engineer who was tutor to the Prince Imperial, had drawn up recommendations for holding two fine defensive positions: on the Frœschwiller ridge in Alsace and around Cadenbronn in Lorraine, and had reconnoitred the ground thoroughly. This plan had not been officially adopted, however. In 1868 Napoleon and General Lebrun had worked on another involving the formation of three armies, one at Metz, one at Strasbourg and one at Châlons, ready to launch an offensive. An order of battle, with the names of officers who would command units in these armies was drawn up and regularly updated, though it bore no relation to peacetime commands. The War Ministry was responsible for all aspects of preparation, but it lacked any central senior coordinating body to set objectives and priorities, and ensure that all departments worked together on a coherent mobilization plan. In the highly centralized government of imperial France that impulse could only come from the very top, as it did in Prussia: but it did not come.

Marshal Niel, though heavily preoccupied with the conscription issue, managed a few useful if modest measures. He simplified administrative arrangements for recalling reservists, which would save valuable time. In 1869 he convened a Central Railways Commission which drew up regulations and recommendations for troop movements, but this exercise bore no fruit. Le Bœuf, Niel's successor, allowed the commission to lapse. Getting troops on and off trains seemed such an obvious exercise that officers and NCOs were not trained in it. The eight directorates at the War Ministry, though each highly centralized and often obsessed with bureaucracy and cost-cutting, tended to work in isolation. For instance, the Intendance, the powerful department responsible for purchasing and supply, transport, pay and the medical service, was independent of field commanders and took orders directly from the Ministry. While it had plenty of material stored in huge central warehouses, plans for distributing supplies from railheads to the troops who would need them were inadequate and would be at the mercy of whatever operational plan was finally adopted. When war broke out the railway companies, instead of working to a well-prepared plan implemented by a single authority, would find themselves receiving separate orders from the Intendance, the artillery, the engineers, and the department responsible for troop movements, ending in confusion that should have been predictable and preventable.

Though she possessed gifted individual staff officers trained at the Staff College established in 1818, France had no equivalent of the Prussian General Staff. Commanders too often used the staff assigned to them as glorified clerks and messengers and did not take them into their confidence. Staff officers usually had little regimental experience and (like officers of the Intendance) were resented in combat units as a gilded elite who won promotions in comfortable jobs. Collectively, staff officers did not bear the responsibility for planning and coordination exercised by their Prussian counterparts, or enjoy comparable authority and status in the chain of command.

Even at best, French war planning was partial and disjointed, with too much reliance placed on improvisation and 'muddling through' to cover critical gaps in a very complex operation. System D – *débrouillez vous* ('muddle through somehow') – became, in the words of one officer 'the great excuse for incomplete orders, superficial studies and half-organized services'.[17] Yet some deficiencies were too deeply rooted to be remedied by any amount of last-minute improvisation. With some shining exceptions, the standard of general and professional education of French officers was well below the average of German officers. The prevailing ethos was that such mundane matters as administration and supply were beneath the consideration of warriors eager for *la gloire* who expected to win promotion through bravery. They and their troops had plenty of practice in drill, but almost none in field manoeuvres or how to organize a route march. Maps were in short supply, and junior officers were expected to buy them from their allowances once a campaign began. Even then, few officers had practice in reading them, and many had little idea even of the topography of areas where they had been garrisoned for years.

Many French soldiers would pay a heavy price for the failure to reform the French army medical service after the lessons of the Crimean and Italian wars. Although a new Army Medical School had been opened at Strasbourg in 1856, still there were insufficient doctors to meet even the army's peacetime needs. Hospital doctors had officer rank, but little authority over army personnel, and were subordinate to officers of the Intendance. Thus surgeons had only limited say in the location of field hospitals, the food and medicine to be given to their patients and the equipment they needed. The whole system, an English surgeon observed, seemed calculated to reduce any benefit to the troops to a minimum.[18] The wounded would be brought from the front line either by mule drivers or by regimental bandsmen detailed for the purpose.

The Red Cross organization was resented. 'The Intendance and the army medical service spoke of [it] with disdain ... they delighted in making game of the Geneva Convention, which they considered a piece of humanitarian nonsense and the hobby-horse of a few cranks. The emblem of neutrality seemed worthless to them: "Did we need that thing in Italy or the Crimea?" Hospital wagons did not display the Red Cross banner, nor did officers of the army medical corps adopt the armband.'[19] The French Red Cross Society was little more than a salon affair, more concerned with organizing fund-raising events than with serious preparation for war, and there was no formal agreement governing its relations with military authority in wartime.

The artillery, like the Intendance and the medical service, suffered from a lack of money, men and horses. French War Ministers could not, like Roon in Berlin, count on generous funding safe from parliamentary scrutiny. Re-arming the infantry with the Chassepot and producing the *mitrailleuse* were so expensive that the Legislature reduced funds requested for other arms. In any case, Le Bœuf, an artillery expert whose handling of the 1858 model muzzle-loading rifled bronze cannon had helped win Solferino, saw no reason to change it. He was comfortable with the 12-pounder, a weapon the Emperor himself had helped to develop and which had proved its worth in the American Civil War. Le Bœuf knew from Stoffel what the Germans were doing with breech-loaders and considered the matter in 1868 when Krupp, ever anxious to fill his order books, tried to interest the French in buying some of his steel guns. Admittedly, Sadowa had hardly proved beyond doubt that they were a miracle weapon. Several accidents with burst steel barrels during the campaign raised doubts whether they were superior to bronze, and they were certainly a great deal more expensive. Le Bœuf was aware that many German officers shared the same misgivings, and he concluded that, pending further tests and the develop-ment of a French steel gun, further action was unnecessary. He believed that the French army had more than enough field guns, though in truth the Germans had over twice as many, and ones with a superior range and rate of fire at that.

Even so, French cannon might have been more effective had they used shell with a percussion fuse that exploded on impact, like the one used by the Prussians. Instead the French adopted more sophisticated time fuses that could be cut to detonate the shell in the air at set distances. This system, which made it safer to transport shells, was favoured by the Emperor. Supposedly it simplified and speeded up the gunner's task, but in practice the choice of pre-set ranges available was too limited. This inflexibility would be compounded by poor tactics, for French practice did not allow for massing of batteries early in an engagement for maximum effect. Once again it was the Prussians, the victims of Napoleon I, who had learned his style of warfare better than his military heirs. In this field, as in so many others, the French were much further behind the Germans than they imagined, despite the spur of continuing tension between the two countries.

That tension manifested itself in minor incidents, despite official declarations of peaceful intentions by both sides which might have been more convincing had they been less often repeated.[20] In February 1868 Bismarck protested against the exiled King of Hanover being permitted to muster his Legion in Alsace, and the French acted to disperse it. On 16 September there was a brief panic on the Paris Stock Exchange when an abbreviated news telegram gave the false impression that King Wilhelm had made a bellicose speech at Kiel. More serious was the reaction of the Paris press to the Belgian railways imbroglio of February 1869. Even after its rebuff over Luxembourg, the French government had not given up its designs on the region. Seeking economic penetration of the Low Countries, it backed the takeover by a French company of the Luxembourg rail network, which had branches into Belgium. A similar deal with a major Belgian railway was very close to completion when the Belgian Parliament quickly passed legislation to block the move. The French were livid. Paris newspapers were full of menaces against the Belgians, and accused Bismarck of again working covertly to thwart France, using the Belgians as his cat's-paw. Napoleon, who had never taken the idea of Belgian nationality seriously, momentarily contemplated the possibility of an invasion of Belgium. Such a move, he wrote to Niel, would restore French prestige. He outlined the strategic advantages occupying a country that, in the event of war with Prussia, 'would open the doors of Germany to us', and, he thought, add 100,000 Belgians to his army. If Germany tried to interfere, 'she would be the provocateur' and 'if this opportunity passes, when shall we find another? It isn't easy to find occasions to declare war when all the right is on one's side.' For Napoleon believed that 'Prussia will carefully avoid giving us plausible pretexts [to declare war on her]. She advances stealthily, like a wolf, always in such a manner as to show us up, if we grow angry, as the instigators of war and enemies of the unification of Germany.'[21]

Though he was glad to see the French in difficulties, Bismarck was not behind the Belgian refusal. The Belgian government had reasons enough of its own to stand firm in defence of its neutrality and political independence, which would have been gravely compromised by French economic domination. Belgium had no wish to become the battleground between France and Prussia, and received British diplomatic backing for her stand against French intimidation. Once more disappointed in her ambitions, France backed down. The Belgian affair had highlighted her suspicions of Prussia, the sensitivity of French public opinion, and the uneasy equilibrium between the two powers. The substantial issue between them remained how far France would tolerate further Prussian gains in Germany, gains which she felt diminished and threatened her own power.

The South German Question

In 1866 Napoleon III had insisted that the four German states lying south of the River Main should retain an 'independent national existence' – wording included in the Treaty of Prague despite Bismarck's attempt to drop it. The Luxembourg confrontation made it less likely than ever that imperial France would accept peacefully the creation of the enlarged and powerful German state that would result from a union between North and South. Bismarck was therefore wary of mounting pressure from Liberals and nationalists in the North who wanted to push him towards more active pursuit of the goal of national unification, or at least the 'Little German' version of it. Besides, the South was politically and culturally very different from the North, and at first he had more than enough to do consolidating the North German Confederation without attempting the impracticable task of absorbing the South simultaneously. Nevertheless, he was initially optimistic that union with the South would be only 'a matter of time',[22] and he set about promoting stronger ties.

The conclusion of offensive-defensive alliances with the southern states before the Treaty of Prague was even signed was a bold opening move, but their publication made Prussia even more unpopular in the South. The realization that they would have no say in decisions of war and peace disturbed many southerners, and fear of being drawn into a war over Luxembourg in the spring of 1867 by a Prussian-dominated North more than counterbalanced enthusiasm for union among middle-class commercial circles. Over the next three years resentment deepened as the financial and social costs of absorption to Prussia's military system hit home. The adoption of Prussian-style discipline and drill, conscription and higher taxes made sense to southern governments and military authorities as defensive measures, but many of their citizens feared that union with the authoritarian and militarized North simply meant that they would have to 'pay up, join up and shut up'.[23]

Yet, sandwiched uncomfortably between three rival great powers, what alternative had the southern states? The revelation of France's ambitions in the Rhineland made her appear a predator rather than a protector. The opportunity France had in the 1820s to pre-empt Prussia and make clients of the southern states by bringing them into her customs system had been missed because of French protectionism, and now membership of the German Customs Union was an economic necessity to the South. Bismarck knew this and attempted to use it as a lever to attach the South more firmly to the North. He devised a plan for a Customs Parliament consisting of members of the North German Reichstag and elected representatives from the South. The South German states had reluctantly to accept the plan, but elections there in 1868 showed how strong separatist sentiment was. Catholics, who made up 5 million of the 8.7 million people of the South, feared union with the Protestant North; many conservatives, peasants and workers saw in it a dangerous threat to their way of life and remained strongly loyal to their states. Of the eighty-five members of the Customs Parliament democratically elected from the South and sent to Berlin, forty-nine opposed greater unification and used their power to block northern moves in that direction. Seeing the Customs Parliament determined to confine itself to economic issues and unwilling to play the political part he had cast it for, Bismarck lost interest. Other expedients he explored were no more fruitful. A proposal for a loose political federation and hopes that the South German states might join together in a single entity that would help dissolve particularist sentiment and facilitate ties with the North were resisted by the South. With apparent resignation, Bismarck famously wrote to the frustrated Prussian Minister to Bavaria in February 1869:

> Arbitrary interference in the course of history ... has only ever resulted in the shaking down of unripe fruit. That German unity is not at this moment a ripe fruit is obvious in my opinion ... We can put the clocks forward, but time does not move faster on that account, and the ability to wait, while the situation develops, is a prerequisite of practical politics.[24]

Of the four southern states, only the government of the Grand Duchy of Baden was amenable to closer union, largely because its Grand Duke was Protestant and the son-in-law of King Wilhelm of Prussia, and ruled a state bordering the Rhine, so had most to fear from French invasion. Military integration therefore proceeded more smoothly than in the other states. In February 1870 a Liberal deputy in the Reichstag proposed admitting Baden to the North German Confederation, but Bismarck opposed the move as ill-timed. French reaction would be hostile, and he had no intention of allowing the National Liberals in the Reichstag to provoke war or dictate the pace of unification in a way that would increase their powers. If Prussia's best friend in the South were admitted prematurely, it would make winning over recalcitrant Württemberg and Bavaria even harder. Indeed, resistance in those states was becoming stronger rather than weaker by 1869–70, as election results and a monster petition against conscription in Württemberg demonstrated. Local 'Patriot' parties were everywhere in the ascendant over German nationalists, and arguments over closer union were throwing southern politics into dangerous turmoil.

Early in 1870 Bismarck made one further effort to promote the national idea. He floated a proposal that King Wilhelm, instead of being styled President of the North German Confederation, should assume the title of Emperor. But this idea too fell flat. The National Liberals in the Reichstag wanted concessions on ministerial responsibility that Bismarck was unwilling to yield. The other German princes, including the kings of Württemberg and Bavaria, made known their displeasure at one of their number being elevated above them.

For all Bismarck's efforts, his many opponents in the South could rejoice that, in the words of a Bavarian journal, the Prussian engine had been halted at the line of the Main. Union between North and South, let alone one legitimized by popular votes, looked even less likely in the spring of 1870 than it had in the autumn of 1866. It needed no genius to see that the only circumstance in which the South German states would willingly join with the North would be that of an unprovoked attack by France which would activate the military alliances with Prussia. That alone might overcome separatist sentiment and rally all Germans to the national cause. Bismarck occasionally spoke of the possibility, even inevitability, of war with France, though disclaiming any desire to bear the responsibility for bringing it about. It was, nevertheless, at a juncture when prospects for promoting voluntary union with the South looked bleakest that he secretly set in train an initiative that had the potential to lead to a major diplomatic crisis with France.

Chapter 4

The Crisis

The Liberal Empire

The year 1870 opened on a note of optimism and renewal in France. After months of political uncertainty, a Liberal ministry took office on 2 January. The most prominent figure in it was the eloquent, well-intentioned but inexperienced Émile Ollivier, who embarked on an ambitious programme of constitutional reform with the support of the political centre in the Legislature. Gambetta might rail at the new administration that 'You are nothing but a bridge between the Republic of 1848 and the Republic to come, and we shall pass over that bridge!'[1], but for the moment republicans remained a noisy minority.

The new government showed its determination to deal firmly with disorder from the Left. On 10 January a hot-tempered cousin of the Emperor's, Prince Pierre Bonaparte, shot dead a republican journalist, Victor Noir, who had struck the Prince while delivering a challenge to a duel from a radical editor whose insults to the Bonaparte family had incurred the Prince's wrath. Noir's employer, Henri Rochefort, who had been party to the war of words preceding this incident, boldly attacked the dynasty in his paper, *La Marseillaise*, declaring, 'I have been so weak as to believe a Bonaparte could be other than an assassin! ... For eighteen years now France has been held in the bloodied hands of these cut-throats, who, not content to shoot down republicans in the streets, draw them into dirty traps in order to slit their throats in private. Frenchmen, have you not had quite enough of it?'[2]

Funerals were favourite occasions for political demonstrations in France, and Noir's on 12 January threatened to spark revolution. Some 100,000 people gathered in the western suburbs of Paris. The more violent revolutionaries, followers of Auguste Blanqui, tried to lead the funeral procession into the centre of the capital to start an insurrection. But the government deployed troops, and more experienced republicans like Delescluze, seconded by the timid Rochefort, concluded that the procession should go instead straight to the Neuilly cemetery, so averting violent confrontation. In February Rochefort was arrested at a meeting, charged with insulting the Emperor and inciting civil war, and imprisoned for six months. Some 450 radical activists were also arrested. With even-handedness, Prince Pierre was put on trial, though the court found that he had acted in self-defence and acquitted him.

The government had passed its first test confidently, but hostility from the Right would prove more insidious and eventually fatal. That hostility was deep-rooted among loyalists of the authoritarian Empire, who wanted restoration of Napoleon's personal rule. They resented seeing power wielded by politicians who in many cases were Liberal monarchists still loyal to the Orléans dynasty, and who had opposed the coup d'état of 1851. When Ollivier set about reforming the Senate as a step towards introducing genuine parliamentary government, a committee of senators led by Rouher suggested to the Emperor that such a change to the constitution approved by the plebiscite of 1852 required popular endorsement. Napoleon was persuaded, and in April announced that a plebiscite would be held asking whether or not voters approved of the Liberal reforms he had introduced since 1860. The question was cleverly posed, for in endorsing reform voters had also to endorse the Empire. The decision to hold a plebiscite disconcerted the Centre Left, who saw a direct appeal by the sovereign to the people as incompatible with the introduction of parliamentary sovereignty. Two ministers resigned over the issue, including Count Daru, the Foreign Minister.

After a lively campaign, the vote was held on 8 May. Although some opponents of the regime abstained, enough voted to show that Paris and other big cities remained irreconcilably hostile to the Empire. In the country as a whole it was a different story. The national vote was 7,358,786 in favour, 1,571,939 against, with 1,894,681 abstentions. It was hard to deny that it was a major triumph for Napoleon after his recent difficulties. It seemed that the veteran political operator had not lost his touch after all. 'The enemies of our institutions have made an issue between revolution and the Empire. The country has decided,' he pronounced. The eventual succession of the Prince Imperial seemed assured. Gambetta was devastated, confessing privately that 'the Emperor is stronger than ever', and he thought that the Empire might last another ten years.[3]

Republicans could take solace from the apparent effectiveness of their propaganda among troops stationed in the cities. A sixth of the army voted 'no' in the plebiscite. Publication of the results for the armed forces conveniently informed the Germans that the French army had 299,494 men present for duty.

One of the Ollivier ministry's first foreign policy initiatives had been to sound Bismarck secretly about possible mutual troop reductions. Ollivier himself believed in the principle of nationality and thought peaceful co-existence with Germany possible. 'The moment to halt Prussia has passed, irrevocably passed,' he wrote just before taking office, and in February 1870 he told the

Cologne Gazette that, so far as he was concerned, 'There is no German question.'[4] Rather than approach Bismarck directly, that month Daru used the good offices of the British Foreign Minister, Lord Clarendon, to broach the disarmament question. Bismarck rejected the proposal, arguing that as Germany held a central position between three strong powers she had to be able to defend herself, and that King Wilhelm would not countenance changes to his military system. Despite this rebuff, the French proceeded with plans to reduce their annual contingent by 10,000 men to 90,000, and the Liberal Empire seemed to have ushered in an easing of Franco-German tensions.

Following Daru's resignation and the plebiscite, Napoleon cast around for a new Foreign Minister, and eventually chose Duc Agénor de Gramont, a career diplomat who had served eight years as French ambassador to Austria. Bismarck and others in Germany interpreted this as a hostile move by a strengthened Napoleon. Gramont, an aristocrat who had rallied to the Bonapartist regime, believed that further Prussian ambitions should be checked, and was a known advocate of alliance with Austria.

Napoleon, who in foreign policy as in other fields took secret initiatives without informing his ministers or ambassadors, had been pursuing an alliance with Austria since 1867, and expected Gramont to be helpful in this regard. Talks with Austria had continued sporadically in 1868 and 1869, but had produced little more than expressions of goodwill between the sovereigns. The Austrians wished to maintain good relations with France, but feared that they had more to lose than to gain by joining too eagerly in any war of revenge against Prussia. They avoided giving any formal commitment. Attempts to bring Italy into a triple alliance foundered on continued French occupation of Rome. Yet Napoleon, regarding the treaty as 'morally signed',[5] persisted in assuming that Austria would not stand aloof if a Franco–Prussian war did come – for instance, in the event that Prussia should attempt to seize the South German states by force. In March 1870 the Austrian Archduke Albrecht visited Paris and Napoleon discussed with him the strategy to be pursued in such a war. On 19 May Napoleon expounded to Generals Le Bœuf, Frossard and Lebrun the resulting plan, whereby French troops would advance into Bavaria and join with the Austrians and Italians before marching on Berlin. His generals were concerned that such a scheme could work only if the allies mobilized simultaneously.

Yet when General Lebrun, the Emperor's aide, travelled to Vienna in June to discuss the military details of this strategy, Albrecht made clear that he regarded such planning as a theoretical exercise only, insisting that Austria would need six weeks to mobilize before declaring war. Albrecht's calculations, like Napoleon's, seriously underestimated the likely speed of German mobilization and the numbers they could bring to bear. Moreover, Emperor Franz Josef emphasized to Lebrun that he desired peace, and would only make common cause with Napoleon if he were to arrive in South Germany with his armies 'not as an enemy but as a liberator'.[6] If war broke out, in other words, the Austrians would wait on the sidelines until the French were winning.

Lebrun returned to Paris, saw the Emperor, and submitted his formal report on 30 June – by chance on the day that Ollivier justified the reduction in the annual military contingent by declaring to the Legislature that 'the government has no anxieties, and that at no time has the maintenance of peace in Europe appeared to us better assured.'[7] June was indeed a languid month. French farmers were worried by drought caused by the hot weather, and at the prospect of a bad harvest the War Ministry had begun to sell horses. In Germany, Bismarck, Moltke and Roon escaped the heat of Berlin to spend the summer on their country estates. On 1 July the Emperor Napoleon was examined by five eminent surgeons, who were divided on whether an operation was necessary for his chronic bladder complaint. Next evening, news reports reached Paris from Madrid that Prince Leopold of Hohenzollern-Sigmaringen, a cousin of King Wilhelm's, the son of a former Prussian Minister-President, and a serving Prussian officer, had been offered the Spanish throne.

Spanish Complications

In September 1868 Queen Isabella II of Spain had been overthrown. For the Spanish generals who seized power in the faction-ridden kingdom, finding a new monarch proved a frustrating business, complicated by Great Power interests. France, for instance, objected strongly to the candidacy of a son of King Louis Philippe of the Orléans dynasty. Attempts to put Portuguese or Italian princes on the Spanish throne were no more successful, due to a combination of internal politics, the reservations of France and Britain about a possible union between Spain and Portugal, and the reluctance of the candidates themselves when considering such a precarious honour. Among several candidates discussed in Madrid from the autumn of 1868, Leopold of Hohenzollern-Sigmaringen had much to recommend him. Leopold was in his prime, an army officer, and married to a Portuguese princess. Though a Hohenzollern, he was Catholic: his branch of the family had stayed on their ancestral estates in south Germany when the other branch had set off in the Middle Ages to find lands and fortune in Brandenburg to the north.

The French became aware that Leopold's name was being aired in Madrid. Napoleon had no quarrel with the Sigmaringens. He was related to them on his mother's side, had supported Charles, Leopold's elder brother, in his successful bid for the Rumanian throne in 1866, and had even recommended Leopold himself for the Greek throne in 1863. But all that had been before Sadowa and Luxembourg. To have a Prussian prince on the throne of France's southern neighbour was quite another matter. Napoleon believed that France would not stand for it and that it must be prevented.[8] In March 1869 Benedetti, the French ambassador, told the Prussian Foreign Ministry that the possibility 'interested the Emperor's government too directly for it not to be my duty to call attention to the fact'. In May Benedetti sounded Bismarck on the issue, and Bismarck commented that, were the Spanish to make an offer, both King Wilhelm and the Sigmaringen family would be against Leopold's embarking on such a hazardous adventure.[9]

King Wilhelm and Prince Karl Anton, Leopold's father, had already exchanged views to this effect, and held to them when the Spanish made a preliminary approach to the Sigmaringens in September 1869. Karl Anton told the Spanish negotiator that the consent of both Napoleon and Wilhelm would be necessary if European peace were not to be imperilled.[10] Five months passed before the Spanish, thwarted with regard to other candidates, renewed their secret approaches more formally in February 1870. It was only at this point that Bismarck took up the Hohenzollern candidacy in earnest. He drew up a report to the king urging the advantages to Germany and the Hohenzollern dynasty. A military ally on France's southern border could force her to detach an army corps to deal with that threat in the event of a war with Germany. Moltke advocated this argument, and had envisaged Spanish support in his 1869 military plan. Spain as an ally would provide a counterweight to the possible French alliance with Austria and Italy. Conversely, if the Spanish became allies of France, they might free French troops by providing the garrison for Rome. There would also be prestige for the Hohenzollern dynasty in supplying a king for Spain, elevating it to a status not seen since the Habsburg Emperor Charles V in the sixteenth century. Besides, a refusal might offend the Spaniards and cause them to turn to the Bavarian royal house instead – or, worse, open the way to a republic. Bismarck also alleged great commercial advantages.

King Wilhelm was sceptical of this reasoning, but called a special meeting for the evening of 15 March to discuss the matter. Those present included the Crown Prince, Karl Anton and Leopold, Roon and Moltke. Bismarck presented his case, which was strongly supported by Roon and Moltke. Wilhelm was unmoved. He considered Spain too unstable to justify the risk, quite apart from the possible reaction of other powers. As head of the family he would not encourage or support Leopold's candidacy, but at most would give his reluctant consent if Leopold really wanted to go. Leopold did not. Nor, it transpired during April, did his younger brother.

Bismarck kept negotiations with Spain's rulers going anyway, assuring them that the obstacles could be overcome, but by mid–May it looked as if Wilhelm's objections had brought the matter to an end. On 13 May Bismarck, wracked by bouts of illness, lamented, 'The Spanish business has taken a wretched turn. Unquestionable *raison d'état* has been subordinated to the private inclinations of the princes ... The ill-feeling caused by it has weighed heavily on my nerves for weeks.'[11] Within a fortnight, however, his persistence bore fruit. His agents were busy both in Spain and at persuading Karl Anton and Leopold to change their minds and to seize the opportunity that might soon be lost. For years afterwards Bismarck would maintain the fiction that he had had no interest in the candidacy, that there had been no March meeting, and that the matter was purely dynastic rather than the concern of the Prussian government. Yet in the spring of 1870 he worked to convince the reluctant dynasts concerned that Germany's vital interests required Leopold's acceptance. Such arguments, mingled with family pride and ambition, won over Karl Anton by the beginning of June. Leopold, obedient to his father, became convinced that national interests required him to sacrifice his personal inclinations.

King Wilhelm, cross to discover that a matter he had thought closed had been pursued behind his back, gave the candidacy his consent on 21 June 'with a very heavy heart'.[12] A coded telegram sent from Berlin that day by the Spanish negotiator, Salazar, announced that he would return to Madrid on 26 June with news, indicating that the Spanish parliament – the Cortes – should be kept in session so that the candidate could be elected. The telegram was wrongly decoded: perhaps deliberately by an opponent of the candidacy in the German embassy at Madrid. As deciphered, it said that Salazar would not return until 9 July: too long to keep the Cortes waiting in the intense heat. Marshal Prim, head of the government, prorogued it and retired to the country. When Salazar returned to Madrid and found neither Prim nor the Cortes waiting for him, he could not resist telling people about the success of his mission. When Prim returned to Madrid on 1 July he was horrified to learn at the railway station that the secret of the Hohenzollern candidature had become common knowledge. He had intended to broach the subject with Napoleon III during July, once the Cortes had voted the election. Now he realized he must act quickly. On 2 July he called in the French ambassador, opening with the words, 'I have to talk to you about something that I fear will not please the Emperor, and you must help me to keep him from taking it in too bad part.'[13] It was thus that the news reached Paris officially next day.

Because the Hohenzollern candidacy led to the Franco-Prussian War and because, despite his denials, Bismarck was a prime mover in promoting the candidacy between February and June 1870, argument over his intentions has been intense. Can the strategic and dynastic reasons he gave in March be taken at face value, as his admirers urge? Or did he aim from the beginning at provoking war, as the French always believed? Although documents captured in Berlin after the Second World War proved that Bismarck's professions of not being involved in the candidacy were disingenuous – to use no stronger term – there is no conclusive proof of his motive. There is almost no mention in official documents of likely French reaction, though this aspect of the matter concerned Karl Anton, who predicted in February that a Hohenzollern on the Spanish throne 'would give rise to a wild outcry in anti-Prussian Europe'.[14] That Bismarck did not see this at least as clearly as Karl Anton is improbable, even if he could not foresee the exact timing and sequence of a confrontation with France. In his memoirs Bismarck, doubtless tongue in cheek, affected surprise that Napoleon should object to having one of his relatives on the Spanish throne.[15] Yet from the outset German strategic interest in Spain was aimed at countering French interests. Bismarck had commented in October 1868 that 'a solution agreeable to Napoleon would hardly be the useful one for us.'[16] In June 1870 Karl Anton raised further concerns with Bismarck's agent and friend, Major Max von Versen of the General Staff, about his son's candidacy giving rise to 'complications' with France. Versen replied, 'Bismarck says that is just what he is looking for.' Karl Anton rejoined, 'Yes, Count Bismarck may want it, but is it really in the interests of the State?'[17]

What did 'complications' mean? War? Another confrontation with France like the one over Luxembourg, that would reawaken the national movement in South Germany? A resulting revolution in France that might topple Napoleon and bring a regime more disposed to accept German unity? No one can say with certainty. In any event, the flexible Bismarck could exploit the situation to Germany's advantage and, crucially, he operated in the confidence that Germany was militarily prepared and France relatively weak. As he told the Russian ambassador in March 1868, 'We believe ourselves equal to a war against France alone.'[18] However peaceful Bismarck's utterances to politicians at home, in February 1869 he had speculated to the Russian ambassador that, in the event of a war involving Russia in Eastern Europe, 'complications might lead to a war between us and France.' 'Nothing would be easier,' he said, 'than to compel the French government to mobilize to avoid the consequences and the effect on public opinion in France of measures he had in mind to take in Germany.' France would thus have to 'assume the role of aggressor against Germany'. Bismarck stressed to the Russian that this would be the option of last resort, and that he would prefer that the South German question were further advanced.[19] In his own record of the conversation, Bismarck wrote that in such a scenario 'we would try to create a situation which would force

France to attack or, at least, threaten Germany. Troop movements, national manifestations in Germany and Italy, our relations with Belgium or even with Spain, would give us the opportunity of a diversion which would bring about our intervention without giving the appearance of an aggressive Cabinet war.'[20]

This specimen of Bismarck's thinking in 1869 is not proof of his motives in 1870, but it shows that he had ruminated on how war with France might be provoked without Germany being the aggressor, something he preferred to avoid. That he was tempted to advance German unity by somehow exploiting the Hohenzollern candidature is probable. That he did not foresee a strong French reaction once the candidature was announced strains credulity. He may have calculated that the French would back down once more, but his own analysis of French politics was that the French Right was awaiting its opportunity where Germany was concerned.[21] In the conditions of nineteenth-century diplomacy, particularly given recent tensions between France and Germany and the state of armaments, any confrontation carried a high risk of war. At the very least, Bismarck accepted that risk when he secretly promoted the Spanish project. It has become customary to stress his skill at keeping his options open, but by June, and perhaps much earlier, the option of conciliation with France had evidently ceased to be useful or attractive to him. He would demonstrate this beyond doubt during the coming crisis.

'The Devil is Loose at Paris'

The term 'media frenzy' had not been coined in 1870, yet those momentous thirteen days between news of the Hohenzollern candidature spreading around Paris on 3 July and the effective French declaration of war on Prussia on 15 July were a disastrous instance of that phenomenon. The crisis that escalated with astonishing speed over those sultry days was primarily a Parisian event, with newspapers fuelling popular hysteria in the capital. Voices of moderation certainly existed but were soon drowned out, or found themselves drawn into the vortex. Initially rational demands for satisfaction built to a pitch where war was imperatively demanded as the only conceivable release from an intolerable situation.

Leading the pack in violence, though not in circulation, was Paul de Cassagnac, editor of *Le Pays*, son of the authoritarian Bonapartist Deputy Adolphe Granier de Cassagnac and like him a ferocious duellist. He boasted on 21 July, 'The press has preached a crusade. From the pulpit of our editorials we called the people to arms, and the people came.'[22] Prominent also were the war cries of Émile de Girardin, pioneer of the cheap press in France and an influential press baron. Already by 5 July an overwhelming chorus of voices in the capital insisted that France could not accept Leopold's nomination, which was seen as a deliberate provocation by Prussia. All the pent-up fears of Prussian aggrandizement since 1866, the failure of the government to reassert France's position, and the insouciance with which Bismarck was seen to have inflicted successive humiliations on France, now came to a head. Injured vanity at seeing a parvenu power initiating changes in Europe without French permission played its part, but France had cause for grievance. There was widespread shock at the sudden revelation of the Spanish succession intrigue, for by diplomatic convention France might have expected to be consulted by Spain. As the London *Times* put it in considering the intense excitement in France, nobody liked being tricked. Such proceedings were 'grossly discourteous to foreign Powers. The whole transaction too has the air of a vulgar and impudent *coup d'état* of a kind that is sure not to be successful.'[23] In the view of Prime Minister Gladstone, the strict secrecy of proceedings was 'inconsistent with the spirit of friendship or the rules of comity between nations'.[24]

The outrage felt in France deepened when, in response to the French enquiry as to what the Prussian government knew of the affair, the Foreign Office in Berlin coolly replied that it knew nothing of the matter, which did not exist officially so far as it was concerned. This flat refusal to negotiate only increased the impression that Germany was bent on provocation. On 5 July the Duc de Gramont told the British ambassador, Lord Lyons, that the Hohenzollern candidature was 'nothing less than an insult to France' and the government 'would not endure it'.[25] Next morning the Prussian ambassador told a colleague, 'The Devil is loose at Paris: it looks very much like war.'[26]

After the war ended so disastrously for France, her leaders in the crisis, Napoleon III, Gramont and Ollivier, all strove to show that they had been helpless in the face of public opinion. Ministers felt that they had a tiger by the tail. Gramont wired ambassador Benedetti on 10 July, 'You can't imagine how excited public opinion is. We are overwhelmed by it, and are counting the hours.'[27] Later republican myths that street demonstrations were whipped up by the imperial police were merely a convenient way of making a scapegoat of the fallen regime.

Nevertheless, for all the ink spilled in later denials, the imperial regime rushed towards the brink of war, and would have enjoyed the accolades had the conflict ended victoriously. The handsome, haughty and excitable Gramont demonstrated none of the restraint shown by the deceased Moustier during the Luxembourg crisis. Gramont rightly suspected that Bismarck was behind the Spanish scheme and believed he was the man to stand up to him at last. Both he and Napoleon took a number of initiatives to persuade other European governments and monarchs to intercede with Spain, King Wilhelm and the Sigmaringens to withdraw the candidacy, but, rather than give these efforts time to succeed, raised the stakes by publicly threatening war almost immediately. If the Cabinet became the victim of popular passions in the capital, it could largely thank its own reckless efforts to court and outbid them. It was the Minister of the Interior who on 4 July dined with Girardin and invited him to write an article making the case for war with Prussia.

A marked escalation came on 6 July, when the Cabinet met to discuss the statement Gramont would make to the Legislature. The first draft was restrained, but was given a cutting edge by a strong final paragraph drafted by Ollivier, endorsed by Napoleon and unanimously adopted. Ollivier's respect for German nationality had never been unqualified: 'One rebuff [from Prussia] means war,' he had said before the crisis.[28] He was as sensitive to national honour as Gramont, and wished his Liberal administration to be seen to be as firm in foreign affairs as in domestic. Proud of his eloquence, he seemed unable to gauge the effect of his words on foreign powers. Gramont read the amended declaration to the Chamber that afternoon. After a dutiful bow to Spanish sovereignty, he continued:

> 'But we do not believe that respect for the rights of a neighbouring people obliges us to suffer that a foreign power, by placing one of its princes on the throne of Charles V, may disturb to our disadvantage the present balance of power in Europe ... (*Loud and enthusiastic applause*) ... and place in jeopardy the interests and honour of France. (*Fresh applause and bravos.*)
>
> 'We firmly hope that this eventuality will not be realized.
>
> 'To prevent it, we count both on the wisdom of the German and the friendship of the Spanish peoples.'
>
> [Adolphe de] Cassagnac: 'And on our resolve!' ...
>
> Gramont: 'If it should be otherwise, gentlemen, strong in your support and in that of the nation' ...
>
> Laroche-Joubert: 'You won't find it lacking!'
>
> Gramont: ... 'We shall know how to fulfil our duty without hesitation or weakness.' (*Long applause. Repeated cheering.*)[29]

Protests from the Left were shouted down and the session was soon adjourned. A troubled deputy reproached Gramont, 'But this means war! You've thrown down the gauntlet to Prussia!' Gramont replied, 'It is peace if it's still possible; it's war if it's unavoidable.'[30] Yet in the language of the day his words were clearly understood as a threat. A majority of Paris newspapers approved Gramont's firm line, but both North and South Germans now feared that France was bent on war on any pretext. Imperious and hasty, Gramont was burning his diplomatic bridges and had dangerously reduced the space for compromise. To the Austrian ambassador's suggestion that he was seizing his opportunity for either a diplomatic success over Prussia or a war against her on grounds unconnected with German national issues, Gramont replied, 'That expresses it perfectly.'[31] Next day he wrote to ambassador Benedetti that unless the candidacy were withdrawn, 'it's war', and spoke of immediate mobilization. Gramont instructed Benedetti to accept no prevarication from the King of Prussia.[32]

King Wilhelm was at his residence at the spa town of Ems, taking the waters like any wealthy German in summer. Bismarck stayed far away on his estate at Varzin, maintaining that this was a purely dynastic and Spanish matter. This gave the French a promising opportunity to approach Wilhelm directly, and at first it bore fruit. Wilhelm found the furore caused by Leopold's candidacy disagreeable: 'I have to thank Bismarck for this; he made light of it, just as he did in many another case,' he complained.[33] Over the following days he had talks with Benedetti, who had the sense to moderate Gramont's instructions, but Wilhelm held to the line that, as he had not ordered the candidacy, he could not countermand it. Nor, after Gramont's speech, would he be seen to give in to French threats of war. Privately though, influenced by foreign monarchs and by Queen Augusta, Wilhelm pressed the Sigmaringens to withdraw the candidacy. After it became clear that the Spanish had had a change of heart in the face of such uproar, Karl Anton reluctantly agreed. On behalf of his son Leopold, who was on a walking holiday in the Alps blissfully unaware that his name was about to start a major war, Karl Anton withdrew the candidacy on 12 July. To get the news to Paris as quickly as possible, he wired it to the Spanish ambassador there.

The first reaction of both Napoleon and Ollivier was that this was enough to save the peace. Foreign diplomats shared the judgement of veteran French ministers that this was a major triumph for France. Ollivier started spreading the news in the lobbies, only to discover that the Right was in no mood to take such an optimistic view. Bonapartists saw war with Prussia as a means of simultaneously restoring French prestige and the authoritarian Empire, and of bringing down the despised Ollivier ministry. A Deputy named Clément Duvernois, who had once been close to the Emperor and blamed Ollivier for his fall from favour, tabled a question asking the Cabinet what guarantees it planned to demand 'to avoid the recurrence of further complications with Prussia'.[34]

Gramont was adamant that notification from Spain of the withdrawal of Leopold's candidacy was no substitute for the public statement from the Prussian king that he aimed at. Recent history, including the seizure of the Rumanian throne by Leopold's brother Charles, showed that indirect disavowals were of little value. Now Gramont wanted a guarantee from Prussia that the candidacy would never be renewed. Majority opinion in the capital backed Gramont in believing that Karl Anton's gesture on its own was derisory. That afternoon, without consulting the Cabinet, Gramont went to see the Emperor to argue for demanding guarantees. Napoleon backed him and later, having met with his cousin Jerome David and Adolphe de Cassagnac, sent a note to Gramont strengthening the points to be demanded of Wilhelm. Gramont telegraphed instructions that evening to Benedetti, who attempted to carry them out early next morning.

So on 13 July occurred the famous scene in the Kurgarten at Ems. Wilhelm, out for his morning walk with his attendants, was relieved to see that news of the withdrawal was in the newspapers, and sent a copy over to Benedetti with his compliments, believing the incident closed. Benedetti, seeking to carry out his new instructions, intercepted the king as he went to leave the park. The ambassador pressed the demand for a guarantee almost to the point of impertinence, Wilhelm felt. Irritated by this importunity and breach of protocol, the king remained courteous but would give no guarantee. Only later in the day did Wilhelm send Benedetti messages putting off a further audience but confirming his approval of the withdrawal – news that would have been crucial a week earlier, but which was almost lost sight of in what followed.

Wilhelm also told Privy Counsellor Heinrich Abeken to send a report of the day's events to Bismarck, with authorization to publish it. Abeken wired an account from Ems that was accurate but quite sharply worded, betraying the annoyance of Wilhelm and his entourage at the further French demands.

Bismarck had now arrived in Berlin. He had from the start seen French demands as 'insolent', and after Gramont's declaration of 6 July he contemplated summoning the Reichstag to demand 'explanations' from France – a euphemism for an ultimatum from which war might follow. He had wanted to persist with the candidacy, was downcast at its withdrawal, and later confessed that he thought of resigning at the greatest Prussian humiliation since Olmütz. In view of 'the growing exasperation of public opinion over the presumptuous conduct of France' – exasperation Bismarck had vigorously stoked with press stories from the start of the crisis – he wired Wilhelm on 13 July on behalf of himself, Moltke and Roon advocating a 'summons' to France, and requesting Wilhelm to return to Berlin.[35]

Soon afterwards, Bismarck received Abeken's telegram, saw his opportunity, and took it with gusto. His abbreviation of the 'Ems Telegram' gave the impression that King Wilhelm had curtly snubbed the French ambassador's demands, sending an aide-de-camp to inform him that he had nothing further to say to him. While this was not, as some French writers later alleged, a forgery, it put a brutal gloss on the facts, and was intended to 'have the effect of a red rag upon the Gallic bull'.[36] To maximize the provocation, Bismarck communicated it to the press and German representatives abroad. For it was not the French alone he sought to inflame. In Germany too crowds were soon in the streets, furious at the insult to the king and as determined as Bismarck that their new nation would no longer tolerate dictation from the French. In Berlin, hurrahs for the king were mixed with shouts of 'To the Rhine!' in an explosion of pent-up anger.

In Paris, the momentum for war was building even before the 'Ems Telegram' became known, and would have been difficult to stop. On 13 July the Cabinet agreed not to treat the demand for guarantees as an ultimatum, but in the Chamber Jerome David launched a stinging attack on the 'derisory slowness' of the government's negotiations with Prussia and its failure to gain satisfaction. To declare itself satisfied with Karl Anton's renunciation would quite probably have prompted the overthrow of what Cassagnac's *Le Pays* dubbed 'The Ministry of Shame'.

This onslaught by the Right was encouraged by the Empress, who, mindful of the security of her son's future throne, was all for a showdown with Prussia. The Austrian ambassador thought Eugénie looked ten years younger at the prospect of a political triumph or a war. One of her attendants wrote that 'everyone here, the Empress foremost, desires war so much that it seems to me impossible that we shall not have it.'[37] Some ascribed to Eugénie the Emperor's crucial stiffening of attitude in backing the Gramont declaration and the demand for guarantees. Could a Bonapartist regime survive if it failed to take the lead in a popular foreign war? Eugénie's undoubted bellicosity, like Gramont's, was in tune with the popular mood in the capital at this point. Both took it for granted, as did the entire Cabinet, that France was militarily ready and, with her Chassepots and *mitrailleuses*, had a good chance of winning.

Marshal Le Bœuf had given that advice on 5 July, and repeated it when the Cabinet met on 14 July (which was not at that time the national holiday).[38] Gramont had learned of the 'Ems Telegram' that morning, exclaiming to Ollivier, 'My friend, you are looking at a man who has just been slapped in the face.' Driving through the violently excited crowds and entering the Cabinet room, he slammed his despatch case on the table and said, 'After what has just happened, a Foreign Minister who cannot make up his mind for war is not fit to retain his office.'[39] During the afternoon the decision was taken to call up the reserves: by now both governments were alarmed at the other's military precautions. Le Bœuf was anxious that France was losing precious time by delaying mobilization, and left to attend to it. Still there were hesitations and even talk – ten days too late – of calling a European congress: but finally the decision to mobilize was upheld.

That evening, as late editions carried news of the 'Ems Telegram', demonstrations reached fever pitch on the boulevards. A mob had to be turned away from the Prussian embassy. Crowds chanted 'À Berlin!' and sang the Marseillaise, hitherto banned as a republican and revolutionary song. Smaller counter-demonstrations were overwhelmed. Next morning, Friday 15 July, as excitement grew, the Cabinet resolved unanimously on war, and went to the Chamber that afternoon for approval. During the debate Ollivier let slip the unfortunate phrase that he went to war 'with a light heart', and would spend the next four decades insisting that he had meant 'with a clear conscience'. Throughout the crisis Ollivier had proved excitable. He had neither the power nor personality to keep Gramont under control, and had shown little capacity to shape or lead opinion. It was left to Thiers to make the most coherent protest that a mistake was being made and that the occasion was ill-chosen: 'Do you want all Europe to say that the substance was gained, but that you have decided to shed torrents of blood over a question of form?' He pointed out that the Prussians would have appeared the aggressors had they ever attempted to renew the candidacy, and no time had been given for Europe to work for a peaceful settlement. To Gramont he said, 'You began things badly and you have ended them badly.'[40] But Thiers was out of step with the ebullient mood of the Chamber. Hastily interrogated during an adjournment, Le Bœuf insisted that the army was 'absolutely ready' and that time was essential to forestall the Germans. Backed by Ollivier, he asserted that France had eight to ten days' lead over the enemy, and that there was nothing to fear.[41] Le Bœuf believed that, if war was inevitable, it was better to fight before the Germans adopted an improved rifle, and before the Legislature ruined the army by further budget cuts.

After eleven hours of debate, the Legislature voted overwhelmingly, by 245 to 10, for initial war credits of 50 million francs. In the end both Thiers and Gambetta swallowed their mistrust of the regime and voted for war. Only a handful of republicans voted against, fearing that military victory would entrench the authoritarian Empire for another generation.

On that same 15 July in Germany the king's return from Ems to Berlin became a triumphal procession, with cheering, waving crowds giving him an ovation at every station. Bismarck and Moltke travelled out to Brandenburg to intercept him, carrying the mobilization order. They were joined by the Crown Prince, and assured him that the strength and condition of the French army were 'in reality far less imposing than was hitherto imagined, making our prospects more favourable than has been supposed'. When they joined Wilhelm on the train all three urged him that not a moment must be lost in decreeing full mobilization. At Potsdam station news came through that the French had decided on war, overcoming the king's last reservations. He gave the order for mobilization from the waiting room; the Crown Prince went out and made the announcement to the jubilant crowd on the platform, and father and son embraced. The ride to the Royal Palace was 'one unbroken storm of cheers' as they moved with difficulty through the singing multitude. Wilhelm had to show himself on the balcony again and again as the crowd with one voice chanted 'The Watch on the Rhine'.[42]

The Declaration of War

France declared war upon Prussia formally on 17 July, almost as an after-thought: the Navy Minister insisted that he must have legal clarity before enemy shipping could be seized. The declaration was delivered in Berlin on 19 July, the day the Reichstag met to vote war credits. His voice trembling with emotion, Wilhelm addressed it on the theme of German unity. In past centuries, he reflected, Germany had suffered many wounds because her divisions prevented her from being strong, but today 'the bond of moral and legal union, a bond which our wars of independence began to establish, binds together all members of the German family with a unity that will be as close as it will be enduring. Today Germany's armaments leave no door open to the enemy; Germany has the will and the strength to defend herself against this fresh violence from France.' Enthusiastically echoing his appeal to the God of battles, the Reichstag expressed the hope that 'The German people will find at last, in a territory respected by all nations, a free and peaceful unity.'[43]

Bismarck had already called on the southern states to fulfil their military treaty obligations. Bavaria and Baden duly mobilized on 16 July, Württemberg on the 17th. French hopes of finding allies in the South simply evaporated. The French assumed that the South German states would be the battlefield in the coming campaign, so would not offer them neutrality. On the same assumption, the South prepared to defend itself with Prussian help. By taking the role of aggressor, France had consummated German unity at the popular, emotional level even before a shot was fired. 'This is the way I always hoped and wished to see it,' said Bismarck.[44] Most South Germans now saw Prussia as the champion of the national cause. Her critics found themselves heavily outvoted in their legislatures and their newspapers dwindled in circulation.

Thus a Franco-Prussian War became immediately a Franco-German War, waged by the Germans in a spirit of national self-defence, national independence and cultural self-assertion against the old oppressor. Symbolically, Wilhelm revived the Order of the Iron Cross, instituted in the War of Liberation against

Napoleon I, and visited the tomb of his mother, Queen Louise, whose spirit in the face of French invasion had been indomitable.

On the French side, the war was begun in hot blood for 'national honour'. In his proclamation of 23 July Napoleon blamed Prussia for her disdain of French goodwill after 1866: 'Launched on an aggressive path, she has awakened widespread mistrust, has necessitated excessive armaments everywhere, and has made Europe an armed camp where uncertainty and fear of the future reign.' The latest incident had been too much to bear, and now France sought a peace that would guarantee her security.[45]

Neither side announced territorial objectives, though there had been much newspaper talk in France of the left bank of the Rhine, and in Germany of Alsace and Lorraine. Such aspirations would be elaborated as the fighting progressed. The first aim in each case was the military defeat of the enemy in order for the victor to impose his will. In one sense this war between 38 million French and 40 million Germans would be but another episode in what Alfred Cobban called 'the millennial struggle of the West and East Franks'.[46] At its rawest it was a struggle for primacy in Europe. The new German contender had challenged the incumbent, France, and France had chosen to fight rather than accept relegation. Bismarck embraced war as a means of breaking the deadlock over German unity. In France Gramont was bent on the humiliation of Prussia. The crisis gave the Right the chance to reassert its strength by revenging itself on the Ollivier ministry, and the Empress and her camarilla the chance to strengthen the dynasty. In both countries the war party won over the sovereign. War was welcome to the officer class on both sides as their *raison d'être* and as a chance to win distinction. Mutual popular antipathies by no means made war inevitable (otherwise France and England might have fought as readily as France and Prussia), but they provided ever ready tinder for unscrupulous or short-sighted leaders in pursuit of their goals. Gramont and Bismarck must bear the heaviest responsibility in equal measure.

France and Germany would fight out their quarrel alone. The French declaration of war left the other nations of Europe amazed and indignant. The Russians had interceded with Wilhelm to persuade him to drop the Hohenzollern candidature, and to calm French anxieties they were planning a European guarantee that it would never be renewed. It was too late. When Alexander II heard of the French demand for guarantees he raged at the French ambassador: 'I have taken much trouble to avert war; do you want it then?' When the French ambassador spoke of French honour, the Czar snapped, 'Your honour! What about others' honour?'[47]

Unwilling to see a French victory over Prussia, Russia warned the Danes to stay neutral. With German forces near their frontier, the Danes needed little persuading, and anyway France failed to follow through on plans for a landing in Denmark. Russia also, as she had promised Bismarck, advised Austria-Hungary that she would mobilize if Austria attacked Prussia. But there was no appetite among either Austria's German or Hungarian populations for a war of revenge. France had declared war on an issue of no concern to Austria, and Chancellor Beust complained to his ambassador in Paris that Gramont 'without consulting us or giving warning, rushes boldly ahead on the question of war ... presuming, as if it were already agreed, that it suffices merely to inform us for us to mobilize ...'[48] Austria declared her neutrality on 19 July, assuring France that she would review the situation as events unfolded. Italy did likewise. Although Napoleon and Gramont clung to the waning illusion of a grand alliance against Prussia, after the first French defeats they received only expressions of sympathy from Austrian and Italian diplomats.

The British government had used its influence for the withdrawal of Leopold's candidacy, believing that would satisfy France and end the crisis. Exasperated by Gramont's demand for guarantees, it concluded that France was bent on provoking war after all. *The Times* savaged Napoleon for wantonly and wickedly starting a war 'of which no man can see the end'.[49] British anger at Napoleon as the major disturber of the peace was redoubled when Bismarck sent *The Times* Benedetti's draft treaty from 1866 for the French annexation of Belgium, giving the impression that it was more recent and claiming that Prussia had been duly horrified. Although Gramont had already promised to respect Belgian neutrality, Britain now asked both combatants to sign a treaty pledging to uphold it during hostilities. Prussia signed on 9 August, France on 11 August. By that time, the opening battles of the war had been fought.

Chapter 5

The Armies Mobilize

German Mobilization

In Germany transition to a war footing progressed in a well-ordered sequence: mobilization, transportation of men to the front and the concentration of the armies. Reservists received notices to join their unit and reported to their district depot where they were equipped and armed. Some regiments were ready by 21 July, most by 24 July. Roon thought this period while units organized the quietest he could ever remember at the War Ministry. Then began the great railway operation, so long and well prepared. Moving at precisely regulated intervals, an average seventy trains a day began moving complete units south-westwards towards the region adjoining the French frontier.

Enthusiasm for the war, the Crown Prince noted, was 'positively indescribable': but, from prince to private, as men said emotional farewells to their families many privately wondered 'Which of us will come back?'[1] Wherever the trains stopped bands played, crowds cheered, and troops were regaled with cigars, food and wine, which came as a welcome relief from the stifling heat of late July. Meanwhile volunteering was brisk. Ferries from Dover to Ostend were crammed with Germans who had been working in England returning to fight for the fatherland, even as English tourists on the Continent scurried back in the opposite direction. From the USA came telegrams of encouragement from German-Americans, and even volunteers.

The euphoria was not quite universal. There was some discontent in areas conquered by Prussia in 1864 and 1866. The Crown Prince admitted that 'highly treasonable expressions' were being uttered in Hanover.[2] Nor was the process of concentration by any means as flawless as the German official history would later suggest. Nevertheless, the immense operation was a staggeringly successful feat. By 1 August 384,000 fighting men, plus non-combatant personnel, 152,000 horses and 1,206 field guns had been assembled in three armies on a hundred-mile front broadly from Trier near the Luxembourg border to Karlsruhe. From north to south, these forces were:

First Army, consisting of two army corps and one cavalry division, with a combat strength of 60,000 men commanded by General von Steinmetz, a brave but bull-headed veteran;

BELGIUM

PRUSSIA

KOBLENZ

MÉZIÈRES Sedan

LUXEMBOURG Trier
I

R. Nahe

MAINZ
II

Montmédy
Thionville
Briey
Verdun
R. Aisne

METZ
4
3
G
2
5 Bitche

PALATINATE
Saarbrücken
R. Lauter

Kaiserlautern

Speyer
III

6
CHÂLONS
R. Marne

Bar-le-Duc

Toul

NANCY

LORRAINE

Lunéville

Wissembourg

1

KARLSRUHE

R. Aube

R. Meuse

R. Moselle

ÉPINAL

STRASBOURG Kehl

ALSACE

Vosges Mts

COLMAR

R. Rhine

BADEN

7 Mulhouse

Belfort

*The Concentration
of the Armies*
31 July 1870

II *German Armies*

3 *French Corps
G : Imperial Guard*

SWITZERLAND

0   50   100
Kilometres

Second Army, consisting of six army corps and two cavalry divisions, with
a combat strength of 194,000 men commanded by the king's competent
nephew, Prince Friedrich Karl;

Third Army, consisting of four army corps, the Baden and Württemberg
Divisions, and one cavalry division, with a combat strength of 130,000 men.
It was commanded by Crown Prince Friedrich who, being an enthusiast
for German unity and the revival of the Reich, mixed satisfaction at his
command of South German troops with pessimism as to how they would
perform by Prussian standards.

First and Second Armies faced Lorraine, while Third Army covered the north-
eastern border of Alsace.

On 31 July the Royal Headquarters train left Berlin. Ironically, there was
a hitch at the station. Colonel Karl von Brandenstein, who had planned and
supervised all troop movements by rail so efficiently, found that his allocation
of the General Staff to carriages according to their military function had been
overturned by an official of the royal household, who had reseated everyone
in order of social precedence. Brandenstein having made clear in no uncertain
terms that *ancien régime* etiquette must make way for the demands of war
direction in the railway age, matters were rectified. The train reached Mainz on
2 August, accompanied by Bismarck and a great gaggle of German and foreign
dignitaries and newspaper correspondents.

Moltke would write in his history of the war that no plan of campaign
survives the first collision with the enemy.[3] In 1870 he actually modified his plan
even before the enemy was sighted. It was known that the French were hurrying mobilization, sending units forward without waiting for their reservists
to join them. This, and the hasty declaration of war, suggested that they must
be preparing a sudden thrust across the frontier to disrupt the concentration
of the German armies. While Moltke was confident, and more so with every
passing day, that he could deal with such a threat, he was sufficiently cautious
to disembark Second Army much further back from the frontier than he had
planned, and he strengthened the perilously thin cordon of cavalry whose
job was to screen the German deployment until everything was ready for the
advance.

Apprehensions of a French thrust persisted for a few days. On the first day
of the war the Baden authorities disabled the main bridge across the Rhine at
Strasbourg, and all ferries and boats were brought to the German side. The
railway bridge to the city was blown up on 22 July, and barges were sunk in
the Rhine to deter French gunboats. Plans were in place for German railways
to be dynamited if the French invaded. Third Army Headquarters remained

cautious on 30 July, when Moltke impatiently ordered it to begin the advance. The reply came that it would not have all its troops and supplies ready until 3 August. Meanwhile the men of Second Army, laden with heavy packs and eighty rounds of ammunition each, had to march the final miles towards the frontier in intense heat down narrow roads that wound through the forested mountains of the Palatinate.

Already in the last week of July German cavalry patrols had penetrated French territory, disrupting communications and spreading alarm. The first men died in skirmishes between German horsemen and French customs posts or cavalry outposts. What were the French main forces doing? Intelligence had pinpointed the location and strength of their units with fair accuracy, but their intentions remained inscrutable and their passivity unaccountable. The only certainty was that, much to Moltke's surprise and relief, they had allowed him time to complete his concentration unhindered.

French Mobilization

On 6 July Marshal Le Bœuf advised the Emperor that field forces of 350,000 men could be assembled in fifteen days from the order to mobilize.[4] The order to call up the reserves was given on the evening of 14 July. Yet by 2 August, the nineteenth day of mobilization, France had gathered only about 255,000 men on her frontier. Of the 173,500 reservists expected, scarcely half had reached the front even by 6 August. Thus the Germans began the campaign with a superiority of more than three to two. Moreover, the French arrived wretchedly supplied, and still had not completed their organization by that date.

Yet the effort of the French railways was hardly inferior to their German counterparts. The Eastern and Northern railway companies performed prodigies of improvisation, running on average fifty-five trains a day to the front from 16 July. The scale of their achievement has sometimes been lost in descriptions of the general chaos associated with that second fortnight of July 1870 in France.

The confusion of French mobilization had many layers, all due to poor planning. In France as a matter of policy regiments were not based on local districts. Troops were considered more reliable for keeping civil order if they served far from relatives and friends, and regular rotation of garrisons was intended to prevent regiments getting too close to communities, as well as to promote a national outlook. A consequence of this practice was that a regiment's depot might be hundreds of miles from where it was stationed; and its reservists might come from anywhere in France. When war broke out, reservists reported to their local centre where they were formed into detachments and transported to their regimental depots. Regiments themselves meanwhile were sent straight to the front, despite being well below strength, on the promise that their reservists and equipment would be forwarded to them once they got there. On 19 July the Garde Mobile too was mobilized, though almost no preparation had been made to organize and equip it. The result of attempting general mobilization and concentration of the field army simultaneously was a bedlam of troops going to the front, reservists going to their depots or chasing after their regiments, and Gardes Mobiles going to their local mustering centre.

Not everything went as spectacularly wrong as some accounts later suggested. Many regiments departed in an orderly fashion. There was logic in troops from north-eastern France being despatched to form the northern portion of the French line; those from Paris and central France going to form the centre; the Army of Africa, debarking from Marseilles, being sent to Alsace to join troops already in the area; and those from south-east France forming the southern end of the line, while troops from the west formed a second line at Châlons. Yet all was marred by the prevalence of confusion and disorder that wasted precious time as reservists criss-crossed France by rail in a way that beggared common sense. In an extreme case, reservists from northern France travelled to Marseilles then embarked for Oran in Algeria to reach their regimental depot. From there they sailed back to Marseilles to join their unit in Alsace, a round trip of 2,000 kilometres.

Nor was the quality of many reservists reassuring. Many had received only minimal training thanks to budget cuts, and those who had done their service before 1867 were untrained in use of the Chassepot. Many resented being called away from their homes, and stations became crowded with men who either genuinely did not know where their units were or who were in no hurry to find out, and spent their travel allowance in getting uproariously drunk. Many junior officers seemed to think it the duty of their NCOs or railway officials to embark their men, and as a result bands of deserters took to pillage and begging in French cities for weeks without much attempt by the authorities to suppress the evil. In Strasbourg Rodolphe Reuss observed that the reservists were 'all drunk, or nearly so; it was a disgusting spectacle to see them staggering in the streets', and he complained that they were begging from house to house.[5] Seventy-year-old Frédéric Piton, the city's librarian, was old enough to draw a telling comparison with an earlier invasion: 'I was astonished by our soldiers' lack of enthusiasm; I can remember very well that in 1814 and 1815, despite the gravity of our situation, there were lusty cries of "Long Live the Emperor! Long Live the Emperor!" Nothing of the sort today. But then, what a difference between the spirit of Napoleon I and that of his nephew.'[6] A general in Marseilles thought of shipping 9,000 rowdy reservists to Algeria just to be rid of them.[7] As for the Garde Mobile, instead of taking on garrison duty to relieve the regular army, as the *Landwehr* did in Germany, its lack of training made it at first a huge distraction during mobilization. The Paris Garde Mobile mustered at Châlons Camp proved so hopelessly undisciplined and mutinous that nothing could be done with it.

The mayhem of mobilization caused by lack of an efficient transportation plan was overlaid by the chaos of central planning. Though nobody seemed to be in command, plenty of people were giving orders, and those orders changed almost daily. Napoleon III brought to military affairs the same irresolute and vacillating approach that he practised in politics, with wretched results. We have seen that in 1868 he had drawn up with General Lebrun a plan for three armies, to be commanded by Marshals MacMahon, Canrobert and Bazaine, and the War Ministry had planned on that basis. But on 11 July Napoleon called in Le Bœuf to tell him that there would be but one field army, the Army of the Rhine, and that he would command it personally. Some ascribed the change to the Emperor's desire to ensure unity in the first stages of the offensive. Others strongly suspected dynastic motives and Eugénie's influence: a Napoleon needed to lead his army and reap the laurels of victory, which otherwise might be gleaned by his marshals. Whatever the motive, the War Ministry had to work night and day hastily to redraw the entire order of battle. It was also decided that the three marshals should as consolation each command an enlarged army corps of four infantry divisions rather than the corps of three divisions commanded by generals. Thus the army undertook a major reorganization even as it mobilized.

Wartime appointments bore no relation to peacetime territorial commands, so commanders went to unfamiliar units and had to get used to staff officers they did not know. Le Bœuf himself was taken away from his functions as War Minister at a crucial time to act as chief of staff. On 23 July Napoleon sent him a lengthy and detailed list of services to be organized; in itself an admission of what had been left undone since 1866.[8] Meanwhile, the War Ministry required every regiment, while mobilizing, to reorganize by creating a fourth battalion to receive reservists at the depot while other battalions left for the front. Yet supplies of equipment and orders specifying when and where reservists were to be despatched were frustratingly slow in arriving at regimental depots, all losing more time.

When units reached the front there was frequent befuddlement about their designated concentration point and much plodding back and forth around the countryside as regiments, squads of reservists, and sometimes commanders went in search of their units. Worse still was the disorder of supplies. Essentials of all sorts were despatched in abundance from central depots to the marshalling yards of Metz, but because longer platforms planned there before the war had not been built and because of a labour shortage, unmarked goods wagons remained unloaded in sidings for days or even weeks, and then carts were lacking to carry supplies to units that needed them, when anybody knew their location. The army service corps, like the cavalry and artillery, was seriously short of horses. Most regiments were short of essential items, whether spare parts for their Chassepots or harness for much-needed transport. Amidst these chronic difficulties, officials of the Intendance remained so wedded to bureaucratic routine that on 17 July an order had to be issued threatening them with exemplary punishment if they denied troops needful supplies on the pretext of regulations.

Telegrams from harassed commanders to the War Ministry, which was expected to decide the most trifling details, tell their own story: 18 July, 'There is no sugar, coffee, rice, brandy or salt in Metz, and little bacon or hard tack. Send at least a million rations to Thionville urgently'; 21 July, 'The depot has sent enormous bundles of maps which are useless for the moment, we have not a single map of the French frontier'; 25 July, 'I have neither hospital orderlies, labourers or administrators, nor hospital wagons or field-ovens ...'; 27 July, 'The detachments joining the army are still arriving without cartridges or camping equipment'; 29 July, 'General de Failly urgently requests camping gear: shelter-tents, blankets, canteens and mess-tins are all in short supply. The men joining 5 Corps are arriving almost without camping equipment and cooking pots. He estimates that he needs equipment for 5,000 men.'[9]

The troops had set off in high spirits, meeting the same enthusiastic reception and hospitality at stations seen in Germany. The Marseillaise was roared out everywhere. In the fields labourers waved hats and handkerchiefs at passing troop trains. The men remained confident that they were more than a match for the Germans. But shortages and the evident confusion and indecision among the high command soon caused grumbling. Overburdened troops began to throw away such items as shakos, heavy knapsacks, ammunition and even rifles in the hot sun. Nor were the troops cheered by the address Napoleon issued to them on 28 July.

The Emperor, looking pale and ill, left his palace of Saint-Cloud by rail that oppressively overcast morning, departing without passing through Paris. He made the Empress Regent in his absence. On reaching Metz that evening he took up residence at the Prefecture, some distance from the fevered atmosphere of Army Headquarters at the Hôtel de l'Europe, which swarmed with gold-braided officers all demanding information or orders and sharing rumours as they rubbed shoulders with civilians and reporters amid a total absence of security. In his proclamation, Napoleon assured the troops that they were defending liberty and civilization, and that 'Whatever road we take beyond our frontiers, we shall be following in the glorious footsteps of our fathers. We shall show ourselves worthy of them.' But he predicted a long, hard war against 'one of the best armies in Europe' in an area (South Germany) bristling with obstacles and fortresses. He also spoke of defending French soil – a necessity that had hardly dawned on anyone in the ranks.[10]

Napoleon was disturbed to find how few men he had at his command, at their continuing unreadiness, and the disorder around him. The French high command still believed that it was ahead of the Germans, but seemed at a loss what plan to adopt. The Paris press was clamouring for an early offensive, and a reconnaissance in force across the German border was decided upon.

On the morning of 2 August divisions from three French corps crossed the frontier to storm hills shielding the town of Saarbrücken. On the parade ground atop one of the hills, soldiers of the small German garrison were smoking and gossiping in the sun while their officers sipped Rhine wine under the shade of the trees, when they saw the glint of a long line of bayonets and dense lines of scarlet-legged infantry approaching their positions. Overwhelmed by a storm of Chassepot and *mitrailleuse* fire, the Germans withdrew as they had been ordered to do if attacked by a superior force, though not before inflicting nearly ninety casualties on the French, about the same number as they suffered themselves. The French fired some shells after them into the town, of which the Germans were to make much in justifying their own bombardment of French cities. A Breton soldier admitted, 'It was a heart-rending spectacle to see the maddened inhabitants fleeing their blazing homes', while a junior officer from Mulhouse was disgusted to see some of his men behaving like barbarians, pillaging houses and destroying what they could not use – acts for which he punished them.[11]

For all that has been said of French deficiencies in numbers, supply and discipline, Napoleon had managed to launch an offensive before Moltke – but there was no follow-up. The French did not even attempt to hold Saarbrücken, let alone to press beyond it. Nor was Napoleon any wiser as to what the Germans were doing, French cavalry having proved unenterprising in reconnaissance.

Saarbrücken at least made a splash in the newspapers across France and raised hopes of a quick victory. The war continued to command wide support, even if Paris republicans jeered at the exploits of the 14-year-old Prince Imperial, who had watched the action with his father, when Ollivier published a private telegram from Napoleon to the Empress: 'Louis has just received his baptism of fire. He showed admirable coolness ... Louis has kept a bullet that fell next to him. There were soldiers who wept at seeing him so calm.'[12]

The French army remained strung out over 250 kilometres (155 miles) of territory, far too extended given its inferior numbers and reliance on a few railheads for supplies. The army deployed eight corps from northern Lorraine to southern Alsace, divided by the barrier of the Vosges. From north to south these formations were: 4 Corps under General Ladmirault around Thionville; 2 Corps under General Frossard around Forbach; 3 Corps under Marshal Bazaine around Boulay east of Metz; the Imperial Guard under General Bourbaki in Metz; 5 Corps under General de Failly around Bitche; 1 Corps under Marshal MacMahon around Strasbourg; 7 Corps under General Félix Douay around Belfort and Colmar, and finally 6 Corps under Marshal Canrobert to the rear at Châlons Camp.

For all its problems, the French army might yet have held its own had it not been so dispersed, with major units trying to do the job of cavalry by covering all approaches, while remaining mostly too far from each other to provide support if one were attacked close to the frontier. A few days might make a difference as more reservists came up and the supply muddle was sorted out, but those few days were denied.

Chapter 6

The Invasion of Alsace

Wissembourg

Strasbourg, the 'Queen City of Alsace' was France's great bulwark on the Rhine, dominated by the citadel built by Vauban after Louis XIV entered the city in triumph in 1681. In late July 1870 the city was again a hive of military activity. Dr Henri Beaunis, who taught at the university and the Army Medical School there, remembered the city's squares overflowing in the evenings with 'ladies all dressed up, officers of all ranks and arms in glittering uniforms, the cafés lit up and full of customers, lively discussions punctuated by jokes and laughter, the clank of sabres and glasses and, dominating all, military bands blaring out the national refrain like a challenge that was taken up by thousands of voices'.[1] This was, after all, the city where the Marseillaise had been composed during the Revolutionary Wars. Amid all the drinking and excitement, one of Beaunis's colleagues noted, 'Everyone had his plan of campaign and his inside news, but above all the blindest confidence prevailed. Everyone had forgotten Sadowa and talked only of Jena ... You can't imagine how much nonsense was uttered.'[2]

Marshal Maurice MacMahon arrived in the city on 23 July to take command of 1 Corps. With a commanding presence enhanced by his white hair and moustache, he was confident in his troops, who included a solid core from the Army of Africa. Second perhaps only to Canrobert as France's most renowned warrior, MacMahon had won distinction in Algeria, the Crimea and Italy. He had been born at the chateau of Sully in 1808, a descendant of men who had fought for the Stuarts at the Boyne and Culloden. Although his family connections were royalist, he had served the Second Empire loyally, if with some diffidence. In 1858, after the Orsini bomb attempt on Napoleon III, MacMahon had been the only senator to vote against a stringent security law introduced by the government, believing it to be unconstitutional. His prestige was such that this did him little harm, and the Emperor turned to him in 1861 to represent France at the coronation of King Wilhelm I of Prussia, a role MacMahon fulfilled with aristocratic dignity and style. Now he had been recalled from the Governorship of Algeria for what the Emperor assured him on 21 July would be only a short campaign.[3]

At Strasbourg, the centre of the southern portion of the French line, MacMahon found himself beset by the same difficulties as his fellow corps commanders, with men and supplies agonizingly slow in arriving. To his south, at Belfort, General Félix Douay commanding 7 Corps had even greater problems. Some 7 Corps units were still back in Lyon and one brigade was still in Rome. Meantime, persistent reports of German troop movements east of the Rhine made Douay hesitant about sending any of his units northwards to MacMahon in preparation for the offensive that the Emperor supposedly was preparing.

Pending the development of that offensive, MacMahon followed his orders from Le Bœuf to watch the Rhine crossings and the passes through the Vosges, as well as the River Lauter, which separated French from German territory at the northern frontier of Alsace. As soon as they were ready, MacMahon started funnelling his forces into northern Alsace but, like the French army as a whole, they were widely dispersed: MacMahon did not suspect any imminent German threat. When Edgar Hepp, Deputy Prefect based at the frontier town of Wissembourg, wired nervous reports of a large enemy build-up north of the Lauter, MacMahon directed his 2nd Division to move up there, and planned to go and see the situation there himself on 4 August. Meantime that division was put under the orders of his second-in-command, General Ducrot, who commanded his 1st Division and knew the country well.

Before the war Auguste Ducrot had been a vocal prophet of the danger from Prussia. He considered French acquiescence in Prussian expansion cowardly, and had predicted in 1869 that 'the Emperor will smoke his cigarettes and twirl his moustache; revolution will take hold, and one fine day Prussia, having become arbiter of Europe, will put her jackboot on France, annexing Alsace and Lorraine to the greater German Empire while disorder and anarchy bring down our own poor country.'[4] Ducrot could be remarkably prescient at times, but he had been far from wanting to avoid war. During the Hohenzollern crisis he had correctly predicted that Prussia would not risk her leadership in Germany by backing down in the face of French threats, but he approved his own government's firmness.[5] He welcomed war as 'a necessary evil, which alone allows truly strong spirits to show their brilliance'. War with Prussia was 'not only inevitable but highly desirable; ... it is the only way of warding off the dangers that threaten France, and one might say the whole of European society!' An ardent Catholic, he believed that only a 'violent crisis' could rescue the virtues of self-negation and patriotism in a religiously confused and decadent society.[6]

Always insistent on the superiority of his own strategic ideas, when hostilities broke out Ducrot wanted to throw bridgeheads across the Rhine opposite Strasbourg. MacMahon restrained him, pointing out that there were not yet enough troops at hand, and that the move played no part in the Emperor's plan. Yet, for all Ducrot's pre-war prophecies about Prussian preparedness, he was contemptuous of civilian reports from Wissembourg of a German threat. He assured MacMahon on 3 August that 'The Bavarian threat appears to me to be pure bluff,' and that, having studied the area around Wissembourg through a telescope, 'I am convinced that nowhere in the vicinity is the enemy in force.'[7] The orders Ducrot gave 2nd Division were typical of French commanders at this period: precise instructions for placing battalions, leaving no discretion to his subordinate, but without reference to the enemy or guidance as to whether to accept combat. Ducrot was more concerned with finding bread in Wissembourg to feed the men than with an enemy attack.

The commander of 2nd Division was Abel Douay, brother of Félix: a third Douay brother had been killed at Solferino. On 3 August Abel Douay marched his men up to Wissembourg where they arrived in darkness and pouring rain. Next morning, on Ducrot's orders, he sent one regiment back, leaving himself 6,500 men.[8] A telegram came from MacMahon passing on intelligence from army headquarters that the Germans might be about to launch a general offensive. Douay was not alarmed. He had sent out a reconnaissance at dawn but it had seen nothing – unsurprisingly as it had hardly ventured beyond the frontier. The first inkling he had that the Germans were in force north of the Lauter came at about 8.15 a.m. when shells started raining down on Wissembourg.

On the afternoon of 3 August the German Third Army had been ordered to begin the invasion of Alsace next morning, the twentieth day of mobilization. At dawn heavy columns headed for the River Lauter with orders to cross it and drive back the enemy wherever found. The leading units of three army corps were within supporting distance of each other as they descended on Wissembourg, a historic town which had seen fighting between French and Prussians during the Revolutionary Wars but which had been declassified as a fortress in 1867. General von Bothmer's division of the Bavarian II Corps dashed through hop fields and vineyards to try to seize the town, but soon found itself in a stiff fire-fight with Douay's men, who fired from the ramparts and took cover in the meadows bordering the Lauter, in roadside ditches and gardens, and around the railway station.

With his men fighting doggedly around the town, it became apparent to Douay by mid-morning that he was being attacked in overwhelming force. While the Bavarians, distinctive in their light blue uniforms and crested helmets, were being held at bay in his front, the Prussian V Corps was forcing his right flank and the arrival of XI Corps threatened to overlap it altogether. Douay ordered a retreat. He had ridden over to a battery of *mitrailleuses* on a hill above Wissembourg marked by three poplars, when a shell-burst knocked him dying from his horse. Below, his troops managed to extricate themselves and headed south for the hill that dominated the town, the Geissberg.

One battalion under Major Liaud was left stranded in Wissembourg, having received the order to evacuate too late. Liaud led a desperate defence of the town gates, leading men from one side of town to the other as the Germans bludgeoned their way in with hatchets and cannon fire. Finally it came to close-quarter fighting in the winding, smoke-filled streets, Liaud went down with a leg wound and his successor, at the urging of the town's mayor, had to acknowledge his hopeless position and to capitulate soon after 1 p.m.

Meanwhile, on the Geissberg above the town several hundred French troops held out in a solidly built chateau, from which they shot down waves of German infantry who proved too eager to take it by storm and paid the price of their bravery. But the French were running low on ammunition, and once artillery was dragged up the steep, rain-sodden slopes of the Geissberg to pound them they were forced to surrender at about 2 p.m. Their stand had at least enabled what was left of Douay's Division to retreat southwards. The Germans were too winded to mount an effective pursuit.

By now MacMahon and Ducrot had arrived at the natural observatory of the Col du Pigeonnier four kilometres to the south. Watching smoke rising from fires in Wissembourg through field glasses, they concluded that it was too late to send any troops to the rescue. MacMahon could only declare, 'The Germans have taken the first trick; we shall take the second.'[9]

The first major encounter of the war was of limited strategic influence. In disabling one dangerously exposed French infantry division out of the twenty-six then forming the Army of the Rhine, the Germans had taken the first pawn. In terms of morale, however, they had the fillip of a first victory, with laurels shared between Prussians and Bavarians – even if the performance of the latter had confirmed Prussian prejudices about their fighting quality. Conversely, the defeat and Douay's death sent shockwaves through France. In tactics, the battle prefigured the pattern of the war. German units had shown the ability to support each other and to find and turn the enemy's flank. On their side they had initiative, numbers, and powerful artillery, but the boldness of officers in launching frontal assaults had proved costly. On the French side, the quality of their infantry could not compensate for lack of numbers, faulty dispositions, careless reconnaissance and inferior artillery – and the *mitrailleuse* proved vulnerable to accurate German shelling.

Wissembourg cost 274 German dead and 1,186 wounded, for French losses of over 2,000, nearly half of them prisoners. Some French civilians, including women and children, had been killed in the shelling. About forty men of the town, many of them ex-soldiers, had fought in its defence, and when the Germans entered the town they made arrests and imposed draconian requisitions, setting a grim pattern for the invasion. They considered Alsace to be rightfully 'German', but this was to be no liberation.

The Germans were also infuriated by the French use against them of Algerian troops, the 'Turcos', who had borne the brunt of the combat. The Crown Prince claimed that they 'proved themselves veritable savages, for they shot wounded men and shammed dead, to open fire again from behind; so the German soldiers will give them no quarter henceforth.' The Bavarians reportedly bayoneted some wounded Turcos being treated in the town.[10]

On the evening of the battle, a white officer of Turcos, Lieutenant Louis de Narcy, was haunted by the horrible images of the day: the deafening noise and blinding smoke of combat, the sight of grass streaked with blood and a bloody foot lying in the roadway, the demonic dying grin of one of his men pierced by a bullet. Most of all, he bitterly mourned his comrades: 'Poor friends, so cheery and full of smiles this morning, you have been annihilated at the will of a man with a "light heart"! ... And for what result?'[11]

Frœschwiller

In Lorraine Napoleon III had been shuffling around his divisions in the hope of covering every possible avenue of invasion, issuing orders and counter-orders but achieving little more than wearing out his heavily laden men. The impression among the troops that the high command did not know what it was doing was reinforced when their generals kept whole divisions on the alert all night at the least alarm, or ordered them to march off just as their meal was cooking, causing the food to be thrown away. Marches were so poorly organized that men at the rear of columns were kept standing in ranks all day until the head of the column had cleared the road. Nor were marching and posting pickets the only military skills to have decayed in the French army since the Napoleonic Wars. At the astounding news of Wissembourg, the Emperor decided at last to launch an offensive beyond the River Saar, only to abandon the idea when General Wolf, the Intendant General of the Army, advised him that there were insufficient supplies to maintain an army in Germany for more than forty-eight hours.[12]

Napoleon had come to realize that managing the whole army from one headquarters was cumbersome. He reverted to the idea of two wings, one under Bazaine in Lorraine and one under MacMahon in Alsace, though without authorizing army staffs for them. Thus MacMahon had 5 Corps to the north and 7 Corps to his south put under his orders, and immediately used this authority to order General de Failly of 5 Corps to send his divisions down from

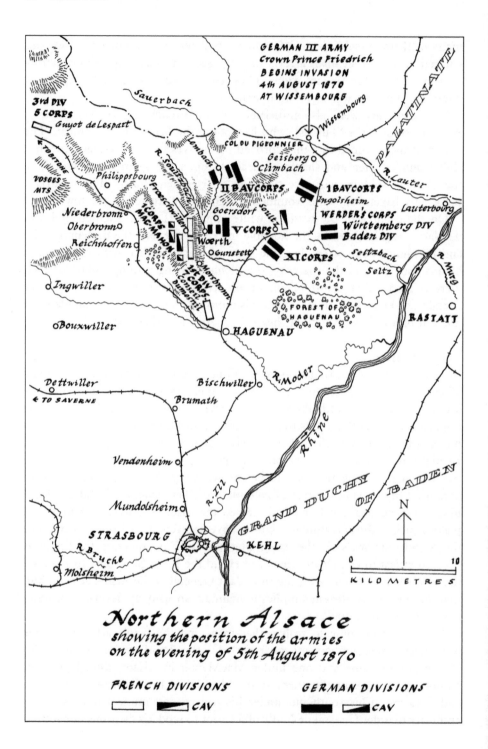

Northern Alsace
showing the position of the armies
on the evening of 5th August 1870

FRENCH DIVISIONS   GERMAN DIVISIONS
CAV   CAV

Bitche to join him. With three corps combined, MacMahon thought it would be possible to go over to the offensive. Yet, despite the urgency of MacMahon's instructions to join him, Failly hesitated and delayed. Like most of his fellow generals, he was obsessed with the dangers of abandoning his own sector of frontier – as if Napoleon I had never lived and the French army had reverted to eighteenth-century notions of positional warfare. Failly sent only one of his divisions to MacMahon. It would arrive too late.

On 5 August MacMahon took up a 'fine position' on the imposing Frœschwiller ridge, a line recommended by General Frossard before the war. Here, 40 kilometres north of Strasbourg, he believed that he could either defend himself or strike the Germans in flank if they attempted to pass him. All four infantry divisions of his 1 Corps plus his cavalry gathered there during the day. One division of 7 Corps arrived too, though without its artillery. Squads of disoriented, ill-trained reservists were still reaching the army that evening. Carl Klein, the Protestant pastor of the village of Frœschwiller, was struck by the indiscipline produced by hunger, for there was not enough bread to go round:

> The soldiers were no longer civilized men but famished hordes who pillaged and robbed without restraint. Woe to our potato patches, our gardens, our fruit trees, our bee-hives, our hens, our geese, our farmyards and our cellars. Woe betide anything else not protected by stout bolts! They arrived and got into everything, seizing whatever came to hand with laughter, swearing or threats. But how could we begrudge it to them? The poor fellows were perishing of hunger.[13]

The troops' temper was not improved by a heavy overnight thunderstorm, with torrential rain that prevented them getting much sleep. Yet they were supremely confident and, according to Ducrot, MacMahon 'trusting in his lucky star and in the excellent troops which composed 1 Corps, was rather too contemptuous of our enemies and believed them incapable of taking a vigorous offensive immediately'.[14] Ducrot claimed that he suggested that the men should entrench their position, but that other generals opposed tiring the troops.

The Marshal expected no battle on Saturday, 6 August. His orders for that day were for his troops to rest and be issued with double rations. However, two of his division commanders, Ducrot and Raoult, were uneasy and early that morning urged him to withdraw into the Vosges passes. They were joined by Count Paul de Leusse, a Deputy who had been among the most eager for war and was also mayor of nearby Reichshoffen. They urged that one corps was insufficient to hold the Frœschwiller position. MacMahon had about 48,000 troops with him,[15] whereas his own estimate put the German strength at 80,000, and they appeared to be nearby in force. Moreover, despite its steep northern and eastern faces, the Frœschwiller ridge fell away in gentler slopes to the south.

MacMahon seemed persuaded of the need to withdraw when increased firing to the front signalled serious fighting. He broke off the discussion on the grounds that it was too late. He expected a division of Failly's men to reach him soon. He may have reasoned that it made no sense to abandon Strasbourg to the enemy without a fight. At any rate, acting on the motto that legend attributed to him in the assault on the Malakoff Redoubt at Sebastopol, 'Here I am and here I stay', MacMahon decided to accept battle at Frœschwiller. That decision would cost France Alsace.

The German Third Army had lost contact with the French after Wissembourg, but as it moved south into Alsace on 5 August, unhampered by any French cavalry screen, it soon picked up the trail. By evening German scouts saw large numbers of French tents to their west, on the Frœschwiller ridge beyond the little River Sauer that flowed past the large village of Wœrth at its foot. The Crown Prince determined to concentrate his forces next day with a view to attacking on 7 August. He thought MacMahon's position too strong to take by frontal assault, so planned a flanking manoeuvre, but 'I am in constant apprehension lest, considering the fighting spirit of the Vth Army Corps, the smallest accident may bring on a pitched battle, so upsetting my well-laid plans.'[16] That is just what happened.

On his own initiative, a brigadier of V Corps sent a reconnaissance across the Sauer early in the morning of the 6th, only to have to withdraw it when it discovered that the French were still there in strength. But the sound of cannonading had carried northwards, where the Bavarian II Corps took it as a signal that the French were attacking and dutifully advanced through thick forest against the French left flank. Though Ducrot's men drove the Bavarians off, the sound of combat determined the Prussians to renew their attack. Each imagining that they were supporting the other, Prussians and Bavarians thus set rolling a great unplanned battle that raged for 7 kilometres along the banks of the Sauer. The Prussians seized Wœrth, and further downstream waded the river at fords or improvised bridges from hop-poles, planks and felled trees. They established footholds on the western bank but were unable to advance in the face of spirited French counter-attacks both around Wœrth and over meadows to the south. German troops 'maintained their positions with great difficulty against the murderous fire and the repeated and violent onslaughts of the enemy'.[17]

Conversely, the French held the Germans back but, try as they might, could not dislodge them. Massing their batteries along the hills east of the Sauer, the Germans quickly established artillery dominance, outranging and overpowering

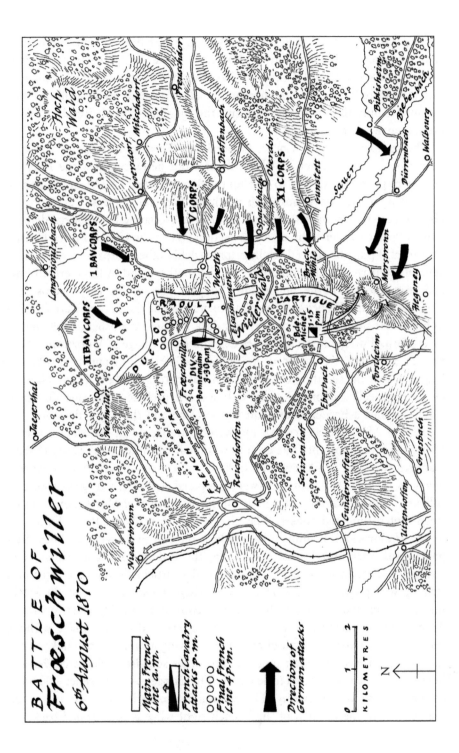

BATTLE OF
Frœschwiller
6th August 1870

Main French
Line a.m.

French Cavalry
attacks p.m.

ooooo
Final French
Line 4 p.m.

Direction of
German attacks

0   1   2
KILOMETRES

N

French batteries. French troops well to the rear were baffled at being targeted by an unseen enemy. 'There was firing all around,' wrote one, 'grape-shot, shrapnel, shells ... It was a frightful thunder! We disappeared in a cloud of smoke ... When it cleared I searched the horizon ... Not an enemy to be seen! ... Only the forest; only the great dark firs and the motionless birch trees! ... Were these men we were fighting?'[18]

The commander of V Corps, General von Kirchbach, had his arm in a sling from a wound taken at Wissembourg, but he exemplified the Prussian offensive spirit. His will not to give up the fight matched MacMahon's, and he persuaded both the Bavarians to his north and General von Bose's XI Corps to his south to support his attack, arguing that the escalating fight superseded the Crown Prince's order to break off the action. When the Crown Prince himself arrived at 1 p.m. he agreed, calling forward his other corps and ordering a general offensive. By that time Bose, at the southern end of the German line, had seen and taken the opportunity to pass part of his corps across the Sauer beyond the French right flank to turn it. While the French were fighting to hold their position in front they saw dark lines of skirmishers deploying to their south. Two infantry companies defending the village of Morsbronn at the French far right were forced to retreat before the advancing Prussians. Realizing that the situation of his division was critical, at about 1 p.m. General de Lartigue called upon the cavalry. It was the prelude to an episode which would become a French equivalent to the Charge of the Light Brigade.

General Michel's cavalry brigade went charging down the slope towards Morsbronn like a torrent. The ground was totally unsuited to a cavalry charge, scattered with tree trunks and hop trellises and cut by ditches. No sooner had Michel's men set out than they were peppered with German grapeshot and rifle fire. Two squadrons galloped down the main street of Morsbronn, with its steep-roofed timbered houses. The Germans were ready for them, lining the upper windows and manning a barricade at the exit to the village. They fired point-blank, their muzzle-flashes scorching the uniforms of French riders. The sound of bullets hitting steel breastplates, said a participant, was 'like hailstones striking windowpanes in a storm',[19] and when the smoke cleared the street was a heap of dying men and horses. Survivors were quickly taken prisoner. Another group met the same fate at the western end of the village without getting within sword's length of an enemy, leaving a sunken lane choked with the corpses of men and their mounts. The other squadrons charging German lines outside the village fared little better. The charge cost the French 800 men, at minimal loss to their enemy. Though at a disproportionate price, it covered the exhausted infantrymen of the French right wing as they pulled back.

The Germans were not long delayed, and the battle was turning in their favour. The flanking units of XI Corps regained contact with their comrades in the centre and fought their way through a bitterly contested stretch of forest called the Nieder-Wald. French officers, their kepis on their swords, repeatedly led their men in old-fashioned dense formations into withering fire. In the intense fighting here and around Wœrth several French regiments lost over 1,200 men each, well over half their strength.[20] The impetuously led German V Corps hardly suffered less.[21] Like a pair of giant nutcrackers, XI and V Corps steadily squeezed the French centre. Through his telescope MacMahon, who had been directing the battle from in front of a walnut tree on a hillock, saw the Germans pushing into the heart of his position. The valley of the Sauer below him was now thick with masses of infantry in dark blue uniforms. They looked, said an officer present, 'like a cloud hugging the ground and moving ever forward'.[22] Still there was no sign of the leading division of 5 Corps on which MacMahon had been counting.

By 3 p.m. the Germans were firmly astride the Frœschwiller ridge and had eighty guns targeting French resistance around the blazing hamlet of Elsass-hausen. More and more German troops came up, and those who had become detached from their units in the heat of the fighting simply joined in the great semicircle of fire around the French.

Retreat was MacMahon's only option, but he needed to stem the German tide if he was to save his army. He turned to Bonnemains's heavy cavalry division. In their religiously burnished breastplates these socially elite riders held it as an article of faith that theirs was the decisive, battle-winning arm, and that nothing could withstand their shock. Yet the ground over which these cuirassiers had to charge was even worse than that encountered by Michel's men two hours earlier, cut with ditches and cultivated with orchards, hedges, vineyards and hop-fields with wooden posts and wire trellises that could bring horses and riders crashing to earth. MacMahon was dismissive of such obstacles, and sent the units of Bonnemains's Division hurtling down the slopes towards Wœrth in a series of charges.

Some regiments were caught by German artillery even before they set off: one colonel was decapitated by a shell in the act of raising his sabre to order the charge. Cuirassier Georges de Moussac, having crossed himself as he started down the slope, was gathering speed when he realized that a comrade had collided with a tree. Then he felt a blow to his head: 'We had come to a hop-field, from which came a very heavy fire; it was impossible to get at the enemy. The Germans were almost invisible amidst all these poles and foliage.' Men were falling all around him. Similarly Firmin Guillouet was halted at a ditch when beneath some trees he saw masses of men 'who from their cover fired at us almost point-blank. The bullets flew past our ears, making a sound like a swarm of flies. All our officers save one were toppled.' Withdrawing, his unit charged again. Guillouet sabred a German who had bayoneted him through the thigh, but despite supporting *mitrailleuse* fire he and his comrades were forced back by shelling and the fire of oncoming German columns. Their unit was in tatters. From the debris of another squadron the only man to get close to the German line was a bugler whose eye had been shot out and who was carried forward, blinded and screaming, by his maddened horse. When a comrade galloped forward and grabbed the horse's reins to turn it around, the Germans refrained from shooting. As the pair withdrew, the wounded man begged to be finished off.[23] Five hundred of Bonnemains's men had been shot down or captured. The Germans pressed forward doggedly.

Next MacMahon ordered up his reserve artillery to bombard the Germans who had taken Elsasshausen, but the gunners were felled by rifle fire within minutes. Then he sent in the 1st Algerian Sharpshooters (popularly known as Turcos), still a formidable unit despite their loss of 500 men at Wissembourg. They ran forward into clouds of smoke. Louis de Narcy could make out only spiked helmets ahead of him and a wall of dark uniforms beyond that. Converging fire wrought havoc in the Turcos' closely packed ranks, and they paused to re-form behind a crest. Fixing bayonets, they charged ahead with 'long, savage cries' in Arabic, and for a moment they looked unstoppable as they retook Elsasshausen. Beyond it they were caught in a crossfire, and could find no one to bayonet: 'Our soldiers were packed together, forming visible groups and standing upright, heads high, looking for the enemy columns. But the Prussians lay under cover and laid us low without showing themselves.'[24] After a further vigorous effort to charge the German guns that were decimating them, the Algerians were finally halted by a hail of shells. As they fought to hold their position, Narcy watched one of his men use his knife to cut off his smashed thumb, which was hanging by a shred. Eventually, the Turcos were forced to retreat to avoid encirclement, leaving 800 men behind them, half the regiment's strength.

On the French northern flank Ducrot had held his ground all day against the relatively timid Bavarians, and had been able to send units to reinforce threatened points to the south. However, another Bavarian corps had come into line and his left flank was being turned, forcing him back. By 4 p.m. the Germans occupied three sides of a box around the French, to the north, east and south, and were massing men and guns for a final assault. MacMahon organized a last-ditch defence around the village of Frœschwiller to protect the westward retreat.

There was pandemonium in the village as shells fell. The larger buildings – the chateau, the church, the town hall – were all being used as hospitals. The church caught fire and the wounded had to be rapidly evacuated. In the town hall Dr Charles Sarazin, an Assistant Professor of Surgery at Strasbourg before the war, had been operating since morning. Sarazin had volunteered as chief surgeon of Ducrot's division, but had found medical supplies so short that he had had to beg chloroform from the civilian hospital. On 27 July he had ridden out of Strasbourg with all the equipment he could find in a hackney cab, thinking that 'if it weren't so sad, it would have been quite laughable!'[25] Finally his wagons and orderlies had arrived, and he and his team were working at full stretch in Frœschwiller. Sarazin had had the foresight to have buckets filled with water early in the day, which was just as well as a German shell soon destroyed the pump in the street. Others occasionally penetrated the building, killing patients and starting fires that had to be quickly extinguished. As the wounded poured in Sarazin learned that stories of performing major operations under fire were myth. Amid the noise, 'when I asked for forceps or a knife they passed me a sponge or a thread for ligature.'[26] As he bent down to tend his patients he suffered acute back pain and fatigue as the sound of battle raged outside.

> All of a sudden the bombardment ceased. I was occupied in staunch-ing the bleeding from the forearm of an infantry lieutenant whom I had anaesthetized. I was on my own, without help, on my knees in the straw. Next to me a major who had been shot through the chest gave a low groan and suffocated. Further off, an officer whose forehead had been opened by a shell fragment died in convulsions. With that ability peculiar to people under stress, I developed a dual personality: the surgeon was entirely absorbed in the delicate operation he was performing, while the man was thinking of his wife and child who – would you believe – was exactly seven weeks old at that hour. In this Hell I held on to that little corner of Heaven, and dreamed that I would be lucky enough to see them again.

Just as he was tying up an artery,

> a long, doleful, unfamiliar bugle call broke the silence that several minutes ago had succeeded the din of the bombardment. Oh, that accursed bugle! Better a hundred times to endure the crackle of bullets and the hissing and bursting of shells! Everyone stopped. The wounded raised themselves up. We looked at each other without saying a word. Some covered their faces; everybody understood. Oh how hard is the first defeat!

> Outside there were frenzied hurrahs, commands in German, a few shots, and thousands of German soldiers rushed headlong into Frœschwiller, surrounding the hospital. They looked wild-eyed, suspicious, fierce, and were black with powder.[27]

MacMahon, having had one horse shot beneath him during the day and his clothing nicked by bullets, was among the last French troops to leave Frœschwiller before the victorious Germans swept in at about 5 p.m. Ducrot conducted a fighting retreat as the defeated and disorganized French crowded down the forest road to Reichshoffen and then on to the town of Niederbronn. There, at last, they met the leading division of Failly's Corps, which was able to beat off German cavalry whose slashing attacks had provoked panic among desperately fleeing troops and teamsters. As night fell MacMahon fainted and fell from his horse, but after being revived with brandy wired the Emperor from Niederbronn, 'I have lost the battle.'[28]

Frœschwiller had been a bloodbath for both sides. French losses were approximately 19,600, of whom 9,200 were captured. The loss of 630 officers was a particular blow to the army's organization. Among the dead were a division commander, General Raoult, and MacMahon's chief of staff. As befitted the marshal's style of warfare, French accounts of the heroism and sacrifice of individual units would read almost like modern variants of Froissart's chronicles of chivalry. Yet fighting the battle with a single corps in isolation proved a costly mistake. The strength of some of the best units in the French army had been squandered. MacMahon's personal bravery and determination had been conspicuous, but his strategic and tactical judgement had proved questionable. French counter-attacks had been piecemeal and prodigal in lives, whereas earlier coordinated attacks by all arms might have had more effect and have allowed a less costly retreat.

For the Germans, who cheered the Crown Prince as he entered the village, Frœschwiller was a hard-fought and bruising victory, costing 1,589 dead, 7,680 wounded and 1,373 missing, for a total of 10,642. Of these, officer casualties totalled 489, including the wounded General von Bose. The improvised nature of the battle amply demonstrated German initiative and determination to win, but the premature offensive had increased losses, and opportunities to cut off the French retreat were lost. The Crown Prince had been exasperated by the slowness of the Bavarians in the north. The lead units of the Württemberg Division which he had ordered to cut off the French retreat had instead been diverted into the fighting for Elsasshausen. Still, the enemy was in full retreat and the Germans were masters of Alsace.

The terrified citizens of the area where the battle had been fought had sought refuge in cellars or the forest. A few who stayed in their villages were killed by stray shells or bullets. A handful lost their minds permanently from their experiences during those August days. Others met a brutal fate. From their entry into Alsace German troops had mixed anger at the French declaration of war with suspicion of the population. Fearful of poison, they customarily accompanied demands for drink with insistence that the donor first drink some himself. There was paranoia concerning French civilians firing at German troops. A few instances did occur, magnifying German fears, but any shot fired from an unseen source too often was attributed to civilians rather than to French troops firing from cover. During the heat of battle on 6 August a rumour took hold among the Germans that their wounded had been mutilated in the village of Gunstett. Enraged soldiers shot or beat to death at least five inhabitants. In other villages citizens who emerged too early from their cellars risked being shot as *francs-tireurs*. Others were arrested, beaten and maltreated for days on suspicion of sniping. As passions cooled, however, and as local dignitaries interceded with senior German officers, most of these hapless people were released. Appeals to the Crown Prince seldom failed to meet with a merciful response.[29]

Once the battle ended, famished and thirsty German troops, having risked their lives in combat all day, pillaged Frœschwiller for every morsel of food and wine, sometimes threatening anyone in their way with death. Within hours, however, German officers restored discipline more effectively than their French counterparts had done before the battle.

The day of battle was only the beginning of the local people's ordeal. Besides shortages of food and water and ruined or damaged buildings, the dead had to be interred. Villagers were drafted to dig burial pits in which French and German corpses were laid indiscriminately, by the dozen or the hundred. The gruelling work took days, and though the weather turned cold and wet the smell became nauseating. As it proved almost impossible to move the hundreds of dead horses littering the field, most were dug into the earth where they lay. German military police also supervised the clearance of battlefield debris, and heaps of spiked helmets, breastplates and bayonets were piled up for collection. The emptied pockets and slit haversacks of the dead and wounded testified that battlefield marauders had already done their work.[30]

Every effort was made to bring the wounded under cover, but for some this took two or three days while they lay exposed to heat and rain. For many, help came too late, and months after the battle bodies were found in undergrowth and gullies. Even those brought inside were often packed into buildings with roofs holed by shells. Many died for lack of attention because there were too few doctors. 'My heart was close to breaking,' confessed Pastor Klein, 'at hearing the screams and lamentations of these poor victims of the battle, whose haggard faces and eyes burning with fever seemed sinister and terrifying in the half-light.'[31]

Every building in the area became a hospital as exhausted doctors worked for days performing operations. On the French side anaesthetic had run out. Sarazin, for instance, could give some amputees only spirits. He grudgingly acknowledged that help given by German doctors and their well-organized stretcher teams was invaluable. A French volunteer admitted, 'Our wounded lived by the generosity of our enemy.'[32] If battle and its aftermath showed the worst of human nature, it also brought out the best. Within days help and desperately needed supplies flowed in from Germany, France and Switzerland, and cartloads of food were sent by villages in the region that had suffered less severely.

With the help of the International Society (the 'Red Cross'), most wounded were evacuated to Haguenau, the nearest large town, by 10 August. In the over-crowded conditions of field hospitals many wounds had become foul. Sarazin observed:

> Often, because the wounded were unable to raise themselves up and did not get timely help from hospital orderlies who were too few in number, their evacuations of every sort were mixed with the damp and bloody straw on which they lay.
>
> For transport we had only the peasants' carts. They were very uncomfortable and ... exposed the wounded to new tortures. Imagine if you will a man suffering from broken bones as a result of a gunshot to the lower limbs, or even an amputee. Every jarring, even a light one, provokes the sharpest pain. What will a journey of three hours be like for him, with hard and continual jolts from a vehicle without suspension, on an uneven road rendered almost impassable by the passage of an entire army with much artillery? Nevertheless, it was in just these conditions that the evacuation of the field hospitals from Frœschwiller to Haguenau was carried out.[33]

Despite better facilities in Haguenau, infections spread rapidly. French surgeons were more reluctant than their German colleagues to accept antiseptic practices, and their amputees had a mortality rate of about 80 per cent. The stench of putrefaction became unbearable. Such conditions convinced Doctor Henri Beaunis that it was 'better for a seriously wounded man to be treated in a village by a mediocre surgeon than by a prince of the art in a large hospital'.[34]

Meanwhile, the war went on. A French aid worker in Frœschwiller watched seemingly endless enemy columns tramp by: 'The onward march of the German invasion continued for three days without interruption. All the roads were black with troops, like a busy, fast-flowing swarm of ants.'[35]

The Retreat

The retreat from Frœschwiller on the evening of 6 August was 'a dream, a frightful nightmare', a French staff officer recalled.[36] Men's heads ached and their ears rang from the concussion of gunfire. Amid the chaos of men, horses and wagons, wrote an infantry major, 'All the units jumbled up and in confusion formed an indescribable mob. Shells whistled into the midst of this throng, ploughing bloody gaps.' Haunted by the pitiful sights of the corpse-strewn road and the pleas of the wounded not to be abandoned, the beaten army marched through the night.[37]

From Niederbronn most of the retreating French headed south-west to Saverne, though enough turned north-west towards Bitche to produce the accidental benefit of throwing the Germans onto the wrong scent. The Germans assumed that MacMahon would attempt to rejoin the rest of the Army of the Rhine directly, just as they were anxious to regain contact with the left wing of their Second Army in Lorraine. Although they captured great quantities of men, equipment and guns amid scenes that reminded one cavalryman of the aftermath of Königgrätz,[38] they failed to pursue the French hard enough to turn a disordered retreat into rout. In fact, they soon lost contact with the enemy altogether.

MacMahon might have attempted to defend the pass through the Vosges Mountains at Saverne, or have continued into southern Alsace to join the rest of 7 Corps and threaten the flank of the advancing Germans. He might have moved north via Nancy to rejoin the Emperor at Metz, or have halted at the line of the Meuse. But he, with Napoleon's concurrence, had but one thought: to get the battered remnant of his force far to the rear, to Châlons Camp on the River Marne, where it could both regroup and cover Paris. So he passed through the Vosges into Lorraine. When engineers asked for orders to blow up the railway tunnel through the mountains, MacMahon said no: the French might need it if they returned to the offensive. When the Germans reached Saverne they were surprised and relieved to find the tunnel intact. It would be of great service to them.

The French retreated through eleven days and 350 kilometres, the last 170 kilometres to Châlons being by rail. The conditions of the march deepened the demoralization begun by defeat. The troops were utterly exhausted and hungry, most of them having had to leave their knapsacks behind on the battlefield. The

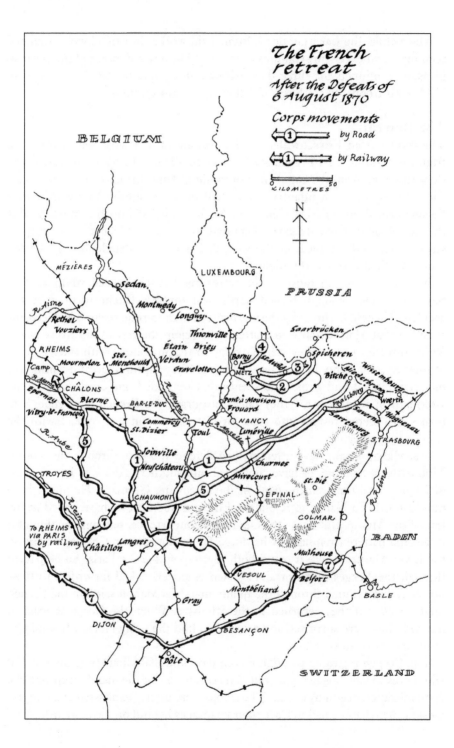

The French retreat
After the Defeats of 6 August 1870

Corps movements
← ① → by Road
← ① → by Railway

Intendance seemed incapable of organizing enough bread to feed them all, either at Saverne or any of the other towns they passed through. In some places the inhabitants were generous, but often the men lived by begging, foraging in orchards and potato fields, or pillaging the farms and villages they passed through. Many got drunk on wine, fell out of ranks and became insubordinate. One officer of MacMahon's staff was grossly insulted by drunken soldiers who proceeded to hurl abuse at officers who could afford to sit in cafés eating and drinking.[39] Another had to draw his revolver on two Zouaves who tried to rob him of his purse.[40] On top of this, from 9 August it rained heavily for days, soaking men to the skin and condemning them to sleep in fields of liquid mud.

MacMahon thought his army could not make a stand in its miserable state. Attempts to reorganize at Saverne had very limited success. Yet the state of the troops owed much to command failures. The men needed time to rest and eat properly, but they were not allowed it. So pervasive were fears of close German pursuit and ambushes that units were ordered to make night marches. Staff work had broken down badly, leading to ill-planned marches, crossing of routes and wrong turnings, often on roads shared by dejected families fleeing with their possessions on carts. Major David wrote that on 7 August,

> I passed a frightful night full of bitter reflections on the war and the train of horrors and sufferings that accompany it! And then, I was denied any sleep. I kept marching like a drunken man, stumbling at every step and bumping into men who were as benumbed as me. In my rare lucid moments I saw squads of soldiers, unable to endure the lack of sleep any longer, lay down ... [by the roadside] to slumber. I would have done the same, had I been a private.[41]

Yet at 1 a.m. they were allowed only one hour's rest before marching on. MacMahon continued the illogical practice of keeping his infantry between his cavalry and the enemy, instead of sending his horsemen to find out what the Germans were doing and to drive off their scouts, whose presence was the source of so many alarms.

From this time Louis de Narcy saw 'indiscipline spread rapidly and badly damage our military spirit and respect for authority'.[42] The Germans were taken aback by the bitterness of French prisoners against their officers, hearing them denounce MacMahon as 'a pig' and Napoleon as 'an old woman'.[43] Major David saw his men as 'Poor peasants without education or training, amongst whom the concept of patriotism struck little chord! They were conscious of having done their duty. They were ready to fight again if someone would just feed them, and they thought no further than that. Such are the vices of a recruitment system which is not borne equally by all classes of society.'[44]

On 9 August the demoralized troops learned that theirs had not been the only defeat on the 6th. On the Lorraine frontier General Frossard's 2 Corps had been attacked on the Spicheren heights, overlooking Saarbrücken. The Germans had made a series of clumsy frontal assaults on French positions and paid with 4,871 casualties. By evening though, fearing that his isolated corps was being flanked after losing 4,078 men, Frossard had pulled back, and the French army in Lorraine retreated on Metz.

MacMahon's men reached the railway at Neufchâtel on 14 August and boarded trains which transported them to Châlons over succeeding days. An anonymous staff officer of 1 Corps, who had become bitterly disillusioned at MacMahon's lack of grip on his army, recalled spending two nights and a day on a train:

> And why were we crawling along at the speed of a freight train in a siding? Here's why. At Joinville we received a telegram, a telegram from a *high* public official, a booking clerk, no less, telling us that the line had been cut at Saint-Dizier. You would have thought that someone would have telegraphed to Saint-Dizier to find out whether this was true or not. No such thing! It was much simpler to return to Chaumont. Once there, someone thought of sending a telegram, and found out that the track had never been cut at Saint-Dizier, from which the Prussians were still far distant. It was then decided to set forth again. In sum, it was a day lost because of a stubborn reluctance to find out information. One officer sent forward the day before to ride over our route would have avoided these marches and counter-marches that tire out the men, antagonize them, and make them laugh at their leaders and regard them as pitiful.[45]

Nevertheless, the movement of 1 Corps, consisting of only 22,000 infantry, 5,500 horses and 500 artillery pieces or wagons, was completed by 17 August, twenty-four hours before the Germans really did reach the railway.[46]

General de Failly's 5 Corps had joined the retreat. During the day of 6 August his soldiers had expected to be led towards the sound of gunfire, but Failly had hesitated. When word came that MacMahon had been defeated and that the Germans were at Niederbronn, he ordered a headlong retreat across the Vosges at night, needlessly abandoning supplies and equipment. Some of his units covered 120 kilometres in thirty-eight hours. Failly's precipitate withdrawal to avoid being cut off invited bitter comparisons with the sloth of his divisions in coming to MacMahon's aid when needed. His men, good troops who mostly had not seen the enemy or fired a shot, became disaffected and surly in retreat, particularly when they came into contact with 1 Corps units and like them suffered hunger. The Emperor, having quickly forgotten that he had put 5 Corps under MacMahon's orders, sent it confusing and contradictory instructions which led to zigzagging and counter-marches. Failly, as ever, tried to set his own strategic agenda and separated himself again from 1 Corps until head-quarters gave him peremptory orders to entrain for Châlons. A staff officer wondered acerbically, 'Have our generals sworn an oath to fight alone and not to support the others? Does each of them aim to win a battle all by himself, so that he can be made a duke or a marshal? That's how it seems.'[47]

It was an understandable reflection on the French conduct of the campaign so far, though Failly's movements had always been away from the enemy. His corps reached Châlons between 17 and 19 August.

Meanwhile, after the news of Frœschwiller, the rest of Félix Douay's 7 Corps had been withdrawn from Mulhouse in southern Alsace to Belfort. Here too, retreat had occasioned 'shameful acts of indiscipline. There were soldiers who did not flinch from scattering their cartridges and throwing their rifles away along the road.'[48] At Belfort the corps at last completed its organization and readied the defences of the fortress 'in profound ignorance' of events else-where.[49] Finally, on 16 August, came orders from Paris to join MacMahon. By 20 August all Douay's men were on trains heading north for Châlons.

Thus the French had all but abandoned Alsace and a significant portion of Lorraine to the advancing Germans. In their wake only a few fortresses held out under siege, notably Bitche, Phalsbourg and Toul. Most important of all was Strasbourg. Only three weeks earlier the capital of Alsace had been regarded as a base for the invasion of Germany. By the second week of August it was cut off from the rest of France, its inadequate garrison supplemented by 4,000 demoralized fugitives from Frœschwiller. The Baden Field Division under General von Werder began a siege, and on the night of 14 August the first German shells landed inside the city. With the departure of 7 Corps north-wards, there was no prospect of any French force coming to Strasbourg's relief.

Chapter 7

The Empire Totters

Power Changes Hands

Paris lived on rumours and its nerves. After hopes raised by Saarbrücken and the dejection of Wissembourg, a rumour hatched in the Stock Exchange of a great victory won by MacMahon swept the city on 6 August. Edmond de Goncourt had never witnessed such enthusiasm; men pale with emotion waving their hats in the air, children leaping for joy, famous singers leading crowds in the Marseillaise.[1] Flags and illuminations appeared in windows.

The truth arrived during the night in a telegram from the Emperor to the distraught Empress: 'We are in full retreat. A state of siege must be declared and preparations made for defence of the capital.'[2] On 7 August, a Sunday Parisians would long remember, official bulletins announcing the double defeats of Frœschwiller and Spicheren produced stupefaction. 'The silence was frightful,' wrote Goncourt. 'On the boulevards, not a carriage moved; in suburban houses, not even the noise of children playing; all across Paris, sound had died.'[3] Alfred Darimon, a Deputy who had spent recent nights in sleepless anxiety, sought news from contacts at the Interior Ministry and his wide political circle of dining companions. Those close to the imperial government betrayed 'the most complete despondency. They didn't believe the Empire could survive [another] defeat.' That evening on the boulevards, 'the surging crowds were tempestuous. You felt it would have taken only a word to push them to anger and revolt.'[4]

For two decades Napoleon III had drawn upon his uncle's legend to pose as the man who could best protect France. When the ageing nephew showed himself incapable of doing so, his political capital drained away. The Legislature, prorogued on 21 July, demanded to be recalled immediately, and the Empress did so without even seeking the Emperor's authority.

A stormy session opened on 9 August. Republican Jules Favre boldly demanded that the Emperor return from the front and that the Legislature form a Defence Committee as the new national executive. Evoking the potent legend of the *levée en masse* during the Prussian invasion of 1792, republicans called for the arming of the Paris National Guard. In revolutionary myth, this citizen militia was invincible, and would incidentally provide republicans with armed support in the capital. However, republicans were not yet strong enough to impose their will. The authorities took steps to prevent the Chamber being disrupted by large crowds of demonstrators outside calling loudly for arms and the overthrow of the Empire.

It was the men of the Right, the authoritarian Bonapartists, who, with the support of the Centre, dealt the death blow to the Ollivier ministry. Baron Jerome David, the Emperor's cousin and a grandson of the revolutionary painter Jacques-Louis David, delivered a crisp and effective attack: 'Prussia was ready but we were not.' The Legislature brusquely dismissed the Ollivier Cabinet, including Gramont, by voting a motion by Clément Duvernois: 'This House, resolved to support a Cabinet capable of providing for the defence of the country, passes to the order of the day.'[5]

There were ironies in Ollivier's fall. Believing himself a principled Liberal, he had contemplated having leaders of the Left arrested and imprisoned. His Cabinet was the first in the Empire's history to be voted out by a parliamentary majority; but one led by diehard opponents of the Liberal Empire who despised parliamentarianism and savoured their revenge. Moreover, these were the very men who had goaded the government into war only three weeks earlier. Ollivier might plead that he was hardly responsible for the errors of the high command, but there could be no political hereafter for men who had plunged France headlong into a war in which her military unreadiness had been so cruelly exposed.

Heading the new ministry as both President of the Council and War Minister was veteran cavalryman General Charles Cousin de Montauban, Count Palikao. Montauban had led the French expedition to China in 1860, but his victory over the Chinese at Palikao had been marred by his troops burning the fabulous Summer Palace. The disapproving Legislature had first shown its independence by refusing him the financial reward proposed by the Emperor. Now the vigorous 74-year-old Palikao would have to spend a disproportionate amount of time managing the Chamber while he tried to direct the war against the Germans. David was made Minister of Public Works and Clément Duvernois Minister of Commerce. Both did creditable jobs preparing Paris for a siege.

Presiding over this reactionary Cabinet, which was much more congenial to her than the old, was the Empress Eugénie. She had been Regent twice before, during the Italian war and again during Napoleon's 1865 tour of Algeria. She had long aspired to the role of co-sovereign rather than consort, urging the chronically sick Emperor in 1866 to abdicate in favour of their son and make her Regent.[6] Now the Cabinet debated whether the Emperor should return to Paris. For the sake of the dynasty and, it was believed, for the perpetuation of her own powers, Eugénie adamantly opposed his return to the capital, which would be seen as a defeat and might well spark revolution.

However, the army wanted to be rid of Napoleon. In his tormented state of health, his inept, vacillating and fatalistic leadership had been a gift to the Germans, and his presence was demoralizing the troops. On 7 August General Lebrun tactfully put it to him that he should return to Paris, leaving command of the army to one of his marshals. Napoleon took no offence but asked, 'Having left Paris at the head of the army, how do you think I could go back there today alone?'[7] So he stayed at the front another ten days, his intentions oscillating between concentrating the army at Metz or Châlons, where he imagined it would have a breathing space to complete its organization. Châlons was familiar ground and covered the capital, but offered no good defensive position. Retreating there meant yielding the lines of the Moselle and Meuse, and indeed most of eastern France, without fighting. The great military city of Metz on the Moselle at least had strong forts, and seemed to offer refuge against an advancing enemy who had already gained psychological dominance over the French high command. Lack of an effective intelligence service to analyze rumours about German numbers and intentions deepened anxiety at headquarters. Any determination to manoeuvre, or to launch a surprise stroke against one of the enemy's columns before they could unite, was conspicuously absent.

Although Napoleon had given Marshal Achille Bazaine command of the corps in Lorraine now withdrawing to Metz, he continued to issue orders to them directly. A combination of the Emperor's vagueness and General de Failly's wilfulness lost the chance to bring 5 Corps directly to Metz. Similarly, Napoleon's indecision as to where he wanted Canrobert's 6 Corps led to much wasteful counter-marching for its still incomplete divisions, and the consequent tying up of the railways. Precious days passed without any clear strategy being formulated or put energetically into action. The Empress and · Cabinet were doing no more than representing strong and widespread public concern when they pressed Napoleon to pass command to Bazaine, who enjoyed an inflated reputation in the country and the army. This popular enthusiasm was based on little more than Bazaine's having risen from the ranks and having been out of favour at the imperial court after his command of the ill-fated Mexican expedition. Napoleon put Bazaine in command on 12 August, commiserating with Le Bœuf that 'We are both sacked.'[8]

Next day, watched by silent crowds, the Emperor set off from Metz with his luxurious convoy of wagons; but he lingered in the vicinity, still trying to act as commander-in-chief and embarrassing Bazaine with his 'wishes' for military movements.

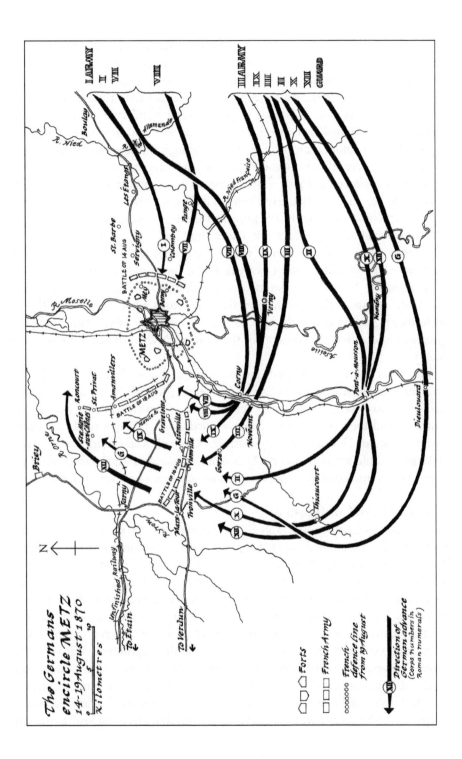

Meanwhile, the German First and Second Armies were approaching the Moselle, sending cavalry patrols across it that created alarm that the French army's flanks were being turned. Napoleon became anxious to continue the retreat of the 'Army of the Rhine' westwards towards Verdun and Châlons without further loss of time. Yet, due to poor planning and staff work, enormous traffic jams developed at the river crossings and in the narrow streets of Metz. It took the army more than two days to file through the city. On 14 August two French corps were still east of the Moselle when an aggressive German brigadier attacked, bringing on a bloody slugging match in the late afternoon and twilight that would be called the Battle of Borny. The French had numerical superiority on the battlefield and might have punished German boldness. Yet Bazaine, for all his personal bravery under fire, could think only of continuing the retreat as soon as possible, in obedience to the Emperor's injunctions. The French suffered 3,614 casualties, the Germans 4,906. Both sides claimed victory.

That night, Napoleon congratulated Bazaine on having 'broken the spell' and spoke to him of the need to keep the army intact while there was still hope of bringing Austria and Italy into the war. When they talked again next day Bazaine noticed that the contents of the Emperor's chamberpot were red with blood.[9]

Finally, at dawn on 16 August, a dejected Napoleon, his face drawn with pain, took leave of Bazaine at the village of Gravelotte, west of Metz, urging him to bring the army westwards on the Verdun road. Then the carriage bearing the Emperor and the Prince Imperial drove north-west, taking a road that would avoid reported German cavalry patrols. General Margueritte's Chasseurs d'Afrique would act as an escort. As Napoleon disappeared, Bazaine 'could not refrain from immediately expressing his satisfaction in no uncertain terms'.[10]

The Châlons Conference

If Bazaine's taciturnity had won him a reputation as a great general, it was General Jules Trochu's eloquence that made him a favourite of the opposition. After the first defeats, Trochu's pre-war criticisms of the army's weaknesses lent him the prestige of a prophet, and his readily expressed ideas caused Paris politicians of the Left and Centre to turn to him as a man with all the answers in a crisis. They favoured his appointment as War Minister, but the intellectual Breton's conscience would not allow him to serve the imperial regime unless he were allowed to denounce its past mistakes to the Legislature. With German armies advancing towards Paris, it was small wonder the Cabinet found this proposal unappealing. Still, some use had to be made of the popular general, who had been sidelined at the start of the war with command of an observation corps on the Spanish border. He had then been designated to lead a seaborne expedition to Denmark, until that plan was aborted. Now he was given command of a corps hurriedly being assembled to swell the numbers of the Army of Châlons. To impress the Germans this was designated 12 Corps, though corps numbered 8–11 did not exist.

As he set off from the Gare de l'Est in Paris on the night of 15 August, the bald, dapper Trochu had other responsibilities in mind. A week earlier he had written a powerful memorandum to a friend in the imperial entourage, who made sure it was seen by the Emperor, warning of the dangers of allowing the army to stay at Metz, where it would inevitably be encircled. Instead, Trochu urged, it should be pulled back to operate in front of Paris, where its supplies were assured and it would be sufficiently strong to prevent the Germans laying a siege.

What he saw at Châlons station on 16 August affronted his strict Catholic sensibilities and confirmed his view that MacMahon's troops were in no state to be led into battle:

> There, in stifling heat, a regiment of Zouaves belonging to Mac-Mahon's army had just arrived and was about to start for the camp. They had been defeated at [Frœschwiller], and an exhausting retreat, accomplished first on foot and then by rail, had brought them to Châlons. The men of this regiment, already ensconced in the carriages, filled the station with their shouting and obscene songs. A dozen of them, stark naked and some clasping bottles, performed dances of revolting indecency on the roofs of the carriages, jumping from one to another! Beside myself with indignation, I rushed onto the platform, interrogating these rascals, seeking their officers and calling on them to suppress this shameful disorder, until the sudden start of the train removed the sickening spectacle.[11]

That evening Trochu's train pulled into Mourmelon, the station that served Châlons Camp, where 1 Corps troops were being disembarked at the end of their retreat. In a train alongside his, Trochu saw the Emperor, seated in a third-class carriage. Having left Gravelotte that morning, Napoleon had reached the railway at Verdun by early afternoon and taken the train. His arrival at the camp could hardly have been more different from Augusts past, when he had come to preside over brilliant military ceremonial.

Next morning Trochu and his chief of staff joined the Emperor in conference to decide strategy, and pressed their views. Trochu had a champion in Prince Napoleon Jerome, a wayward cousin of the Emperor's who strikingly resembled Napoleon I. The Prince was an inveterate opponent of the Empress, sympathetic to Liberalism and nationalism, and had opposed this war as a folly of the political Right. He dominated the meeting, urging that Trochu be made Military Governor of Paris. When Trochu's chief of staff broached the Emperor's need to 'remount the throne', the sovereign sadly conceded, 'Yes, it's true, I seem to have abdicated.'[12]

At this the Prince interjected vehemently: 'At Paris you abdicated the government. At Metz you have just abdicated command of the army. Barring crossing into Belgium, you must take hold of one of them again. Command of the army is impossible. Taking up the government is difficult and dangerous, because it means returning to Paris. But damn it! If we are to fall, let us fall like men!'[13]

These arguments held sway. MacMahon had joined the meeting and contributed little, but vouched to the Emperor for Trochu's reliability. It was agreed that the undisciplined and poorly armed Paris Garde Mobile would return from Châlons to Paris. Trochu, armed with a letter from the Emperor, would return as Military Governor of Paris, with command over its defence forces. He would issue a proclamation preparing the capital for the return of the Emperor, who would follow within hours. MacMahon, appointed to command all troops at Châlons, would bring them back to cover Paris, but would be under the orders of Bazaine as commander-in-chief.

This new strategy was nullified within hours. Trochu, having drafted his proclamation as he travelled back, insisted on seeing the Empress in the small hours of 18 August. She met him with a sarcastic sally at his political sympathies for the previous regime: 'Don't you think that, in our extreme peril, the Orléans princes should be recalled to France?' She was having none of what she saw as an attempted Liberal coup against her authority, and ended the interview with a frosty pronouncement: 'Those who have advised the Emperor on the resolutions you have reported are enemies. The Emperor will not return to Paris.' According to Trochu, she added, 'He will not come back alive. The Army of Châlons will go to join with the Army of Metz.'[14]

Palikao too gave Trochu a hostile reception. He had already telegraphed the Emperor:

> The Empress has communicated to me the letter in which the Emperor announces that he wishes to bring the Army of Châlons back to Paris. I beg the Emperor to give up this idea, which would look like the abandonment of the Army of Metz ... Within three days the Army of Châlons will be 85,000 men strong, not counting Douay's Corps, which will come up in three days with 18,000 men. Can a powerful diversion not be made against Prussian forces already exhausted by several battles? The Empress shares my opinion ...[15]

Napoleon, conceding that to retreat to Paris would be more dangerous than going to fight the enemy, abandoned the idea of returning there.[16] Prince Napoleon Jerome was sent away on a forlorn-hope diplomatic mission to his father-in-law, the King of Italy. As Governor of Paris, Trochu was ignored by the Empress and Palikao. Doubtless they had reason to be wary of his dangerous popularity and unctuous professions of loyalty, but by treating him as a rival and enemy they confirmed him as one, and there would be a price to pay.

With Trochu's plan ruled out, what should the Army of Châlons do? Napoleon told MacMahon that he would no longer attempt to direct military operations: the Marshal should consult Bazaine and Palikao. MacMahon's request to Bazaine for instructions elicited the unhelpful response that the latter could give none, as he considered MacMahon's operations 'entirely outside my sphere of action for the moment'.[17] General Palikao, at least, was not afraid to take a decision. On 19 August, with the support of the Cabinet, he set MacMahon the objective of rejoining Bazaine. MacMahon dutifully replied, 'Please tell the Cabinet that it can count on me and that I shall do everything to rejoin Bazaine.'[18] Yet he harboured doubts. He was reluctant to leave Paris uncovered in face of the rapidly advancing Crown Prince, or rashly to imperil his army, on which so much now depended. Moreover, he was perplexed as to what Bazaine was doing.

The Beleaguered Army

Anxiety mounted at Châlons on 17 August at reports of a great battle fought the previous day. A cryptic wire from Bazaine to the Emperor announced that the enemy had been repelled, but that Bazaine had been forced to draw back towards Metz, alleging a lack of food and munitions. He expected to resume his march in two days' time, heading northwards via Briey. On the afternoon of 18 August came a telegram reporting that the Germans were attacking heavily all along the French line. Finally, at 8.20 p.m., Bazaine announced that firing had ceased. 'Our troops, remaining steadily in their positions ...'.[19] Then the telegraph went dead. The Germans had cut the wire, and their army was firmly across the road from Metz to Châlons.

In fact, the two biggest and bloodiest battles of the war had been fought on the great rolling plateau that extends westwards from Metz. Within hours of Napoleon's departure from Gravelotte on 16 August, leading units of the German Second Army had opened fire on French cavalry who had been heedlessly cooking breakfast in the morning sun by the Verdun road. Believing they were cutting off the French rearguard, the Germans had actually struck the head of the slow-moving French columns. All day long the outnumbered

Germans, hurrying up from the south, fought desperately to keep hold of the highway leading west. By the end of the day they had 64,000 infantry in action, while the French eventually massed some 137,000 troops on the field. Yet the French fought defensively and with little coordination. Bazaine showed that he was as out of his depth as the Emperor when it came to controlling and directing a large modern army. The battle raged back and forth across the Verdun road and the fields and hollows either side of it, swirling round the solidly built Lorraine hamlets of Vionville and Rezonville. The Germans brought up nearly 250 guns to bolster their lines and bought precious time with desperate cavalry charges. At nightfall Bazaine did not press westwards, as he might have done, but abandoned the field to the Germans and swung his army back like a door, with its back to Metz.

His 11-kilometre line, centred on Amanvillers, was a superb defensive position. When the German First and Second Armies attacked it on the afternoon of 18 August with 179,000 infantry and 726 guns, their frontal attacks almost brought them to disaster in the largest battle fought on French soil until that date. On the southern flank, efforts to storm the quarries and farmsteads held by Frossard's riflemen on the hills overlooking Gravelotte reduced the Germans to a state bordering rout by nightfall. At the northern end of the French line, a massed assault over open slopes by the Prussian Guard allowed the French, posted around the village of Saint-Privat, to demonstrate the lethal power of the Chassepot. Only at twilight were Canrobert's men, outflanked and outgunned, without reinforcements and low on ammunition, forced out of the blazing village – though the Imperial Guard stood unused and four million rounds of Chassepot ammunition sat in freight wagons in the marshalling yards of Metz only a few kilometres away.[20] The French position finally unravelled from the north, the troops falling back on Metz after dark.

Moltke had limited success in trying to control the battle, while Bazaine hardly tried to do so. The fighting was directed by unit commanders throughout, and the losses were frightful. Men fell so thick and fast under the intense fire that 'pitching down like at Gravelotte' became a French expression for torrential rain or hail. Including Borny, the three battles around Metz, fought on 14, 16 and 18 August, cost the Germans 10,848 dead, 28,440 wounded and 1,630 missing or captured: a total of 40,918 casualties.[21] The French lost 2,719 dead, 17,667 wounded and 9,258 missing or captured: a total of 29,644.[22] On the German side, everyone from king to private was awed by the extent of the sacrifice and the loss of comrades or kinsmen. On the night of Gravelotte Fritz Hönig heard regimental bands playing 'Hail to Thee in the Victor's Crown' – the Prussian national anthem – and 'Now Thank We All Our God', and brooded that amid such terrible scenes, 'one might have felt inclined to regard this as a parody'. Next day Hönig was sickened as he viewed farms burnt out by German artillery:

> At these points hardly any French were found killed or wounded by infantry bullets; almost all had been destroyed by the fire of the guns ... The ground was changed by the German artillery fire into a desert covered with many corpses. The interiors of Point du Jour and Moscou [farms] were not passable after the battle until they had been cleared.[23]

Among the sad relics in the Gravelotte museum, one perhaps speaks more eloquently of the horror of the fighting than all the monuments and burial plots that dot these fateful battlefields: three Chassepot bayonets fused together by the intense heat of the fire that destroyed Moscou farm and its French defenders.

Although the Germans had paid a terrible price, Bazaine's lack of strategic sense had allowed them to trap his army in Metz. On 19 August they completed a ring around it. A junction between the two halves of the French army, relatively easy only a week before, must now involve a battle with the Germans holding the central position.

Meanwhile, France waited expectantly, starved of reliable military news by censorship. Palikao sought to keep up morale, hinting that victory was imminent and spreading tales worthy of Baron Munchausen of Prussians slaughtered in hecatombs. Such was popular faith in Bazaine that it was believed that his withdrawal into Metz must be part of a clever plan. Howls of treason were raised against journalist Edmond About when he described the drunkenness and disorder of MacMahon's retreating army rather too frankly.[24]

Yet invasion was becoming a reality in eastern France. Fear of it was borne westwards by hordes of refugees fleeing before German cavalry patrols which boldly demanded the surrender of village after village. In the fevered wartime atmosphere wild rumours ran: spy mania was everywhere and sparked ugly incidents. Palikao had one German shot in Paris for passing information to the enemy, and plans were discussed to expel 70,000 German citizens from the capital. Foreigners and minorities came under suspicion. Many an English tourist or newspaper correspondent seen making sketches, consulting a map or asking directions had nasty brushes with mobs and suffered brief imprisonment. In Strasbourg on 7 August a telegraphist saw a man accused of spying beaten to death by a mob, and narrowly escaped the same fate himself, being abused as a 'dirty Jew'.[25]

In Alsace and the south Protestants were accused of being in league with the enemy. In the south-west priests and nobles were eyed suspiciously as conspirators and isolated acts of violence swept the countryside. Deep in rural France on 16 August, at an agricultural fair outside the hamlet of Hautfaye in the Dordogne, a peasant mob shouting 'Long Live the Emperor!' battered, tortured and burned to death a young nobleman whom they mistook for both a 'Prussian' and a hated 'republican'.

By contrast, in large towns where the Empire had never been popular, principally Paris, Marseilles and Lyon, republican activists became restless at news of the first defeats, sensing their opportunity as the regime foundered, but the authorities quickly restored order. An insurrectionary attempt by the extreme Left in Paris on 14 August failed utterly. Wielding pistols and daggers, hard-line followers of the arch-revolutionary Auguste Blanqui attempted to seize rifles at the La Villette firemen's barracks, but were captured after a fight with gendarmes. Bystanders were so out of sympathy with the insurgents that they beat some up, shouting 'They're Prussians!'[26] When it came to suppressing the Commune the following year, the army would remember that the revolutionaries had been fomenting civil strife while it was fighting Germans.

Republican leaders, while keeping up pressure on the government in the Chamber, wanted to give it no pretext for repression, and hastened to distance themselves from the actions of a few violent extremists. For the moment, politics waited on military events. Yet it was evident that the fate of the dynasty, as well as that of France itself, was at stake in the coming campaign.

Chapter 8

The Army of Châlons

An Improvised Army

Arriving at the vast plain covered with white conical tents that was Châlons Camp, MacMahon's men had the look of defeat about them. 'Gaunt, black with dirt, bowed by extreme exhaustion, dull-eyed and dazed looking', they moved one onlooker to exclaim, 'Why, it's the retreat from Russia without the snow!'[1]

They needed time to recuperate, reorganize and re-equip, but the rate of the German advance allowed only a pause. The few days the men spent at Châlons at least allowed them to clean their equipment, eat and rest a little. Some of their losses in clothing, camping gear and equipment were made good, though there were still shortages: in 1 Corps there were only enough haversacks for every other man. Promotions had to be made to fill officer vacancies, which grew more acute when Palikao ordered MacMahon to send forty-two senior officers to Paris to command new formations. Gaps in the ranks were only partially filled, using reservists with little or no experience in handling the Chassepot. Thus 1, 5 and 7 Corps combined demoralized with inexperienced troops, many led by unfamiliar officers.

As MacMahon would command the army, General Ducrot was appointed to lead 1 Corps. Lieutenant de Narcy wrote, 'he passed for a general of energetic bearing, steadfast, educated, and capable of leading a large body of troops skilfully, and there was almost universal confidence in him.'[2] Félix Douay, a competent organizer with Mexican experience, commanded 7 Corps. As for General de Failly, his performance at the head of 5 Corps had aroused such disgust among his men and the public that, unbeknown to him, Palikao had decided on a replacement, who, however, had to travel from Algeria, so the change of command would not be immediate.

The fourth and largest component of the Army of Châlons was the newly formed 12 Corps. Trochu having returned to Paris, this command was given to General Lebrun, who had accompanied the Emperor from Metz. The intellectually gifted Lebrun might have made a better chief of staff for the new army than General Faure, who was assigned to that post. Though his men were unfamiliar to him and he to them, Lebrun took up his command with energy. His troops varied greatly in quality. He had some good regular regiments sent from the Spanish frontier. (For, despite Bismarck's hopes, the Spanish had no intention of becoming embroiled in a war that was only nominally about their throne.) There were infantry and artillery belonging to 6 Corps which had not been forwarded to Metz in time – men and guns Canrobert had sorely missed in the fighting at Saint-Privat. Then there was the Marine Division under General de Vassoigne: the so called 'Blue Division' whose blue-grey trousers contrasted with army red. These *marsouins* (literally 'porpoises') had been so christened by sailors of yore who alleged that Marines hung around ships eating but doing no work. They had been sent to Châlons because they were no longer required for a Baltic expedition.

In contrast to these excellent units, Lebrun had one division of raw troops formed of temporary regiments amalgamated from the fourth battalions of other regiments. Typically these were commanded by lieutenant colonels, with dugout captains leading enlarged companies. These troops represented the government's efforts to summon more manpower: men from the 1869 contingent who had just been called up, plus reluctant reservists who had largely escaped training in previous years. But, while an army might be improvised, soldiers could not. Seeing the men he was to command, General Blanchard protested that 'he asked nothing better than to die defending his country, provided he did so honourably, but not while leading into battle troops entirely composed of recruits who were soldiers in name only.'[3] He promptly got himself a posting to Paris, leaving Lebrun hastily to make another appointment. Worried by the lack of fire discipline French troops had shown so far, Lebrun encouraged efforts by his officers to train his raw men in use of the Chassepot, insisting that each man fire at least five practice rounds.

The army had two reserve cavalry divisions. Bonnemains's heavy cavalry was severely reduced after its exploits at Frœschwiller. The other division would be commanded by General Margueritte who, in addition to his brigade of Chasseurs d'Afrique, had one composed of hussars and chasseurs.

Although the army was under-strength, by 21 August it was drawing rations for 130,566 men and 26,763 horses. Its effective infantry strength (excluding officers) was 106,000, with 12,000 cavalry. With it went 348 guns and 84 *mitrailleuses*.[4] The army had insufficient competent administrators, wagons or field hospitals. Most of all it lacked cohesion and discipline. On 18 August Narcy witnessed an NCO refuse to obey an order from his lieutenant, swearing and turning his back. When the order was repeated the NCO had to be restrained from striking the lieutenant across the face with his sabre, but received only a mild rebuke. Narcy was appalled by how many men made excuses for the culprit: 'A striking example of the progressive indiscipline which the absence of severe punishments encouraged and emboldened!'[5]

At least the worst troops, the rowdy Paris Garde Mobile, were packed off to the capital, to everyone's relief. Their drinking, vandalism, carousing with women they had brought along, their jeers and insults to the Emperor and MacMahon and their disdain for regulars who had been beaten by the Germans had set a demoralizing example: but their behaviour was extreme. When Napoleon and the Prince Imperial rode past 1 Corps on 19 August there were still shouts of 'Long Live the Emperor!'[6] How long such confidence as the troops still had in their leaders could be sustained on campaign would soon be tested. On 21 August MacMahon set his army in motion.

The stimulus to leave Châlons came from an alarmed Colonel Stoffel, former military attaché in Berlin and now the army's one-man intelligence service. On 20 August he learned that German cavalry was 44 kilometres away, and took his apprehensions to MacMahon, who declared, 'Enemy cavalry could, after a night march, be here the day after tomorrow. We must leave tomorrow.'[7] Châlons was no place to give battle against a stronger enemy, but equally a few enemy horsemen were hardly an imminent threat. One officer felt that, in withdrawing, 'We had the appearance of fleeing before the enemy.'[8]

For the army moved neither east towards Verdun nor south against the Crown Prince, options urged by Palikao, but north-west to Rheims, further away from Metz and the enemy. MacMahon, who was vainly seeking further information about Bazaine, explained to Palikao that 'if Bazaine breaks out to the north, I shall be better placed to help him; if he breaks out to the south, he will be too far away for me to be useful to him in any case.'[9]

The march from Châlons to Rheims did not augur well. Men woken in the night stood in line or in the saddle for hours awaiting their turn to move. Wagon convoys crossing columns caused traffic jams. During the long, hot march over the dusty plain of Champagne thousands of men fell out as badly made or poorly fitting boots took their toll. Even the Marines, who had to cover 40 kilometres, were not yet hardened to route marches. Supply arrangements broke down, and even when men got food that evening they lacked kindling wood to cook it. Some took to pillage or deserted. Exhausted stragglers were still finding their way into camp around Rheims next morning. The Emperor, meanwhile, summoned MacMahon to Courcelles, west of the city, to discuss strategy with a visitor from Paris.

The Die is Cast

Since his fall from power in 1869, Eugène Rouher had continued as the guiding spirit of the authoritarian Bonapartists and trusted counsellor of the Empress. As President of the Senate, he had inspired the plebiscite and had worked to undermine the Ollivier Ministry. On 16 July he had delivered a fulsome address congratulating the Emperor in terms implying that the war was premeditated: 'the Emperor has known how to wait; but, for four years, he has carried our armaments to the peak of perfection ... Thanks to your efforts, Sire, France is ready.'[10] Trochu considered Rouher 'the evil genius of imperial France'.[11]

Now, visiting the Emperor unofficially, Rouher urged the views of Eugénie and Palikao for a rapid march to rescue Bazaine and the abandonment of any idea of falling back on Paris. MacMahon countered these political consider-ations with military arguments. There was no further news from Metz. 'It's impossible to go to Bazaine's rescue. Bazaine has no munitions or food-stuffs and will be compelled to capitulate, and we shall arrive too late.'[12] To lead his army eastwards to Verdun or Metz would be to expose it to defeat by overwhelming German forces. Far better to conserve it as a nucleus for the organization of a force of 250,000 to 300,000 men in front of Paris. By moving to Rheims, MacMahon had kept open the option of falling back on Paris, with good defensive positions available to him. Rouher yielded to these arguments, admitting his lack of military expertise. Besides, he saw advantage in placing all forces around Paris under the command of the loyal MacMahon, so under-mining the mistrusted Trochu. He drew up proclamations accordingly and returned to the capital.

Next morning, 22 August, MacMahon gave orders for withdrawal towards Paris. Then a despatch arrived which changed his mind entirely. It was from Bazaine, dated 19 August, and had been smuggled through the lines. It reported that his troops were tired by their battles and needed two or three days' rest, but 'I still count on heading north via Montmédy and so regaining the main road to Sainte-Menehould and Châlons, if it isn't too strongly occupied. If it is, I shall continue towards Sedan or even Mézières to reach Châlons.'[13]

MacMahon's sense of duty momentarily overcame any strategic doubts. If, as Bazaine's message indicated, a breakout from Metz was imminent, how could he not go to the aid of a brother officer? Moreover, rather than embarking on a suicidal mission eastwards straight into the heart of the German positions, heading for Montmédy would keep him on their northern flank and provide a diversion that could help Bazaine and perhaps make junction with him possible.

MacMahon immediately cancelled orders to fall back towards Paris and issued new ones for an eastward march. He sent a reply to Bazaine: 'Received your despatch of the 19th. Am at Rheims; am heading for Montmédy; will be on the Aisne the day after tomorrow, whence I shall act according to circum-stances to come to your assistance.'[14]

He wired his intentions to Palikao. His telegram crossed one from the War Minister to the Emperor. The Cabinet, unanimously rejecting Rouher's recommendations, insisted that 'Not to help Bazaine would have the most deplorable consequences in Paris.'[15] Napoleon communicated the gist of the message to MacMahon, which only fortified the decision he had already taken.

Only after the war did a controversy blow up about a more tentative message from Bazaine dated 20 August: 'The enemy is continually gathering strength around me, and to rejoin you I shall very probably follow the line of the northern fortresses, and shall advise you of my route, if, however, I can undertake the march without compromising the army.'[16]

This message reached headquarters, but neither MacMahon nor his staff officers remembered having seen it. Colonel Stoffel would be accused by a military court of having suppressed it in order not to weaken MacMahon's resolve, though he protested his innocence so strongly that he received a prison sentence for contempt of court. In any event, the despatch was overlooked. MacMahon later gave contradictory views on whether the element of doubt it introduced might have modified his decisions. Like much about the wisdom of the campaign, the question must remain a matter of speculation.

Was MacMahon's eastward march doomed from the outset? Palikao and others would argue that the best chance to rescue Bazaine had already passed. Had MacMahon marched directly from Châlons to Verdun on 21 August, they asserted, his army could have arrived in four days and beaten the German covering force nearby as a prelude to breaking the blockade of Metz while the Crown Prince was still to the west. No one can say with certainty whether this could have succeeded had the army moved fast, covered by an effective cavalry screen. Ducrot was in favour of such a bold stroke. A Napoleon I, leading a veteran army, might conceivably have carried it off. Yet the odds against its success were long, and MacMahon's scepticism was understandable. He was no Napoleon, and his army was an imperfect instrument. Besides, the success of Palikao's plan depended unduly on good luck; on the Germans being off their guard and remaining passive for several days while the French advanced, rather than concentrating against them. It ignored the fact that the Germans around Metz were strong enough to contain Bazaine while holding off the Army of Châlons until the Crown Prince could return to their aid. Even if, by great good fortune, MacMahon managed to join forces with Bazaine, they would still be in the presence of German armies that outnumbered them. The risks of the French being trapped and crushed by superior numbers were therefore much higher than Palikao allowed. Would the more northerly route offer any better chance of success, allowing as it did for the option of escape to the north? Only with boldness, speed, secrecy, skill in manoeuvre and deception, and a generous helping of luck, could the operation to relieve Metz have any chance of success. In all these the French would prove sadly lacking.

The March to the East

From Rheims to Montmédy, MacMahon's objective, is about 100 kilometres as the crow flies: five days' march. Yet six days after setting out on 23 August the Army of Châlons had covered scarcely two-thirds of the distance.

The advance began confidently, despite leaden skies, cold driving rain, and the usual traffic snarls caused by poor planning. But, although MacMahon had ordered the troops to carry four days' rations, supply arrangements broke down before the end of the first day, particularly in 5 and 12 Corps. On the army's southern flank, meanwhile, men of 7 Corps could see huge columns of smoke rising from Châlons Camp, where cavalry had been detailed to evacuate what stores they could. The rest was burned 'in anticipation of the approach of the Prussians, before the eyes of an army which, from the following day, would be short of everything'.[17]

Pillage was rife at Châlons, and also at Rheims in the army's rear, where four hundred deserters joined by civilians ran amok for several hours before being rounded up. The aftermath was witnessed next day by Dr Sarazin who was returning to the army after tending the wounded at Frœschwiller and having been transported through Germany and repatriated under the Geneva Convention. At Rheims station, 'A food convoy had been pillaged by troops; at some points the track was soaked in wine and littered with the remains of packing crates and stove in barrels. Stragglers and drunkards belonging to all arms of the service were swarming on every street and filling all the bars.' Among the citizens of Rheims 'we heard nothing but complaints and recriminations and, of those we questioned, some were preparing to take flight, others to receive the Prussians, who were about to arrive and would be in Rheims before midday. We were told that they ... were giving over to pillage and flames every town and village that resisted them; that it was very lucky that the French army had departed, and as for the remaining *francs-tireurs*, they would be forced to clear off or to give themselves up without firing a shot. The thermometer of patriotism stood at zero.'[18]

On the march too pillage resumed as men ran short of food. Henhouses were raided, potatoes dug up and orchards stripped of unripe fruit, which caused stomach upsets. Fatal accidents occurred as men fired recklessly at hares. Stern orders were issued against marauding, and the following days saw instances of officers putting pistols to their men's heads in an effort to halt it, but to little effect. One officer confessed after attempting this that 'It was repugnant to me to fire my first cartridge at a soldier of the French army.'[19]

On 24 August MacMahon diverted north to the railway at Rethel where supplies were issued. Thus a day was lost, and on the 25th many units made short marches or marked time. Next day the army left behind the chalky plains

Wilhelm I (1797–1888).

Otto von Bismarck (1815–98).

PRINCE BISMARCK.

Albrecht von Roon
(1803–79).

GENERAL VON ROON, MINISTER OF WAR.

Helmuth von Moltke
(1800–91).

GENERAL VON MOLTKE.

Napoleon III (1808–73).

NAPOLEON III.

Agénor de Gramont
(1819–80).

M. LE DUC DE GRAMONT

Dragoon.
Cuirassier.   Hussar.   Landwehr Infantry. Pioneers.
Uhlan (Lancer.)   Jäger.   Horse Artilleryman.
Rifleman of Infantry of the Line.

PRUSSIAN TROOPS.

Prussian Troops by Richard Knötel.

South German Troops by Richard Knötel.

WÜRTTEMBURGERS.
Cavalry.   BAVARIANS.
Artillery.   Artillery.   Light Horse.
Infantry.   Infantry.   Cuirassier.

SOUTH GERMAN TROOPS.

Mounted Rifles.   Artilleryman.

Garde Mobile.   Infantry of the Line.   Turko.   Cuirassier.   Dragoon.

FRENCH TROOPS.

nch Troops by Richard Knötel.

e Bavarian Assault on Wissembourg, 4 August 1870. Engraving after Ludwig Braun.

Friedrich Wilhelm,
Crown Prince of Prussia
(1831–88).

THE CROWN PRINCE OF PRUSSIA.

Maurice de
MacMahon (1808–93).

LE MARÉCHAL DE MAC-MAHON.

French Cuirassier taken prisoner at Frœschwiller, 6 August 1870. Painting by Édouard Detaille.

The Crown Prince acclaimed by his men as he enters Frœschwiller, evening of 6 August 1870. Painting by Ludwig Braun.

Charles Cousin de Montauban, Comte de Palikao (1796–1878).

Emmanuel Félix de Wimpffen (1811–84).

French Soldiers sketched from life between Stonne and Mouzon, 29 August 1870, by Auguste Lançon.

Bandaging Wounded from Beaumont, 3 p.m., 30 August 1870, by Lançon.

Street in the Faubourg de Mouzon, evening of 30 August 1870, by Lançon.

The Road between Mouzon and Remilly, 31 August 1870, by Lançon.

'The Last Cartridges'. Engraving after Alphonse de Neuville, 1873.

Fighting in a courtyard near Bazeilles, 1 September 1870, by Lançon.

Street Scene in Bazeilles, evening of 1 September 1870, by Lançon.

n street of Bazeilles after the battle.

ic at the gates of Sedan.

Charge of the Chasseurs d'Afrique at Floing. Engraving after Anton von Werner, 1884-5.

...eral Reille delivers Napoleon's letter to King Wilhelm. Engraving after Anton von Werner, 1884.

...otiations for capitulation at the Mayor's house in Donchery on the night of the battle. Painting by ...on von Werner, 1885. From left to right: French; Captain d'Orcet (with bandaged head), Chief of ...f General Faure (seated with back to viewer), General Castelnau, General de Wimpffen (standing ...h hand on table): German; General Podbielski (seated behind table), Moltke (standing at table), and ...narck. German staff officers: Captain Winterfeld, Count Nostitz (with notebook), Major Krause, Lt. ... Bronsart von Schellendorff, Lt. Col. Verdy du Vernois, Major Blume and Major de Claer.

Napoleon III, escorted by Bismarck, goes to meet King Wilhelm on 2 September. Painting by Wilhelm Camphausen, 1876.

French Prisoners of War.

of Champagne and entered the wooded, hilly, difficult country of the Argonne, where narrow roads turned to quagmires under the tramp of men, horses, livestock and vehicles in relentless, pelting rain. Inquisitive enemy cavalry now appeared from the south, but French horsemen, sticking too close to their own columns when they were in evidence at all, seemed incapable of driving them off. Frightened peasants told of large German forces not far behind. General Bordas's infantry brigade was sent to Grand Pré to protect the army's right flank, but after a skirmish Bordas took alarm, wrongly convinced that he faced 'superior forces'. The rest of 7 Corps was put on the alert and spent a cold, weary night 'with our ears cocked', straining for 'the least sound of a man's footstep or a horse's hooves'.[20]

Expecting an attack, MacMahon halted the army's march and had it take positions facing south. At dawn on the 27th he fleetingly contemplated attacking, but the threat failed to materialize. The eastward trek was resumed. Later that day, after a sharp encounter with Saxon cavalry near Buzancy, 5 Corps was similarly halted and held in line of battle before turning its back and marching on its way, much to its men's disgust. The meandering, hesitant and timid way the march was being conducted was stirring their contempt for their commanders. The troops no longer cheered the Emperor.

MacMahon had been strenuously seeking word of Bazaine from the civil authorities in the surrounding region. On the 25th came a report that he had broken out south-west from Metz, but it proved unfounded. Unknown to MacMahon, Bazaine did prepare a sortie eastwards from Metz on the 26th, but abandoned his bungled, half-hearted attempt when it rained heavily. Bazaine seems to have persuaded himself that he was performing a useful service simply by keeping his army intact in Metz. For reasons best known to himself, he chose not to share with his generals MacMahon's message of 22 August (smuggled in rolled in a cigarette) that the Army of Châlons was on its way.

At the little town of Le Chesne Populeux on 27 August MacMahon received confirmation from trustworthy sources that Bazaine had not moved from Metz, where he was blockaded by 200,000 men. Worse, instead of Bazaine marching northwards on the east bank of the Meuse, German forces were reported in that direction, well placed to contest any French attempt to cross the river and reach Montmédy. There were also heavy German columns to the south and astride the route back to Châlons. MacMahon's position must now be known to the enemy through his cavalry.

MacMahon saw that his campaign to join Bazaine could not succeed, but it was still possible to save his army by withdrawing northwards to Mézières and getting his men on trains back to Paris. He decided to do so, setting out his reasons in a telegram to the War Minister that evening. As he was about to send it General Faure cautioned, 'The reply you get from Paris will be such that perhaps you will be prevented from carrying out your new plans. You could leave sending it until tomorrow, when we shall already be on our way to Mézières.'[21] MacMahon reread the message, but sent it anyway. It concluded:

> I have had no news from Bazaine since the 19th. If I go to join him I shall be attacked in front by parts of the First and Second Armies which, using the cover of forests, can conceal a force superior to mine; and simultaneously by the Crown Prince's army which will cut my line of retreat. Tomorrow I shall head for Mézières, whence I shall continue my retreat to the west, according to circumstances.[22]

Faure was proved right. Palikao had been 'boiling with impatience' at the languid pace of MacMahon's advance. He considered the Marshal half-hearted and his own plan 'our only chance of salvation'.[23] Upon receiving MacMahon's telegram he immediately wired the Emperor, 'If you abandon Bazaine, there will be revolution in Paris, and you will be attacked by all the enemy's forces.' He insisted that MacMahon still had an adequate lead over the advancing enemy, adding that 'Everybody here understands the necessity of relieving Bazaine, and the anxiety with which we follow your movements is extreme.'[24]

MacMahon was greatly perturbed. He asked Ducrot if he thought it still possible to reach Montmédy. Despite the dangers, the sanguine Ducrot was persuaded 'that by throwing all our cavalry onto our right wing, we could halt the enemy's advance and achieve a junction with Bazaine'.[25] Whether the vacillating marshal was convinced by this or by Palikao's arguments, he evidently felt that he could not disobey such a forcible directive. His ingrained sense of a soldier's duty prevailed. Reportedly he said, 'Come on then, let's go and get whipped!'[26] He would afterwards be much criticized for not insisting on withdrawing northwards. After all, he was commander in the field. Had he been of a different temperament he might have defied the War Minister and galvanized the Emperor into backing him, threatening resignation. He was to be accused of putting loyalty to the dynasty above his duty to the country. Yet Napoleon himself grasped the dangers of the new course, observing that 'it would perhaps have been better to follow yesterday's plan.'[27]

MacMahon had changed the orders for withdrawal northwards to a resumption of the march on Montmédy even before a further telegram from Palikao arrived on the afternoon of 28 August: 'In the name of the Cabinet and the Privy Council, I demand that you go to help Bazaine, taking advantage of the thirty hours lead that you have over the Crown Prince.'[28] The troops had already started moving north when the new orders arrived, causing much swearing, counter-marching and consequent traffic jams.

On the day the army had set forth, 23 August, Gambetta had made one of his attacks on the government in the Legislature, declaring his conviction that 'this country is sliding towards the abyss without realizing it.'[29] With Palikao's order and MacMahon's passive obedience to it, this prophecy was dangerously close to fulfilment. As his men, soaked to the skin, slogged down muddy roads in the pouring rain watched by ever bolder German horsemen, a 7 Corps officer reflected, 'In all, what an evil day for our army this 28 August was. It had not given battle or suffered losses, and yet a great sense of unease hung over it; everybody was downhearted, our souls were full of apprehension. We had a sort of foreboding that the enemy must have taken advantage of our uncertainties and of all the time we had wasted!'[30] The enemy had.

Chapter 9

The Path of the Invader

The Conflict Deepens

After the war military theorists, not least Moltke himself, would analyze at leisure technical flaws in the German campaign so far. Of six pitched battles in a fortnight only one, Gravelotte–Saint-Privat on 18 August, could be said to have been willed and planned by the high command; and that had gone so awry on parts of the line that at the southern end of the battlefield the Germans momentarily believed they had suffered defeat. The other clashes had been encounter battles brought on by unit commanders which, though ending in bloody victories, had contributed only accidentally, if at all, to the strategic objective of enveloping the enemy's main army. The French had retreated too fast for that.

Nevertheless, Bazaine proved an obliging enemy in the Metz battles by allowing himself to be entrapped. By the only criterion that counts amid the fog and friction of warfare, the Germans had succeeded superbly. Within three weeks of the commencement of hostilities they had the enemy's army snared in Metz while the other great city of the east, Strasbourg, was under siege. Europe was awed by the scale and rapidity of their achievement. Through their willingness to fight the enemy wherever they found him, the Germans had retained the initiative and the momentum of victory.

The procession of specially equipped ambulance trains steaming from the Metz front back to Germany testified to the high cost, and there was consternation as well as grief at home. Yet the dedication and care lavished on the wounded by thousands of German Red Cross workers heightened the earnest sense of national purpose. The losses suffered so far only strengthened German public unity in support of the struggle.

Bismarck, travelling with Royal Headquarters, was perfectly in touch with this mood: one of his sons had been badly wounded on 16 August. Within a week of the Frœschwiller victory he had formally resolved on annexation of Alsace as a German war aim. He encouraged the demand through press articles, but he hardly invented the growing swell of opinion that the blood-sacrifice made by Germans should receive solid recompense. Germany had conquered Alsace, to which many believed she had a historical right. Annexation was particularly favoured in the South German states. Moltke shared such views, and he and his generals believed that the future security of Germany against France depended on possession of the line of the Vosges, even beyond the western limit of German as the majority language.

On 14 August a relative of Bismarck's, Count Friedrich Bismarck-Bohlen, was made Military Governor of Alsace. He was to be assisted by a civil commissioner. A week later, his regime was extended to the occupied part of eastern Lorraine. This was the origin of the German construct of 'Alsace-Lorraine', ruled directly by Prussian royal authority.

The German determination to annex Alsace and then Lorraine came to be seen as the fatal element in making the Franco-German quarrel irreconcilable, converting a 'dynastic' war into a 'national' one. It cost Germany much sympathy abroad, notably in the British press. Yet Bismarck was unconvinced that a peace without annexations could assure French goodwill and moderation and guarantee German security. On the contrary, he thought that the bitterness of defeat would itself drive the French to revenge, just as they had sought 'revenge' for Sadowa. As he told the Prussian ambassador to Britain on 21 August, 'the only proper policy is at least to make somewhat less dangerous an enemy whom we can never win as a true friend, and to make ourselves more secure against him. For that, it is not enough to dismantle those of his fortresses which threaten us; only annexing some of them will suffice.'[1] If Franco-German hostility was to be an enduring feature of European politics, Bismarck sought to ensure that a strengthened Germany would have the advantage.

The very act of fighting was deepening national animosities that underlay the conflict. On entering France King Wilhelm had issued a proclamation, dated 11 August, assuring citizens that 'I make war on French soldiers and not on civilians, whose persons and goods will be safe so long as they do not forfeit the right to my protection by acts of aggression against German troops.'[2] His nephew and son went further, proclaiming to their troops that the quarrel was solely with the detested French Emperor, that 'disturber of the peace'.[3] Yet Bismarck no longer made any distinction between the French nation and its rulers. Within a fortnight, Royal Headquarters gave General von Werder authority to bombard the fortified city of Strasbourg, with the frank aim of hastening its surrender by terrorizing its citizens. In the first few nights of an awesome artillery barrage about eighty civilians were killed, hundreds wounded and thousands made homeless. The city's library, full of priceless medieval manuscripts and artworks, went up in flames along with churches, civic buildings and private homes. A young Protestant fire-watcher in the city, Rodolphe Reuss, watched the roof of the great cathedral burn with a sinister glow: 'Those who lived through those dreadful hours, who, impotent and heartbroken, witnessed this brutal profanation of the masterpiece of Christian art, so dear to every native of Strasbourg, will never forget or forgive.'[4]

The cathedral was saved from complete destruction, and the Germans pointed out that the French had used it as an observation post. Nevertheless, this wanton and terrifying bombardment of their city did more than anything to make the generation of Alsatians who lived through it irreconcilable to German rule. The historian Treitschke could only justify the forcible annexation of Alsace against the wishes of its inhabitants by arguing that 'We Germans ... understand better what is good for the Alsatians than those unfortunate people themselves ... Against their own will we wish to give them back their true selves.'[5]

The bombardment grew a little less intense towards the end of August, not from any German change of heart, but because it failed to produce rapid surrender and because Werder's artillery was using up its stock of shells too quickly. The general resigned himself to the necessity of a regular siege of Strasbourg after all.

Around Metz, which had more modern defences, Moltke saw no need to lay a full siege. He needed only to blockade the city at some distance from its heavy fortress guns, leaving hunger to take care of Bazaine's army. Meanwhile, German troops strengthened their trenches and gun emplacements with every passing day, progressively reducing the chance of a successful French breakout. He would leave only sufficient troops under Prince Friedrich Karl to contain Bazaine. The Guard, IV and XII (Saxon) Corps and 5th and 6th Cavalry Divisions were formed into a Fourth Army, called the Army of the Meuse, which was tactfully placed under the command of Crown Prince Albert of Saxony, who with his Saxon troops had proved a redoubtable opponent of Prussia at Königgrätz in 1866. However, the new army's chief of staff was a Prussian, General von Schlotheim.

Moltke immediately made dispositions for pursuit of MacMahon's forces, which he expected to bring to battle before Paris. Orders creating Fourth Army were issued on 19 August, within hours of the end of fighting at Gravelotte. The new force, counting 86,275 men and 288 guns as of 22 August, would operate on the right of the Crown Prince of Prussia's Third Army, numbering 137,662 men and 525 guns.[6] These two forces, covered by a cavalry screen some 75 kilometres wide, advanced steadily westwards across Lorraine and beyond. The fall of Lunéville, Nancy, Vaucouleurs, Commercy, Bar-le-Duc, Saint-Dizier and Vitry-le-François marked the path of the German armies in the third week of August. When the fortresses of Toul and Verdun resisted attempts to storm them, light forces were left to contain their garrisons in order not to delay the main advance.

German troops appeared better disciplined than the French on the march, but they were beginning to outrun their supplies, and met their needs however they could. Heavy requisitions for money and supplies were levied on communities they passed through. Nervous French mayors tried to negotiate reductions by pleading hardship or resorted to subterfuge, arousing the ire of the invaders. A Frenchman bitterly remembered German soldiers descending like a 'famished horde' or 'swarm of locusts'. They 'demanded everything, took everything ... and what these Germans couldn't carry off they smashed'. Every village had its losses to bewail.[7] In print and image, the spiked-helmeted Prussian was increasingly portrayed as a barbarian beast.

On their side, the Germans noted that the population grew more hostile as they marched deeper into France. Telegraph wires were cut and isolated messengers riding through forests were picked off by small groups of Frenchmen. Even the 'Liberal' Crown Prince of Prussia believed that the German army had no alternative to harsh measures:

> The arming of the inhabitants of this neighbourhood has already assumed greater proportions, compelling us to take energetic steps to enforce the surrender of all weapons. Single shots are fired, generally in a cunning, cowardly fashion, on patrols, so that nothing else is left us to do but to adopt retaliatory measures by burning down the house from which the shots came, or else by [employing] the lash and forced contributions. It is horrible, but, to prevent greater mischief, is unavoidable, and is consistent with our proclamation of martial law.[8]

Many a French village discovered to its cost what this policy meant in practice.

German rage and exasperation at shots fired at them by men without uniforms found vent on 25 August. The commander of a battalion of Gardes Mobiles from the threatened garrison of Vitry unwisely evacuated his men eastwards, hoping to reach the railway and Sainte-Menehould and ride back to Paris. The men carried converted muskets, with which they had little practice. Only their officers had uniforms, while the men simply wore cockades to signify their military status. That afternoon they ran into Prussian cavalry, who made short work of these amateurs, taking them in front and rear. Over a thousand prisoners were taken. The Germans suffered three dead, including a popular officer, while the French had twenty-two casualties. Infuriated by being shot at by men they did not consider soldiers, the Germans lashed out with blows and insults. Possibly only the intervention of Duke Wilhelm of Mecklenburg, who happened to be passing, prevented a massacre on the spot. Eventually the column of prisoners was marched off. As they passed through the village of

Passavant a shot was fired – by whom is disputed – killing one of the escort. Some of the prisoners tried to escape into vineyards. Their guards, a detachment of the 16th Hussars abetted by some nearby Guards Dragoons, then hunted down the prisoners with carbine and sabre, killing or wounding over one hundred unarmed men 'like game' before their officers could stop the butchery.[9]

Next day Bismarck himself harangued the French survivors of what became known as the 'Passavant Massacre': 'You will all be hanged. You are not soldiers but assassins.'[10] The threat was not carried out, but he let it be known that any combatants not recognizable at a distance as soldiers would be subject to martial law: that is, executed. The French imperial government was sufficiently concerned to respond on 30 August that if the Germans refused to recognize the citizen soldiers of the Garde Mobile, reprisals would be taken on prisoners of the German equivalent, the *Landwehr*.[11] Bismarck's press secretary commented that 'It is evident that the war is now beginning, in consequence of the practices of these Francs-tireurs [sic], to take a savage turn.'[12]

The fact of invasion was turning this into a war in which Frenchmen, as much as Germans, felt that the integrity of their nation was at stake. Empress Eugénie's proclamation of 7 August that 'There is amongst us but one party, that of France; and but one flag, that of national honour'[13] was more a plea for unity than a statement of fact: some mayors actively discouraged resistance in order to protect their towns from damage, there was reluctance to join the National Guard in some Departments, and hard-core republicans took satisfaction from the defeat of the imperial armies. Nevertheless, most Frenchmen, including the many who had been untouched by the war hysteria of July and those who cared little for the Empire, saw resistance as a patriotic duty. Voluntary enlistments reached 28,000 in August. Palikao used the language of 'National Defence' and spared no efforts to raise the men and resources to sustain the struggle. Yet for the immediate support of MacMahon he had only the half-formed 13 Corps under General Vinoy, whose leading division set off from Paris to Rheims on 25 August. More time was needed to organize new units, but time was running out as the campaign approached its critical phase.

The Germans Wheel North

As the Germans resumed their westward advance on 23 August they were well informed about the French concentration at Châlons. They knew what units were being organized there, and of the Emperor's presence. They aimed to turn the French southern flank and either fight them before they reached the capital or deflect them from it. 'We can be in front of Paris in about eight days,' wrote Roon expectantly.[14] However, it was soon confirmed that the French had withdrawn to Rheims. On 24 August German cavalry rode into the smoking ruins of Châlons Camp, where they found quantities of stores that had survived both flames and pillage.

Moltke assumed, logically, that the French shift of position was intended to cover Paris and threaten the German northern flank. It seemed most likely that MacMahon would fall back on the capital. Little weight could be attached to a captured letter from a French officer in Metz expressing a hope of rescue by the Army of Châlons. Nevertheless, Moltke's deputy, Quartermaster General von Podbielski, argued that, for political reasons, MacMahon might attempt to relieve Bazaine. Moltke's operations officer, Bronsart von Schellendorff, noted that day, 'The possibility that MacMahon will advance around our right flank must be considered seriously. Indications are to be found in the French and English newspapers.'[15]

Yet on the intelligence available Moltke was disinclined to jump to a conclusion that seemed to him inherently improbable. He wrote later, 'In war it is for the most part with probabilities only that the strategist can reckon; and the probability, as a rule, is that the enemy will do the right thing.'[16] To his mind, a hazardous French attempt to relieve Bazaine would be the wrong move for them. Besides, to change the line of march of 225,000 German troops and divert them into the Argonne where supply would be difficult was hardly to be undertaken on the basis of unsubstantiated reports. If those reports were wrong – or even a French ploy – the advance on Paris would be delayed, the army exhausted to no purpose, and the enemy given time to consolidate. For the moment, therefore, Moltke took only the prudent steps of pulling in his left and warning Fourth Army to send cavalry to probe northwards to establish whether the French were there. Nevertheless, he prepared contingency plans in case a French flanking manoeuvre did materialize. He thought to borrow two corps from Second Army around Metz if necessary to block any French attempt to cross the Meuse. He also drew up march tables for a possible turn northwards. Too tight a turn could send Third Army piling into the transport convoys in rear of Fourth Army and lead to immense confusion. For his left and right wings to keep abreast of each other, all available roads would need to be used and Third Army would need to make a smooth, well-coordinated wheel. Pending positive information about French movements, however, Moltke did no more than prepare to angle his advance towards Rheims rather than Châlons.

Thus for three days the Germans continued westwards while MacMahon, undetected, was advancing in the opposite and parallel direction two days' march to the north. Only late on the third day, 25 August, after Moltke had sat down to his nightly game of whist in the pleasant town of Bar-le-Duc, did the situation become clearer. Copies of French newspapers had been procured

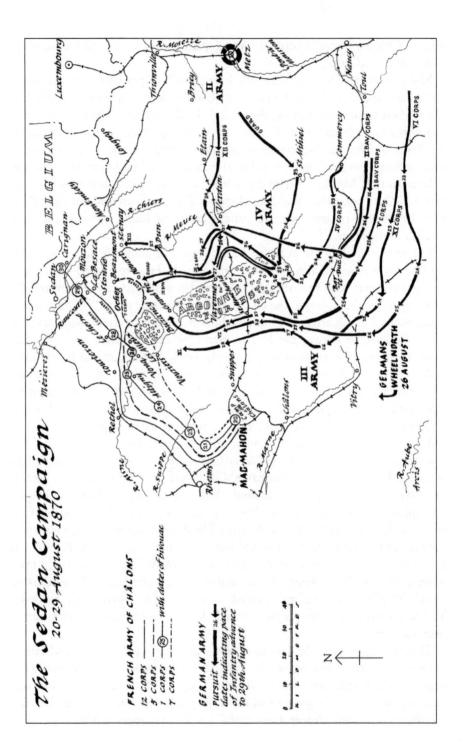

The Sedan Campaign
20-29 August 1870

FRENCH ARMY OF CHÂLONS

12 CORPS ——————
5 CORPS ——————
1 CORPS —————— with dates of bivouac
7 CORPS ——————

GERMAN ARMY

Pursuit ⟶ dates indicating pace
26 of Infantry advance
to 29th August

0 10 20 30 40
KILOMETRES

N

containing reports that lent credence to the idea of a French rescue attempt. Palikao had spoken freely of his plan in Paris and, for all that he would blame MacMahon's sloth for its failure, his own indiscretions and the irresponsibility of the Paris press were equally culpable. There arrived too, via London, a telegram passing on a report dated 23 August from a Paris newspaper, *Le Temps*, asserting that MacMahon had left Rheims that day to go to Bazaine's assistance, and implying that his destination was Montmédy. If this were correct, could Moltke take the risk of continuing westwards, leaving MacMahon in his rear and closer to Metz than him?

Moltke reasoned that if this report were true French forces would be found to the north, around Buzancy and Vouziers. His staff officers were relaxing for the evening, enjoying a sing-song on the benches of the local grammar school, when they were summoned, and hastily buckled on their swords in readiness to ride through the night with messages. Moltke sent orders to Fourth Army to commence the turn to the right next day, subject to confirmation of the French movement by cavalry reconnaissance. He advised Third Army of what was planned, but gave it only discretionary orders. The Chief of General Staff was fortunate that both his army commanders, the Crown Princes of Saxony and Prussia, acted decisively. Both were convinced that the French were attempting a flanking move, and set their columns in motion northwards without delay. It was, wrote one of Moltke's officers, 'a striking proof of how unanimous all were in their views of the situation, and as to the steps to be taken'.[17] In marked contrast to the French, the Germans had a strong sense that the enemy's army, not any geographical position, was their overriding objective.

There was some elation among the German staff, and a sense that the French move was practicable 'only if their troops were quicker in marching than our own, and we ourselves blind'.[18] Crown Prince Friedrich Wilhelm of Prussia thought the French attempt 'foolhardy', observing that Moltke 'even thinks to set a mouse-trap for them and to be able to make prisoner the enemy's Army'.[19]

On 26 and 27 August, as we have seen, contact with the French was re-established, and skirmishes with the French 7 and 5 Corps took place, confirming their position. To the north-west, German cavalry picked up the trail of the French march from Rheims. From the north-east came welcome confirmation that the French had not yet reached the Meuse. Behind the German cavalry, which now clung to the enemy 'like a swarm of flies on a summer evening',[20] the long, dark infantry columns began to stream northwards.

With the gaggle of Englishmen accompanying the headquarters of Queen Victoria's son-in-law, the Crown Prince of Prussia, rode the correspondent of the London *Times*, William Howard Russell of Crimean fame. In Bar-le-Duc on the evening of 26 August, Russell was struck by the sight of 'Count Bismarck standing in a doorway out of the rain whiffing a prodigious cigar, seemingly intent on watching the bubbles which passed along the watercourse by the side of the street'.[21] In the drama now unfolding Bismarck could be only a spectator as hour after hour the men in the ranks put one foot in front of the other in a war of legs. The weather, the bad roads, the mud, the hunger, the weight of their packs, were little easier for them to bear than for the French, but they had a sense that their commanders knew their business, and that if they could catch the French their efforts might bring the war's end closer.

On 27 August the Saxon Corps, the leading German infantry unit, secured the crossings of the Meuse at Dun and Stenay, destroying bridges to block the French route to Montmédy and raising hopes that they could be brought to bay on the west bank of the river. There was some concern lest the French should attack the nearest German units while Third and Fourth Armies remained separated by the densely wooded hills of the Argonne. Fourth Army, forming the weaker right wing, was accordingly cautioned not to provoke a French attack and to keep its leading units on the defensive until Third Army, the left wing, could draw level with it and complete the German concentration. By late on 27 August the German advance was threatening the French sufficiently, as we have seen, to dissuade MacMahon from attempting to continue eastwards, until Palikao's imperative order drove him reluctantly onward.

Chapter 10

Hunter and Hunted

Nouart

On 28 August the French army clumsily resumed its eastward tack, lashed by pelting rain and all too aware that the enemy was close upon its heels. An officer of 7 Corps watched 'Prussian scouts, posted on the hills, observing our march from a distance. They did not attack, to be sure; but there could be no misunderstanding this apparent reserve. If the enemy did not fight us, it was because as yet he had only cavalry to hand. Yet how cleverly he used it to surround us at a distance, like a net that draws tighter every moment, allowing him not to lose sight of our movements, to work on the already shaken morale of our soldiers, and to hinder our march by timely demonstrations!'[1] Failly's 5 Corps was again stalled for several hours by such demonstrations, for want of adequate protection from French cavalry.

Nor was this the only manifestation of enemy activity. In the night sky behind them the French saw a reddish glow as villages they had passed through only hours before were set ablaze. Convinced that shots fired at them by French rearguards or stragglers involved civilians, the Germans retaliated with the torch. In the dry words of the German official account, the village of Falaise 'caught fire' when Prussian cavalry entered it, as did Les Alleux. Next day Vonq was methodically burnt, leaving two hundred houses destroyed, seven hundred people homeless and without horses or livestock. Twenty-six villagers were made prisoner. French civilians looked in vain for their army to defend them.[2]

By now, a French junior officer reflected, 'It was only too true that, thanks to indecision and lost hours, we had become an army that was marching in order to avoid fighting; and every day our troops, far from becoming battle-hardened by continual skirmishes and engagements which would have given them a feeling of strength and accustomed them to fire, were weakened by the demoralizing habit of repeated retreats.' He believed that officers who complained about indiscipline should have tried harder to lead by example; but from them he heard more 'Allez!' – 'Get going!' than 'Allons!' – 'Let's go!'[3]

MacMahon's new resolution was to drive directly east. He told General de Failly, 'It is of the utmost importance that we cross the Meuse as soon as possible ... in the direction of Stenay ... We are marching on Montmédy to rescue Marshal Bazaine.'[4] This plan too was modified at nightfall. Learning that the Germans holding Stenay had destroyed the bridges there, and that he had insufficient pontoons for bridging, MacMahon decided instead to cross the Meuse further north. This meant making a detour to use the bridges at Mouzon and Remilly, then following the east bank of the Meuse towards Montmédy. This would put him in the narrow corridor between the Meuse and the Belgian border, but he hoped for some measure of safety if he could put the river between his army and the Germans. Orders went out, and on 29 August the northern half of the army, 1 and 12 Corps, made better progress.

After a wretched night vainly trying to sleep with rainwater running down his neck, Dr Sarazin was cheered when the weather cleared that morning. Joining a group drying themselves round a fire, he felt 'our Gallic spirit' revive when someone passed round brandy and biscuit. The march of 1 Corps made a dazzling spectacle:

> The sun rose and cleared away the morning mist that mingled with the smoke of bivouac fires in the valley below us. From this bluish haze we saw emerge files of cuirassiers with glittering helmets and breastplates, dragoons, lancers and light cavalry. All these regiments in bright and varied colours were in line to the right of the road and of the little town [Le Chesne], which could be vaguely discerned. To our left, heavy masses of infantry were formed up in lines under arms; they seemed to be getting into motion. In the distance we could make out the red of the Line Regiments and Zouaves, the black of the light infantry battalions and the sky-blue of the Turcos. At intervals we saw the artillery teams and the covered wagons of the hospital trains. All this unfolded as far as the eye could see in magnificent countryside broken by wooded hills, softened by the bluish mists of sunrise. What a striking picture![5]

For the troops in the marching columns it was less picturesque. They struggled through a mighty traffic jam on leaving Le Chesne that morning and ran into another as they entered Raucourt that evening. There was 'frightful disorder' in the narrow streets of Raucourt, wrote Louis de Narcy, despite the presence of generals and officers who dined in houses 'discussing events as if at the close of manoeuvres, without trying to prevent this dangerous situation.'[6] Nevertheless, 1 Corps had covered 23 kilometres and was close to the Meuse. Lebrun's 12 Corps had succeeded in crossing the river at Mouzon, 8 kilometres to the east.

Things had not gone so well for the two southerly French corps. On the night of 28 August MacMahon had entrusted orders to them for the change of direction northwards to a single staff officer. By ill omen, he was Captain George de Grouchy, grandson of the marshal whom Napoleonic loyalists blamed for the loss of Waterloo. Grouchy delivered the orders to 7 Corps safely but then, taking a wrong turn in the dark forest, was captured by German cavalry. He had on him the orders for General de Failly and other important documents.

French changes in direction on 28 August, together with poor visibility in the mist-shrouded hills, had caused the Germans some uncertainty. With these captured orders, however, Moltke would learn the enemy's intentions and direct his columns accordingly.

Failly's 5 Corps continued its eastward march towards Stenay on 29 August under the previous day's orders, unaware of the change of direction and now separated from 7 Corps. In early afternoon, while crossing the marshy valley of the Wiseppe, it collided with the leading division of XII (Saxon) Corps of the German Fourth Army pushing forward from the Meuse. Germans posted near Nouart greeted the French with infantry and artillery fire which was alarmingly accurate, though luckily for the French many shells ploughed harmlessly into mud. French shells, by contrast, fell short or exploded prematurely. Failly deployed most of his men along high ground, and for a while there was heavy skirmishing, coming to bayonet-work in places, resulting in 257 French and 363 German casualties. Neither commander, however, wanted a major engagement, being uncertain of the other's strength. Though Failly had superior numbers, he was content to stand off the German threat. In late afternoon MacMahon's aide-de-camp reached him with a copy of the orders he should have received that morning. After dark Failly had decoy campfires lit to deceive the Germans, then withdrew his men northwards.

After days of marching, lack of sleep and false alerts, his troops were at the end of their tether. The night was dark, the roads glutinous, and the march through woods halting and beset with difficulties. Hunger and thirst added to the men's fatigue, and many fell out to sleep by the roadside. After a seemingly endless night, the 17,000 men of 5 Corps slumped down around the village of Beaumont, 12 kilometres north of Nouart. The last units did not arrive until after daybreak. Everyone was so dog-tired that little attention was given to posting sentinels to guard the camp.

Beaumont

General de Failly was still abed when Marshal MacMahon visited him at Beaumont early on 30 August. Disappointed that Failly could give him no accurate estimate of the forces he had encountered the previous day, before departing MacMahon urged him 'not to lose a moment' in marching on to cross the Meuse at Mouzon.[7] However, Failly judged that his weary men were in no condition for an early start, and that it was better to wait until his wagon-train arrived and rations could be issued that morning. His men needed time to cook and to clean their gear and rifles, which needed attention after all the rain and mud of the past week. Although his troops were spread out in a hollow which was a poor defensive position, there was no expectation of a fight that day. They would start northwards for Mouzon in the early afternoon. The meagre information Failly had about the Germans confirmed his assumption that he had not been pursued. Little credence was given to farmers who came in throughout the morning bearing tales of masses of Prussians in the woods to the south. Madame Bellavoine, who ran a nearby orphanage, eluded a German sentry who shot at her to make her way to Beaumont to warn of an imminent attack. Like most of his officers, Failly was lunching in the village when she was ushered in to see him about midday. He listened politely while she showed him on a map where the Germans were, but reassured her with the words, 'My good woman, that is impossible.'[8]

From the latest reconnaissance and the captured orders, Moltke knew that the French sought to cross the Meuse that day, and he planned to attack them while they were still on the west bank. To achieve the junction of his forces, his orders called for his left wing, Third Army, to make an early start and to advance towards Le Chesne, with the two Bavarian corps on its right bearing towards Beaumont to support Fourth Army. Fourth Army itself would start a little later and drive north towards Beaumont. When Crown Prince Albert of Saxony briefed his corps commanders that morning, he cautioned them to wait until everybody was in line before launching an attack.

Fourth Army moved up the difficult forest roads in four columns, with Gustav von Alvensleben's IV Corps in the van. As its leading division approached the edge of the forest south of Beaumont, scouts reported large French camps ahead. There seemed to be no sentinels, and the French could be seen wandering at ease in their shirt-sleeves in the sun as smoke rose from their cooking-fires. It was too good an opportunity to let slip. The German commander had his men deploy quietly for action, but as they did so a stir in the nearest French camp indicated that the alarm might have been given. Alvensleben now arrived and ordered an immediate attack. At a range of 700 metres, his artillery opened fire at about half past twelve.

The first shells caused mayhem in the French camps. Men were struck dead in their tents or as they pulled on their uniforms. Horses were killed tethered to their picket ropes. There was indescribable confusion in Beaumont as men, horses, wagons and artillery caissons careered pell-mell up the road to Mouzon.

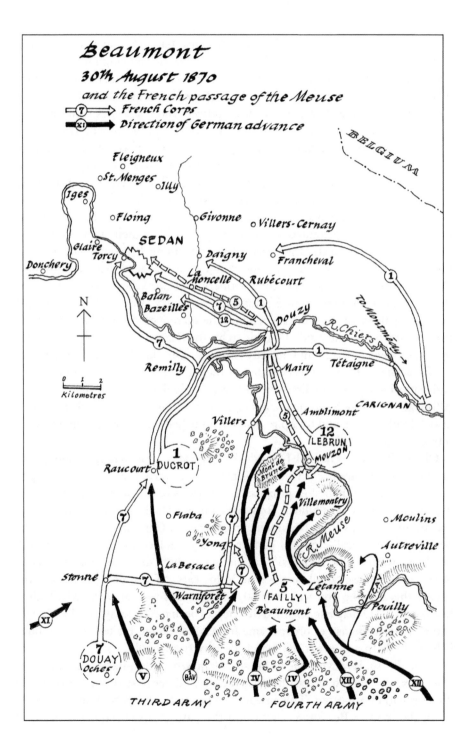

Beaumont

30th August 1870

and the French passage of the Meuse

⑦⟹ French Corps

◆⬛❯ Direction of German advance

BELGIUM

Fleigneux

St.Menges   Illy

Iges

Floing   Givonne   Villers-Cernay

SEDAN   Daigny   Francheval

Glaire   Torcy   La Moncelle   Rubécourt   1

Donchery   Balan   ⑦   ⑤   1   Douzy   R. Chiers   To Montmédy

Bazeilles   ⑫

N

⑦   Mairy   Tétaigne

Remilly   1   CARIGNAN

0 1 2   Amblimont

Kilometres   Villers   5   12
                                    LEBRUN
                                    MOUZON

1
DUCROT   Mont de   Villemontry
Raucourt   Brune

oFlaba   ⑦   R. Meuse   oMoulins

oYonq   Autreville

LaBesace   ⑦

Stonne   ⑦   Létanne

Warniforêt   5
              (FAILLY)   Pouilly
              Beaumont

XI   V   BAV   IV   IV   XII   XII

DOUAY
oches

THIRD ARMY   FOURTH ARMY

Amid this panic-stricken mob Dr Léon Moynac felt a shell explode very near him. Dazed, his eyelashes singed, his vision blurred, choking on powder and smoke, it took him a moment to realize that he was not wounded, and that the blood on him was from the smashed thigh of a soldier who clutched it in agony. To his left, men and horses ran over an officer whose side was split open. As shells and solid shot smashed into roof tiles, walls, and the crowd, Moynac saw 'shreds of human being hurtling through the air, and sprays of blood gushing like lava spouted by a volcano. A great howl rose from this throng, a groaning sound made up of cries of pain, moans and curses. These terrified, unthinking, maddened soldiers rushed up the road to Mouzon ...'.[9]

This panic was only part of the picture for, after a moment's shocked silence, enough French troops rallied to put up a fight. Seizing their stacked arms and steadied by their officers, they greeted the oncoming Prussians with punishing rifle fire. Some regiments advanced and even managed disjointed bayonet charges, while within a short time artillery and *mitrailleuses* opened fire on the Germans from high ground behind their infantry. Alvensleben's men took heavy casualties as they advanced, but the sound of cannon brought fresh troops hurrying to their aid. To their right, the Saxons of XII Corps struggled up over clogged roads and muddy streams. On the left, the approach of the Bavarians of I Corps was heralded by their artillery. As more and more men and batteries came into line, the advantage tilted in the Germans' favour. Although the French put up a contest, they were unable to recover from their initial disadvantage, and by 2 p.m. had been pushed out of Beaumont and were retreating northwards.

Off to the west, General Douay's 7 Corps was approaching Stonne, with German patrols nipping at its tail. His troops had started early that morning to try to make up for their slow progress the previous day. When Douay heard the cannonade he rode up a hillock, from which he watched a semicircle of German fire driving 5 Corps from Beaumont. In contrast to German commanders, who marched automatically towards gunfire, Douay resolved to continue his march north-eastwards. The Marshal's injunction to him that morning, to hasten to cross the Meuse 'at all costs', rang in his ears. 'If you don't get across the Meuse this evening you will have 60,000 Germans to deal with,' MacMahon had warned.[10] Douay later claimed that he had been too far away to help 5 Corps, adding that no change of orders came from MacMahon. He feared an ambush if he tarried. In any event, he marched away from Failly.

As he did so, however, one of his six infantry brigades, including many raw reservists, strayed too far east because the staff officer posted at a crossroads to direct it had disappeared. This brigade, escorting the baggage train, continued down the road to Beaumont, right into the path of an oncoming division of

General von der Tann's I Bavarian Corps. In the ensuing fight the French brigade was taken in front and flank and reduced to a horde of maddened fugitives, leaving its commanders dead or dying. Encountering the fleeing survivors, Douay abandoned all hope of crossing the Meuse at Mouzon and directed his corps northwards towards a safer crossing.

Meanwhile, Failly had withdrawn from the high ground north of Beaumont under German pressure. Contact between the armies was briefly broken, but once the Germans had reformed their columns they pressed the pursuit. A running fight lasted all afternoon as the French defended every hill and copse between Beaumont and Mouzon, 8 kilometres to the north. Eventually the Germans drove them from every position, and by 5 p.m. were fighting for the last high ground south of Mouzon.

As Failly fought to hold the Germans at bay while his men crossed the Meuse, he at least got help from 12 Corps, which was stationed on the east bank at Mouzon. Grasping the seriousness of 5 Corps' plight more quickly than MacMahon, General Lebrun took the initiative in sending some of his troops and artillery back to the west bank to bolster Failly's line. He also had his artillery fire at the enemy from across the Meuse. This intervention, combined with the difficulties of the terrain, stalled the right flank of the German advance. On their left, however, they broke through, forcing the French off Mont de Brune, the last anchor of their line. In desperation Failly ordered the 5th Cuirassiers to charge. They did so, with the usual heroic futility. Firing at will, German infantry emptied over one hundred saddles, stopping the cavalry in its tracks at no loss to themselves. Some fleeing troopers tried to swim the Meuse, only for men and mounts to be lost in its waters.

German artillery wrought havoc among French troops thronging to escape over the stone bridge at Mouzon. Whatever his failings as a commander, Failly showed personal courage in holding together a last-ditch defence. As darkness fell there was fierce fighting in the Faubourg de Mouzon – that part of town lying west of the Meuse. It raged around the church, in the cemetery, in gardens and house-to-house, while fires illuminated an infernal scene of streets littered with corpses of men and horses. Finally, most of the surviving French got over the bridge, which was kept covered by *mitrailleuses* to prevent any German pursuit. In the early hours of the morning remnants of a rearguard regiment, the 88th under Colonel Demange, boldly tried to rush German lines and cross the bridge. Of 223 men who made the attempt, 98 got through, the rest being killed, wounded, drowned or taken prisoner. Demange himself was mortally wounded.

Beaumont had been a calamity for the French. Losses reached 7,500, of whom 4,700 were from 5 Corps and 2,000 were unwounded prisoners. Forty-two cannon and great quantities of material had been lost. The Germans counted 665 dead, 2,717 wounded and 182 missing, for a total of 3,564.[11]

Moltke had caught the French army while it was straddling the Meuse and had mauled it severely: 5 Corps was crippled. Yet, for all the vigour and competence of German operations, he had not succeeded in surrounding the French or preventing their passage of the river. Third Army on the left had not been far enough forward to crush Douay, much to King Wilhelm's frustration. 'The King was very impatient,' noted one of Moltke's officers, 'just as on 18 August. It all goes too slowly for him, and in his enthusiasm he forgets that a real battle does not happen as quickly as a manoeuvre.'[12]

That night, indeed, Douay's 7 Corps was still on the west bank. Continuing northwards to avoid being caught up in Failly's disaster, he made for Remilly. It was here that Ducrot's 1 Corps had crossed that day, some of his men amusing themselves with an impromptu ball in the meadows with local girls while they waited their turn to cross. The fun had ceased when the rumble of gunfire from the south was heard and Prussian scouts appeared on the horizon.[13] Like Douay, Ducrot considered that his duty was to get across the river without allowing himself to be detained by rearguard fighting. Thus he devoted his attention to bridging operations and pushed his leading units onward towards Carignan. When Douay's column reached the riverbank it was growing dark, but the last of Ducrot's men had still to cross, together with Bonnemains's cavalry. Douay waited in acute anxiety, aware that the Germans would be upon them if he did not get all his men over by dawn. The river was high, and the planking of the pontoon bridge was awash. One of Douay's staff watched as Bonnemains's troopers crossed:

> Frightened at being unable to discern this flooring which moved unseen below the water and gave way beneath their hooves at every step, the horses went forward with the utmost reluctance, their necks outstretched, their ears pricked up. The cuirassiers, upright in their stirrups, wrapped in their great white overcoats, passed over silently, as if walking on the water. Two fires lit on the riverbank at either end of the bridge cast their wan light over men and horses. Their flames were reflected strangely in the shiny helmets of these horsemen, and gave this spectacle an eerie quality.[14]

Finally, at 10.15 p.m., 7 Corps began to cross. Occasionally a caisson or terrified horse disappeared into the dark water, but by 2 a.m. the passage was well under way. It was then that Major de Bastard of MacMahon's staff arrived with orders. Douay was to lead his men not south-east towards Montmédy, but north-west to Sedan. At 5 a.m. on 31 August the bedraggled, cold and hungry men of 7 Corps started arriving outside the walls of Sedan. Summoned by Douay, its governor opened the town's gates to them.

The Retreat to Sedan

Shocked and bitterly disappointed at 5 Corps' performance, MacMahon set it and 12 Corps in motion from Mouzon towards Sedan along the roads east of the Meuse. This disorderly night march of 30–31 August only exhausted and demoralized the men further. MacMahon sent Ducrot orders to act as rearguard and to 'invite' the Emperor to withdraw to Sedan.

Ducrot found Napoleon dining with his household in a brightly lit house in Carignan. Unaware of the significance of the day's events, he had telegraphed the Empress at 5.40 p.m., 'There has been another little engagement today, of no great importance. I stayed in the saddle quite a long time.'[15] He was incredulous when told what had happened, repeating, 'But that's impossible!' He was eventually prevailed upon, reluctantly, to take the train to Sedan, where he arrived at the Sub-Prefecture late at night, walking painfully and looking thoroughly ill. He rejected advice to continue to Mézières, refusing to abandon the army.[16]

Rouher had pointedly reminded Napoleon at Courcelles on 21 August that if the Army of Châlons were beaten, 'Your Majesty would have but one course, to hurl yourself amidst the enemy and get yourself killed.' His heroic death would do more for the dynasty than an abdication which many loyalists desired but none dared suggest.[17] Napoleon had at least sent his son away from the army, quietly despatching the Prince Imperial northwards under escort for safety on 26 August. When the Empress heard of this she disapproved. Although her affections and hopes for the dynasty centred far more on her son than her chronically unfaithful husband, she wrote dramatically that she would rather weep for the prince's death or wounding than see him in flight.[18] On hearing of the retreat to Sedan she tried to bolster Napoleon's resolve by wiring him on 31 August, 'The news I have received from various quarters demonstrates conclusively that a vigorous effort towards Metz could give us success ...'.[19]

The 'enormous disorder' of the army in and around Sedan that day[20] made it difficult to share such purblind confidence. A moderately prosperous textile weaving centre of 15,000 inhabitants, Sedan had been notable hitherto only for its fine cloth and as the birthplace in 1611 of Marshal Turenne. Its narrow streets, overshadowed by the houses of successful drapers, now teemed with soldiers, many of whom crowded into bars or knocked on doors begging for bread while their officers dined in restaurants, little concerned with supervising their men. Traffic came almost to a standstill as empty wagons from units seeking rations headed into town, where artillery caissons and baggage trains added to the jam.

To the minority of republicans in the army, the Emperor with his escort and train of vehicles, his household of seventy including forty servants, messengers and cooks, was nothing more than a 'golden ball and chain'.[21] Legend would exaggerate the size of his retinue and the delays caused by its wagons.[22] Yet even sympathizers had come to resent his presence as 'more of an encumbrance than his baggage'.[23] His proclamation that day had a dying fall. Admitting that 'the start of the campaign has been unfortunate,' and that so far success had not crowned the efforts of the marshals he had appointed, he appealed to the men's courage, and to their sense of reputation and duty: 'if there are any cowards, military law and public opinion will do them justice.' Copies of the proclamation were placarded around the town. The few troops who read it felt 'sadness and astonishment'.[24]

MacMahon initially deployed his most reliable troops to face a possible attack from the east by the pursuing Fourth Army. Lebrun's 12 Corps would hold the village of Bazeilles, 4 kilometres south-east of Sedan, and the adjacent heights on the western side of the narrow Givonne valley. Ducrot would extend the line northwards up the Givonne, but his 1 Corps would arrive only after dark. Douay's 7 Corps was to extend Ducrot's line towards Illy, but his men were so shaken and exhausted that Douay asked for them to remain in the rear, on the Algeria plateau north of the town. The battered 5 Corps was placed in reserve at the site outside town called the Old Camp.

That afternoon 5 Corps got a new commander, General Emmanuel Félix de Wimpffen, who relieved a devastated Failly. Wimpffen was an ambitious man who bore a grudge against MacMahon, his former commander. In Algeria Wimpffen had courted popularity with French colonists impatient with government constraints on their expansion. He favoured 'vigorous and direct' repression of dissident southern tribes, and led an expedition in the spring of 1870 that acted ruthlessly and entered southern Morocco against orders. Wimpffen complained bitterly of having his 'hands tied' because MacMahon and the Emperor had tried to limit him to a protective rather than a punitive role and had reminded him of local treaty obligations. Wimpffen considered that he had been denied deserved recognition for a successful expedition. He did not know that MacMahon had interceded for him with the Emperor, who had wanted to recall and suspend Wimpffen for executing fifteen Arabs. He knew only that MacMahon had blocked his succession to the governorship of Algeria.[25]

When war broke out in July 1870 Wimpffen chafed with impatience in Oran as his letters requesting a command in the German war brought no result. However, Palikao needed to replace Failly after his failure to support MacMahon at Frœschwiller. On 22 August Wimpffen received orders to leave Algeria for Paris, where he reported on the 28th. Palikao invited him to lunch, and shared his views on the painfully slow and meandering march of MacMahon's army and the pernicious effect of the Emperor's presence with it. Both thought the army needed a stronger hand. When Wimpffen set off for the front on 29 August he took a letter from Palikao authorizing him to take command in the event of 'any misfortune' befalling MacMahon.[26]

When Wimpffen reached Soissons he showed that he was a soldier of a very different stripe from the marshal. He issued a proclamation to the inhabitants of his native region, invoking the example of 1814–15 and summoning them to resist the invader from behind every hedge, ditch and house. The dangers of that policy were shown that evening as he entered the war zone of burnt and pillaged villages and had his escort ambushed by locals who mistook them for uhlans. Next day Wimpffen reached the front in time to help rally fugitives from Beaumont. In Sedan MacMahon received him coldly, and Wimpffen for his part said nothing of the letter he carried.

In telegraphing Palikao that he had been 'forced to withdraw his troops to Sedan',[27] MacMahon failed to elaborate either his reasons or his intentions. During the 31st he discussed various possibilities, but came to no decision. General Ducrot assumed that the intention must be to withdraw north-westwards to Mézières, where a division of General Vinoy's newly formed 13 Corps awaited them. To that end, Ducrot initially directed his columns towards the high ground beyond Illy, which the map told him was a more defensible position than Sedan and was on the road to Mézières. But MacMahon wrote to him that 'I gave orders for you to move from Carignan to Sedan, and by no means to Mézières, where I have no intention of going.'[28]

Even when, from the walls of the citadel that afternoon, MacMahon saw dust rising from German columns moving towards the Meuse crossing at Donchery west of Sedan, he was unperturbed. He seemed confident that the river gave him security. He did not yet know that his orders to destroy the bridge at Donchery had not been carried out. The demolition party had boarded a train in Sedan which had departed precipitately when the Germans started shelling the station and the station master panicked. The train halted briefly at Donchery to let the sappers off, but then steamed off to Mézières before they could unload their tools and explosives. The bridge remained intact.

Despite the experiences of Frœschwiller and the past week, MacMahon's mind moved in a different time-frame from that of the German high command. He believed that he still had the option of moving on to Mézières, or he might return south-eastwards, to do battle with Fourth Army, beat it and then continue towards Montmédy and Bazaine, whose last message, dated the 27th, indicated that he still hoped to break out. When Douay reported that he intended to have entrenchments dug, MacMahon exclaimed, 'Entrenchments! I don't want to shut myself in, as at Metz; I want to manoeuvre.'[29] To Lebrun he said after Beaumont, 'the situation isn't desperate. The German army facing us numbers 60 to 70,000 men at most. If it attacks us, so much the better; I hope that we shall throw them into the Meuse.'[30]

He did not grasp that he was facing thrice 70,000, and was outnumbered two to one. Although indications to the contrary were multiplying hourly, he believed he was facing just one German army – the Fourth – and that he could beat it and force his way through in either direction. He had no suspicion that the Germans were in sufficient force to block him in both directions, let alone to encircle him.[31]

MacMahon later said, 'I had no intention of giving battle [at Sedan], but I wanted to rally the army and replenish it with food and ammunition.' His orders for next day specified only that.[32] Unfortunately, the same train that bolted from Sedan station with the demolition party aboard had also carried off 800,000 rations that had not been unloaded; but there were still two days' rations, plentiful ammunition, and enough field guns to make up losses at Beaumont. MacMahon would await the result of cavalry reconnaissance on 1 September before deciding what to do. Physically exhausted, he had no conception that, after so many lost chances, his thin final hope of saving his army by retreat northwards was slipping away.

Two of his generals were uneasy. During the afternoon, watching the movement of Prussian columns and receiving a report that the enemy had 'a whole army' marching towards Donchery,[33] Douay redeployed 7 Corps along the heights above Floing, to face a possible threat from the west. He shared his anxieties with MacMahon, who assigned units of 5 Corps to provide a link at the northern hinge between Douay's right and Ducrot's left. Thus by nightfall the French army was spread rather raggedly over a front of nearly 10 kilometres, but occupying a very confined position: 1 and 7 Corps were back-to-back, yet communication was hindered by woods and ravines. The army held two sides of a triangle, of which the River Meuse formed the base. At its apex, framed by two lime trees, was the Calvaire d'Illy, a wayside symbol of the dying Christ on a lonely hilltop looking down towards the village of Illy. To its north, just 8 kilometres away over the first wooded hills of the Ardennes forest, lay the Belgian frontier.

When MacMahon spoke to him of manoeuvring Douay expressed apprehension that tomorrow 'the enemy will not give us time.'[34] That night the commander of 7 Corps asked his chief engineer what he thought of the situation.

'I think we are lost' was the reply. 'That is my opinion too,' replied Douay, 'It only remains for us to do our best before going under.'[35]

Ducrot was more graphic. He saw Sedan, with its outmoded fortifications, as merely a trap for artillery fire. When MacMahon ordered him to defend it rather than Illy he felt despair and rage.[36] That night he pored over his maps, swearing as he marked them with red crayon. Dr Sarazin, his medical director, who knew him well, had never seen him so grim and troubled. Sarazin offered the hope that they would at last have a chance to fight the Prussians. After a pause, the burly Ducrot put a hand on his shoulder: 'Why, my poor doctor, you don't understand at all! We are in a chamber pot and they are about to shit on us!'[37]

The Pursuit

On the night of Beaumont, Moltke set out his strategy in orders to his two army commanders:

> The enemy has retired or been beaten at all points. The advance will therefore be resumed at early dawn tomorrow and the enemy attacked wherever he may be in position on this side of the Meuse, and compressed into the smallest possible space between that river and the Belgian frontier.

The greater part of Fourth Army would cross the Meuse and follow the French, blocking their route eastward, while Third Army advanced against the enemy's front and western flank, taking strong artillery positions on the right bank to harass the French and slow them down.[38]

Crown Prince Albert of Saxony accordingly had XII Corps and the Guard cross the Meuse early on the 31st, both at Mouzon and on pontoons laid upriver. Setting off in typical morning river fog, Fourth Army picked up French stragglers and abandoned supplies as it advanced, cut the railway to Montmédy and skirmished with the retreating enemy. Knowing that Third Army had further to march to get into position, Crown Prince Albert did not wish to press the French so hard that they might flee the trap that was in the making. With his left brushing the Meuse, he extended his right towards the Belgian frontier, barring any French attempt to resume the advance to the east. That afternoon he halted on a line a few kilometres short of the French positions. He would be ready to continue the advance next morning, 1 September, if necessary, but as his men were exhausted after their week of forced marches he would be glad to give them a day's rest if Third Army needed more time to block the French route westwards.

That night Fourth Army saw campfires to the north, lit not by French but by Belgian troops who had been mobilized to protect their frontier. By 30 August Moltke anticipated that the French, hemmed in east and west, might attempt to escape into Belgium or even to manoeuvre through it. That day Bismarck telegraphed to Brussels that German forces would respect the border so long as all French detachments were disarmed there.[39] Moltke's order specified that 'Should the enemy pass over into Belgium without being at once disarmed, he is to be pursued thither without delay.'[40]

For the Belgians, a contest between their two heavyweight neighbours on their very borders was cause for anxiety. Already French civilians pushing their belongings in carts had begun an exodus from the Sedan region into neutral territory. The Belgians were determined to protect their neutrality, guaranteed by the treaties of 1831 and 1839 and reaffirmed by France and Prussia only three weeks previously. Their observation corps, mobilized at the start of the war, received orders on 27 August to repel any foreign troops attempting to cross the frontier, and to disarm and intern any fugitive soldiers entering Belgium. The Belgians answered Bismarck that German intervention would be justifiable only if Belgium proved unable to enforce her rights as a neutral state. Meantime, Crown Prince Albert of Saxony, more sensitive than Moltke to the rights of small nations, passed on GHQ's orders to his commanders with the judicious proviso that 'otherwise any violation of the Belgian frontier is to be scrupulously avoided.'[41]

As Fourth Army advanced along the east bank of the Meuse, the Crown Prince of Prussia's Third Army was marching towards the river from the west. William Howard Russell of *The Times* watched I Bavarian Corps marching through Raucourt. The village, stripped of supplies by the passage of the French army the previous day, had been sacked by the Bavarians.[42] Russell saw campfires built with furniture still burning, and 'women and children, terrified and sobbing . . . huddled together on the doorsteps' bewailing the pillage. After seeing an officer arrest some men, Russell was glad to leave this scene where 'everything was ruin'.[43]

Driving in some French skirmishers who were still on the west bank, the Bavarians reached the Meuse between Remilly and Bazeilles. They opened fire on French troops on the far bank, and an artillery duel across the river got under way, the Germans as usual soon gaining the upper hand. To their left, downstream from Bazeilles, the Bavarians saw a railway viaduct spanning the Meuse, which was about 60 metres wide at this point. MacMahon had ordered the viaduct not to be destroyed, thinking his army might need it for subsequent operations, but at midday, seeing the imminent threat, the French sent a working party to blow it up. Observing the powder barrels being stacked, a company of Bavarian Jäger under Captain Slevogt dashed onto the viaduct under heavy but wild fire, chased off the French, threw the powder into the river and continued to the enemy side. As this fight took on a life of its own, more Bavarians crossed over. Soon they advanced across the meadow to Bazeilles, which until the previous day had been a quiet weaving village of 2,048 souls that had not known the ravages of war for over two centuries.

The Bavarians entered the village in battalion strength before the French mounted a counter-attack. On the hills west of the Meuse Russell had been admiring the view of the river and the sunlit parks, chateaux and walled gardens surrounding Bazeilles. Presently he heard rifle fire, then the roar of *mitrailleuses* from its streets, and saw the flash of French artillery among trees and thick clouds of smoke rising.[44] General Lebrun had sent a brigade of Vassoigne's Marine Division to clear the Germans out, which it did by 3.15 p.m. after a contest which cost the French over four hundred casualties. The outnumbered Bavarians retreated, having lost 142 men including Slevogt, who was killed. Their withdrawal to the riverbank was covered by a sixty-gun bombardment which left several houses in Bazeilles blazing far into the night. Though driven out of the village, the Bavarians kept control of the railway viaduct. At the same time, their engineers were building pontoons near Remilly undisturbed by the French. Learning that Fourth Army had halted and was not close enough to support him, General von der Tann suspended operations for the day, but his I Corps was well placed to renew its crossing when ordered.

West of Sedan, the advance guard of XI Corps reached Donchery that afternoon, meeting no resistance and finding the bridge over the Meuse still standing. Parties were able to cross and cut the railway between Sedan and Mézières while engineers began pontoons to supplement the bridge. Only to their far left did the Germans encounter opposition: as the Württemberg Division reached Flize it clashed with troops sent by Vinoy from nearby Mézières to hinder their crossing. As the columns of XI Corps marched onward they were encouraged by King Wilhelm, who knew how to act as commander-in-chief with his Prussians, bestowing friendly words on officers and men who had been decorated with the Iron Cross.

Meanwhile at Chémery, Moltke met to concert plans with General von Blumenthal, chief of staff and indefatigable military brain of Third Army. Count Albrecht von Blumenthal was a dyspeptic who found relief from his hard toil in his diary. In it he complained about the weather, about his stomach chills and headaches, about being billeted on a Jew or about what he saw as Moltke's too frequent changes of orders which kept him up late at night translating them into meticulously drafted marching orders. That afternoon, he noted, 'Moltke

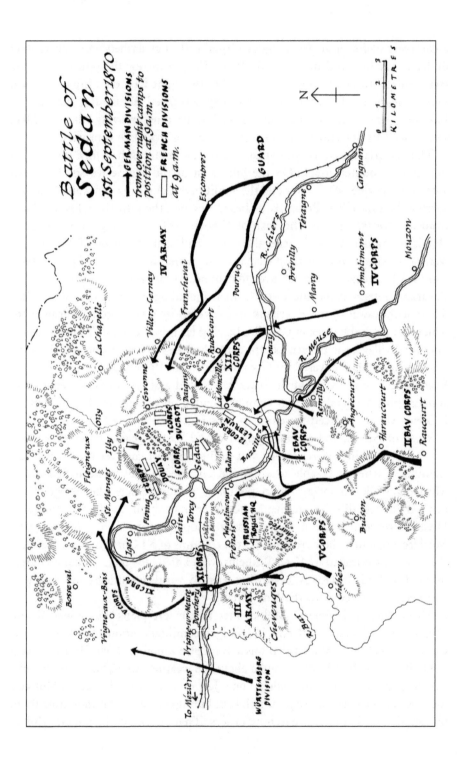

Battle of *Sedan*
1st September 1870

→ GERMAN DIVISIONS from overnight camps to position at 9 a.m.

▭ FRENCH DIVISIONS at 9 a.m.

N

KILOMETRES 0 1 2 3

IV ARMY

GUARD

R. Chiers

Escombres

Villers-Cernay

Francheval

Pouru

Brévilly

Tétaigne

Carignan

Rubécourt

Daigny

La Moncelle

XII CORPS

Douzy

R. Meuse

Mairy

Amblimont

IV CORPS

Mouzon

La Chapelle

Givonne

Olly

Illy

DUCROT

1 CORPS

Remilly

Angecourt

Haraucourt

II BAV CORPS

Raucourt

Fleigneux

St. Menges

DOUAY

7 CORPS

XI CORPS

Gazeille

Sedan

Balan

12 CORPS

LEBRUN

Bazeilles

I BAV CORPS

Bulson

Floring

Torcy

Wadelincourt

Frénois

Château de Bellevue

PRUSSIAN ROYAL HQ

V CORPS

Chéhéry

Glaire

Iges

Villette

Vrigne-aux-Bois

V CORPS

XI CORPS

Vrigne-sur-Meuse

Donchery

III ARMY

Claveuges

R. Bar

To Mézières

WÜRTTEMBERG DIVISION

Bosseval

came in rubbing his hands, with a sardonic smile on his face, and said, "Now we have them in a mousetrap." '[45]

The general plan was clear: XI and V Corps would cross the Meuse next morning at Donchery to cut the road between Sedan and Mézières. The Württembergers would cross to their west at Flize to support them. To thwart any French sally southwards across the river from Sedan itself, II Bavarian Corps would hold the hills overlooking the town, supported by the reserve artillery. I Bavarian Corps would stand ready at Remilly to support Fourth Army. Nevertheless, doubts lingered about what the French would do. Moltke thought a breakout westwards to Mézières their best option. Yet reports that morning had told of troops coming by rail from Mézières into Sedan, and of the wagons running back empty: perhaps indicating that the French were reinforcing for a breakout to the east.

That evening Moltke received a reconnaissance report that caused him to modify the afternoon's arrangements. From Remilly, French troops had been observed moving westwards. Probably these were Ducrot's men filing into their positions above the Givonne, but the Germans misinterpreted it as evidence of a French retreat on Mézières. Fearing this might frustrate his plan, Moltke wrote to Blumenthal asking him to advance the operation by having XI Corps and the Württembergers cross the Meuse that night in order to advance towards the Mézières road by dawn and intercept the French withdrawal.[46]

Blumenthal, who at 9 p.m. had just finished the earlier orders, complied. He also sent word to I Bavarian Corps to fix in place the French opposite him by attacking without waiting for Fourth Army. He let Crown Prince Albert of Saxony know what he was doing, and when Albert received this message at 1 a.m. on 1 September he promptly issued orders for Fourth Army to fall in and be ready to renew the offensive at 5 a.m. As ever, willing cooperation and flexibility were the watchword in the German camps, and they were about to bring an immense reward.

Receiving Blumenthal's orders about midnight, General von Kirchbach set his V Corps in motion towards the bridges at Donchery by 2.30 a.m. General Konstantin von Gersdorff, who had taken over XI Corps from the wounded Bose, had his men take coffee before setting off around 3 a.m. At first the Prussians tramped through the darkness, but as they neared the river towards dawn dense fog enveloped them. Riding along his columns at 4 a.m., Crown Prince Friedrich Wilhelm of Prussia had trouble keeping his men from cheering, explaining to them the need for quiet if they were to outwit the French.[47] Three hours later, the greater part of these two corps was north of the Meuse. The left pincer of the German encirclement was closing on the unsuspecting French.

Chapter 11

Battle

Fighting Begins at Bazeilles

General von der Tann, a massive, grey-haired man with a scarred face, had his Bavarians of I Corps aroused at 3 a.m. An hour later two columns began crossing the Meuse using the railway viaduct and the completed pontoons. Aided by darkness and thick fog, the leading companies of the left column advanced stealthily, hoping to take Bazeilles by surprise. Meeting no opposition at the riverbank, they crossed the meadow, crept into the village and started pushing up its long main street from the south. As they did so, they gave a cheer. It was about 4.15 a.m. when muzzle-flashes from Chassepots pierced the gloom as the first shots rang out.

The French had not left heavy forces in Bazeilles, most of Lebrun's 12 Corps being posted on hills north of the village, but the 3rd Marine Regiment garrisoning it had built barricades and loop-holed the walls of solidly built houses to make them more defensible, and went quickly into action. A struggle of fearful intensity began, with commanders on both sides throwing more battalions into the village 'like coals onto a fire'.[1]

Commanders could exercise limited control over the fighting. Even after daylight came, wreaths of smoke mingling with fog limited visibility and, with the two sides locked in close-quarter combat in narrow side-streets, it was at first hard for the Germans to bring artillery into play. Some Bavarians penetrated to the northern limits of the village, only to be shot or pinned down there by fire from the Villa Beurmann, which the French had turned into a small fortress. As a fresh Marine regiment came up the Bavarians were forced out of the western side of the village, then from the eastern. Major von Sauer, who had led the first wave, was cut off and forced to surrender after stubborn resistance. Eventually General de Vassoigne committed his entire Marine Division, but the Germans clung on to the southern end of Bazeilles.

Marine Louis Rocheron recalled the sheer ferocity of the struggle: 'The enemy was pursued in yards, in gardens, in outbuildings and in houses right up to the attics. It was hand-to-hand fighting: men butchered and killed each other without pity and with equal fury. I'll never forget those terrible moments ... The screams and heart-rending cries of our comrades wrenched our innards and brought tears to our eyes.'[2] He saw maddened civilians running hither and thither, vainly seeking safety. Fires created intense heat and filled the village with suffocating smoke.

General von der Tann now had a second brigade fighting in Bazeilles, and directed a third towards the north-east, both to try to flank the French out of the Villa Beurmann and to establish contact with the leftward units of Fourth Army, which he was assured was coming to his support. The ensuing struggle in the park of Monvillers chateau proved as savage as that in the village. Carl Tanera was a second lieutenant in the 1st Battalion of Bavarian Jäger which charged the park. His men vaulted a ditch and came to grips with the enemy: one crushed a Frenchman's skull with his rifle-butt, a second used the bayonet, the third a knife, while a fourth, having his rifle snatched away by a Marine lieutenant, strangled him, 'as if he were a wolf-hound and the Frenchman a fox'.[3] Yet, despite local Bavarian successes, the French held on in the park.

After catching their breath behind a wall, Tanera's company was directed to take part in an attack around the village of La Moncelle to the north. They came under *mitrailleuse* fire which left ten men riddled with bullets. French artillery fire did them little harm, the shells bursting too high or not at all, but 'The insignificant little pills from the Chassepot were another story: men hit by one heard no warning sound, they just suddenly felt as if their entrails were being torn out, and collapsed in terrible pain that told them clearly that they were mortally stricken. Others felt only a slight sting, but when they went to breathe blood filled their mouths: their lungs had been pierced ... As for those who took the little bullet in the forehead or heart, they came crashing down as if they had been tripped and lay quite motionless.'[4]

By degrees the battle spread northwards, up the mist-filled Givonne valley. The first guns of XII Corps of Fourth Army opened fire from the heights facing La Moncelle just before 6 a.m., but it was another two hours before the whole corps artillery was in action. All the while, German gunners suffered losses from Chassepot fire. With few infantry supports, some Saxon batteries were forced to move back by French sharpshooters; but a cavalry charge against the guns planned by General Lebrun miscarried because orders went astray.

Saxon infantry, marching up from the east, came into action piecemeal opposite La Moncelle from about 6.15 a.m. As fighting extended northwards as far as his front, Ducrot sent a brigade of 1 Corps forward into Daigny in the Givonne valley with the aim of holding the bridge there and seizing the woods beyond to spoil any German flanking attack. The 3rd Zouaves, which had distinguished itself in the Niederwald at Frœschwiller, made several attacks against the Saxon right flank, but neither in numbers nor morale was the regiment what it had been three weeks previously, and it made little headway.

Even so, the thinly stretched Germans facing them had available only the ammunition in their pouches, and were feeling the pressure.

As the sun burned off the cold morning mist, fighting raged along a 4 kilometre front. At about 8.30 a.m. Bazeilles remained a maelstrom of bitter but indecisive fighting, and there was stalemate from thence to Daigny. However, further German supports were coming forward, the number of their guns in action was increasing, and as German gunners began to see their targets more clearly they asserted their superiority in range and accuracy. One by one French batteries found themselves overwhelmed or in severe difficulties and forced to change position. French infantry reserves behind Bazeilles and on the heights west of the Givonne also began taking heavy punishment. And, although they did not know it, German gunners had already thrown the French chain of command into turmoil.

French Changes in Command

MacMahon was awaiting reports from a reconnaissance to the west when he received a note from Lebrun telling him of the attack at Bazeilles. He mounted up to see for himself, galloping from Sedan to where he could observe Vassoigne's men holding their ground. Riding on to find Lebrun, he had paused on the heights above La Moncelle to study enemy positions when a shell fragment tore into his left buttock. 'I thought at first that it was only a contusion,' he recalled, 'but as the horse I was riding had a broken leg, I was obliged to dismount. This movement made me lose consciousness.'[5] It was a little before 6 a.m.

When MacMahon came to he was in great pain, but gave orders that his chief of staff, General Faure, should tell Ducrot that he was in command. Ducrot was junior in rank to both Wimpffen and Douay, but MacMahon believed him best placed to know the enemy's movements. Unfortunately, Major de Bastard of his staff could not locate Faure, so went searching for Ducrot. En route Bastard was felled by a shot which tore away his nose and half his face, so another officer had to take the message. As a consequence, it may have been 7.45 a.m. before Ducrot learned of his unenviable new responsibility.

Amid the din of battle, Ducrot threw up his arms in despair, shouting 'Good God! What did he mean to do here!'[6] Recovering himself, he came rapidly to a decision. He had received word that more German forces (the Guard Corps of Fourth Army) were advancing against the left of his 1 Corps, and thought he recognized the predictable German flanking manoeuvre. Surely they aimed to pin the French down along the lower Givonne while they turned their northern flank. Ducrot determined to do what he had intended the previous evening – to concentrate the army on the Illy plateau to the north-west, where he believed it could better defend itself than in the 'shell trap' of Sedan.

After the war much ink and bile were spilled over whether the army could have escaped to Mézières at this point, so it is well to emphasize that Ducrot did not order a retreat on Mézières, only a regrouping that might precede it. Nor, at this point, did he know of the threat from the west posed by Third Army's advance from Donchery. Ducrot's chief of staff, Colonel Robert, tried to persuade him of the impracticability of conducting a withdrawal under fire, urging that it would be better to fight it out where they were, or at least to wait. Ducrot quoted himself as replying, 'Wait for what? Until we're completely surrounded? There isn't a moment to lose. Enough debate: obey my orders!' An eyewitness heard this as, 'I don't need your advice, f— it! Obey!'[7]

General Lebrun's concerns could not be so curtly overridden. Ducrot rode over and sought to convince him that the Germans were merely toying with them where they were, and extolled the supposed advantages of the Illy position. Lebrun pleaded against a retreat when the Marines were more than holding their own in Bazeilles. Besides, would not a retreat, especially one across broken, wooded country, demoralize the men and soon degenerate into rout? Lebrun asked for a little more time before taking such an extreme step. Ducrot allowed it, but returned half an hour later at 9 a.m. to insist that the retreat begin. Reluctantly, Lebrun gave instructions for the progressive withdrawal of his divisions, including the evacuation of Bazeilles.[8]

Some of Ducrot's own brigades which were not engaged had commenced their rearward movement when Ducrot received a startling note from General de Wimpffen. Claiming that the enemy was in retreat on Lebrun's front, Wimpffen informed Ducrot of his authority and told him, 'I think there should be no question of a retreat at this time ... You are nearer the enemy than me: use all your vigour and skill to bring victory against an enemy who is at a disadvantage ... Support Lebrun vigorously while watching over the line which you are charged with maintaining.'[9]

According to Wimpffen, he had known of MacMahon's wounding for some time but did not immediately produce his letter, naturally though mistakenly assuming that Ducrot was privy to MacMahon's intentions. Wimpffen intervened only to prevent the retreat, which he considered a disastrous mistake. Ducrot galloped over to see him, not to dispute the command, to which Wimpffen's seniority entitled him, but to plead with him to let the withdrawal continue to avoid being outflanked to the north. Wimpffen was in no mood to listen. Palikao had sent him to give the army some backbone, and he told Ducrot, 'What we need is not a retreat but a victory!' 'Oh, you need a victory, do you?' replied Ducrot. 'Well, you'll be very lucky, General, if you have even a retreat by this evening!'[10]

Wimpffen ordered Ducrot to resume his positions then rode over to Lebrun, telling him to halt the withdrawal and promising him 'the honours of the day' if he would retake Bazeilles 'at any cost'. If necessary, the army must force a bloody passage eastwards towards Carignan and Montmédy.[11]

On his way to see Lebrun, at about 10 a.m., Wimpffen encountered the Emperor. Napoleon had set off from Sedan towards Bazeilles at dawn, pausing en route for a few words with the wounded MacMahon who was being carried back to Sedan. After staying awhile with General de Vassoigne, the Emperor sent away most of his household, which was attracting enemy fire, and betook himself with a few companions to a hillock where he lingered an hour on horseback amid shot and shell.

Dr Sarazin could not help but draw a comparison with Napoleon I as he watched 'this little man, a useless spectator on the battlefield, this Caesar who had become a hindrance and to whom we now paid only passing attention; and whom death itself seemed to disregard. This was the successor to the great winner of victories. This was the Napoleon III whom France had chosen as her master, whom it had acclaimed and sustained for twenty years. He had known exile and misery, then extraordinary good fortune during which Europe had always to reckon with him: and there he was, wandering around, ill, almost abandoned and seeking death on a battlefield where his crown and, more indeed, the destiny of the ... country that had confided itself to him were at stake.' Sarazin noted that Ducrot saluted but did not ride over to the Emperor: 'Perhaps, like me, he was thinking of the man in the grey overcoat.'[12] Ducrot expressed himself less poetically. When his chief of staff had suggested that Napoleon should be advised of the retreat, Ducrot snapped, 'F— the Emperor. He's the one who got us into this mess.'[13]

It was a sign of the contempt in which the Paris government held Napoleon that Palikao had not bothered to inform him of Wimpffen's designation as MacMahon's successor, let alone to seek his consent. Now, when Napoleon met Wimpffen, he passed on a warning from an officer who knew the area that the Germans were attempting a flanking movement. 'Your Majesty need not worry,' replied Wimpffen confidently, 'in two hours I shall have thrown them into the Meuse!' One of Napoleon's companions muttered aside, 'Please God it isn't we who are thrown in it!'[14]

The End in Bazeilles

While the French commanders were arguing, issuing orders and counter-orders and riding back and forth behind the front line, the reinforced Saxons and

Bavarians were taking the offensive along the lower Givonne. Fresh regiments turned the tide at Daigny, which was captured after a hard fight about 10 a.m. Paul Déroulède, serving in the 3rd Zouaves, recounted how his company was assigned to protect a battery and beat off assaults during what was at first an orderly withdrawal. Then through mist and dust they saw a long dark line of men emerging from a hollow to their left. They were taking aim when an artillery officer shouted not to fire: these men were not wearing spiked helmets and must be French. He was disputing the point with Déroulède's captain when the advancing line got within three hundred metres and settled the argument with a devastating volley. They were Saxon Jäger. From this point, Déroulède confessed, 'It was no longer retreat, it was flight.'[15]

Caught between two fires, the 3rd Zouaves were driven westwards in disorder, half of them making their way to the Belgian border, whence they succeeded in reaching Paris on 5 September. As French gunners scurried back up the western side of the valley above Daigny they abandoned six guns and three *mitrailleuses*. The French division commander, General de Lartigue, was brought down by artillery fire together with his chief of staff.

To the south, the Germans assaulted the La Moncelle heights and renewed their efforts in Monvillers park. The Saxons and Bavarians were supported by units of the Prussian IV Corps, which had been brought across the Meuse to bolster Tann's men. Against vigorous resistance by French rearguards, the Germans established themselves on the heights by 11 a.m. Troops used their bayonets to hack down hedges in Monvillers park to get at the Villa Beurmann, which was also under renewed attack from within Bazeilles. Finally, the French were forced to evacuate the villa. After nearly seven hours of struggle, most of Bazeilles had fallen to the Bavarians.

Renewed German pressure had coincided with Lebrun's execution of Ducrot's order to withdraw. General de Vassoigne, whose men were hungry and low on ammunition, received that order about 10 a.m. Seeing the losses they were inflicting on the Bavarians, one of his brigadiers was still 'full of hope' for the outcome of the battle when the order came,[16] but his disciplined Marines managed the pull-out skilfully. Vassoigne's men reformed north of Bazeilles and marched north-west with the rest of 12 Corps. On receiving Wimpffen's order to halt the retreat, Lebrun rallied what remained of his corps on the hills above Balan, close to Sedan. Murderous German artillery fire and the advance of enemy infantry made Wimpffen's injunction to retake Bazeilles 'at all costs' a dead letter.

Isolated groups of Marines continued resistance in Bazeilles, defending houses as long as they could. Second Lieutenant Joseph Gallieni described how, after their commander was wounded, his group held out until artillery fire and flames forced them out. They reluctantly decided to surrender rather than leave their twenty-three wounded to burn to death.[17] Similarly, Captain Jean-Baptiste Bourgey with about fifty officers and men barricaded themselves in the modest Bourgerie Tavern at the northern end of the village. They beat off successive attacks for about four hours, inflicting heavy casualties on the Bavarians despite a hail of rifle fire directed at them. From midday, however, the Germans brought up artillery to pound the house, which was now full of acrid smoke and plaster dust. After the pouches of their eighteen casualties had been scoured for any remaining ammunition, the last cartridge was fired by Captain Georges Aubert, whose conduct throughout had been exemplary.[18] Present in the house with an injured foot was Vassoigne's deputy chief of staff, Major Arsène Lambert, a Gascon whose storytelling talents would inspire an acquaintance, the artist Alphonse de Neuville, to immortalize this episode in his striking painting *The Last Cartridges* (1873).

When the survivors emerged from the house under a white flag, a massacre was prevented by a Bavarian officer, Captain Lissignolo, and they were later congratulated on their determined stand by the Bavarian division commander. Gallieni's group too had been spared by the intervention of an officer. Elsewhere, Second Lieutenant Lavenue was agreeably surprised when a Bavarian officer he had just wounded with his revolver stepped in to prevent him being massacred by his captors. Not all groups were so fortunate. Lieutenant Watrin, Second Lieutenant Chevalier and sixteen men of the 1st Marine Regiment were killed after they had surrendered.[19]

Reports of German atrocities against civilians appeared in the British and Belgian press. A passionate 'cry of indignation' penned by the Duc de Fitz-James, a French descendant of the Stuarts and delegate of the French Red Cross, appeared in the London *Times* of 15 September. When the Bavarians entered Bazeilles, he charged, there occurred 'scenes of unspeakable horror and excess which will forever stain those who committed them. To punish the inhabitants for defending themselves, the Bavarians and Prussians set fire to the village ... The inhabitants had taken refuge in their cellars; women, children, all were burned. Of two thousand inhabitants, scarcely three hundred remain, who relate that they saw Bavarians push whole families into the flames and shoot women who tried to escape. I have seen with my own eyes the smoking ruins of this unfortunate village: there remains not a single house standing. An odour of burnt human flesh catches your throat. I have seen the charred remains of inhabitants at their doorsteps.' He accused the Germans of killing for the sake of killing: 'you behaved like savages, not soldiers.' Bismarck's counterblast, communicated to the English press, accused the French government of 'systematic lying', and the people of Bazeilles, including women, of joining in the fighting and of atrocities against 'whole batches' of German wounded. Such acts, he asserted, would have 'fully excused' the burning of the village, but he denied that this had been intentional.[20]

In a public letter of June 1871, General von der Tann defended his men, noting that French figures showed that thirty-nine civilians had been killed in Bazeilles and claiming that fires had been started by the artillery of both sides and as a result of close street fighting.[21] The German official history stressed that 'the inhabitants of the village took an active part in the struggle,' shooting at the Bavarians, sometimes from cellars, and sparing neither the wounded nor stretcher-bearers. Therefore, 'the Bavarians found themselves eventually compelled to cut down all inhabitants found with arms in their hands. In consequence of these circumstances the bitterness on both sides rose to extremes in the long stubborn struggle round the village which was already in flames at several points.'[22]

What lay behind these rival versions? Notwithstanding indignant denials by some French writers, local people admitted to a French army chaplain that some civilians did join in firing at Germans.[23] The number of civilians fighting undoubtedly was magnified by German fears, fuelled by stories of French 'peasants' torturing and killing their wounded.[24] In the heat of a ferocious battle in which they were being shot at from all directions and taking heavy losses, it was hardly surprising that German soldiers fired into cellars where they heard movement or French voices. Every man was fighting for his life, and French Marines were launching bayonet charges with cries of 'No quarter!' Nevertheless, French testimony is consistent that the Bavarians perpetrated excesses that went beyond the justification of self-defence, and that their disproportionate retribution was rough justice when it was justice at all.

The Mayor of Bazeilles accounted for forty-two civilian deaths directly caused by the fighting. Ten were victims of artillery bombardment on 31 August or 1 September, and died in their homes of asphyxiation, burns or shellfire. These included four children and two women aged 75 and 76. Of the remaining victims, only one was female: Uranie Moreau, aged 54, who died of maltreatment and shock a week after the battle, in which she had seen her husband beaten and threatened with death.

The other thirty-one victims were males aged between 25 and 89. A few may have fallen to random fire, possibly including Baptiste Henry, described as a 'poor idiot' who was seen wandering wounded before being killed by a shell. Several bodies were never recovered. Jean-Baptiste Lhuire was seen to have been killed by a sabre-blow as he brought wine from his cellar, but his body was among those consumed by fire. Saint-Jean Jacquet, a wheelwright, was shot as he attempted to flee. Jean Henry, a weaver, may have been killed because he kept ornamental weapons in his house. Monsieur Cuvillier, a deaf Belgian, was among those never found. Others disappeared after being seen as prisoners of the Germans after the battle, and almost certainly were executed.

Several of the bodies found had multiple gunshot or stab wounds or clubbed skulls. Some had their wrists tied, including the one citizen who was fighting as a National Guardsman. The dead included a cooper named Remy, shot three times by a Bavarian officer as he lay ill in bed despite his wife's pleas, and Lambert Herbulot, a farrier cut down by sabre-blows when Bavarians entered the cellar where he and his wife were sheltering. Like many villagers, Ferdinand Pochet, a gardener, had fled to Belgium during the battle but returned on 2 September thinking it safe. He was among those shot following the battle.

The Germans took at least thirty civilian prisoners, male and female, who suffered threats and brutal treatment as they were marched to the railway station with their hands bound. In detention, Jean-François Tavenaux noted that he and other civilians were treated contemptuously by their captors, while French soldiers were shown humanity and even given bread and tobacco. Once tempers had cooled and German officers attempted to establish facts, most of these civilians were released either before or after courts martial.[25]

As for the burning of Bazeilles, the mayor affirmed that four hundred houses were destroyed, leaving only twenty-three standing on the periphery. In thirty-seven instances fires were started by shells: the rest were deliberately burned.[26] In the heat of action houses were torched to smoke out stubborn enemies 'like wasps',[27] and flames spread; but soldiers also systematically set fire to houses under orders from officers. French witnesses insisted that this went on long after fighting had ceased, allegations corroborated by a doctor of the Anglo-American Ambulance. Betraying the self-righteous fury of his countrymen against resistance which they considered illegitimate, the German police commissioner of Sedan referred on 29 September to 'the sentence executed against [Bazeilles] under the rights of war'.[28] Lieutenant Tanera viewed this and the execution of French civilians as inevitable punishment for 'fanaticism', reflecting that 'perhaps in the next war French civilians will be more reasonable: they know what awaits them!'[29]

If these grim facts suggest that French claims of a deliberate massacre of women and children were exaggerated by rumour and overstated for propaganda, it is equally clear that the German official history sought to palliate some ugly deeds. What is beyond dispute is that, for soldiers on both sides and French civilians, the inferno of Bazeilles that day was a man-made hell on earth.

The Battle Spreads Northwards

While Bavarians and Saxons were fighting on the lower Givonne, the Guard Corps under Prince August of Württemberg was coming into line on their right. The guardsmen marched via Francheval and Villers-Cernay along difficult roads cut by ravines, but they hastened their pace as firing ahead grew heavier and they received appeals for support from the embattled Saxons around Daigny. The arrival of infantry and artillery of the Guard's left division helped in the closing stages of the struggle around that village.

Nevertheless, the Crown Prince of Saxony, commanding Fourth Army, did not want the Guard sucked into the fighting on the lower Givonne. His priority was to drive westwards to join with Third Army, and he assumed that the unexpectedly stubborn fighting on his sector was merely a French rearguard action to cover their retreat. The bulk of the Guard therefore pushed ahead, leaving Daigny to their south, driving in French outposts as they went. As the Guard batteries arrived on the heights east of the upper Givonne a terrific artillery duel commenced with the guns of Ducrot's 1 Corps responding from the western side. French gunners found themselves overlooked by their enemies, and before long their pieces were being dismounted or forced back by accurate fire. Opposing infantry skirmished heavily in the valley, the guardsmen seeking to protect their gun-line, the French trying without success to get close enough to drive off the German artillerists. German infantry took the village of Givonne soon after 10 a.m., but it was 11.30 before they forced their way into Haybes, midway between there and Daigny. Shortly afterwards, French skirmishers attempted to recover Givonne. When two French batteries careered into the village they were overpowered before they could even unlimber, the Germans capturing seven cannon, three *mitrailleuses* and 273 men.

Meanwhile, on its northern flank the Guard was hindered by French possession of the village of La Chapelle. Here, as elsewhere that morning, the French might have exploited opportunities to obstruct and delay Fourth Army's approach. But La Chapelle was held only by an isolated battalion of Parisian *francs-tireurs*, who were driven out at 11 a.m. after half an hour of bombardment and assault. Many of the survivors fled into Belgium.

While fighting continued in the Givonne valley, most of 1 Corps remained on the heights west of the stream being pummelled by artillery fire. Louis de Narcy described the ordeal. He had woken up cold and hungry, but his company was called to arms before he could eat the breakfast he had cooked. Although the volume of firing from the south made it evident that a major battle had begun, a mixture of mist and smoke in the valleys hid the action beneath a white shroud. Yet, despite being unable to see their targets properly, he saw

French gunners firing 'so hastily that you would have believed that they were trying to get it all over with as quickly as possible'.[30]

His regiment, the 1st Algerian Sharpshooters, was placed 150 metres behind French batteries on the heights above the village of Givonne. On this open plateau infantry served little useful purpose save to make a target for German gunners once the fog cleared. Narcy observed that his unit could have been spared casualties had it moved 200 metres to its left, but 'none of our generals thought of it, nobody gave us the order; we stayed ...'. They were at least ordered to lie down. Shells exploded at irregular intervals at first, then continuously, with no respite. For three hours they lay there, wondering at the whistle of each approaching shell, 'Who is this one for?' Then came the detonation and the cloud of dust, leaving maybe two, three or four mangled corpses or wounded men crying for help. His men became agitated as this went on and on, demanding why they were not given the order to advance. Despite Narcy's efforts to maintain his composure, his heart was racing, he burned with thirst, and he saw his hand shaking involuntarily. One by one he saw good comrades hit; here with a broken leg, there with a smashed thigh. Five paces away Lieutenant Bourdoncle lay face down in a pool of blood, the top of his skull blown off. Next to Narcy his native lieutenant, Salem ben Guibi, a 'civilized and intelligent negro' who had survived the Mexican campaign, was killed by the same shell as two sergeants. Spattered with earth, blood and brains, Narcy turned away so as not to have to look. Time seemed to crawl as shells rained all around them and men tried to make themselves as small as possible. Narcy was struck by how several comrades, normally carefree, hardened soldiers, had experienced a presentiment of death before the battle, and how often such feelings were fulfilled in the brutal lottery of bombardment.

Without firing a shot, his regiment suffered over two hundred casualties while they lay exposed in this way. The regiment in front was suffering as badly: its men too had been ordered to lie down, but the sun glinting on their neatly stacked rifles pinpointed their position to the Germans.[31]

Much of 1 Corps had suffered similarly and began to lose cohesion before it had struck a blow. Eventually most of its units, approaching the limits of endurance under such attrition, pulled back south-west into the Bois de la Garenne (literally 'Rabbit-Warren Wood') which seemed to offer cover, only to find that the Germans could still inflict significant damage at ranges of nearly 4,000 metres. Thus by midday the Germans had thoroughly shaken Ducrot's men and were in control of the crossings of the Givonne. Once the Guard had cleared La Chapelle, its cavalry probed north-west to try to establish contact with Third Army. For, looking westwards from his headquarters atop a hill

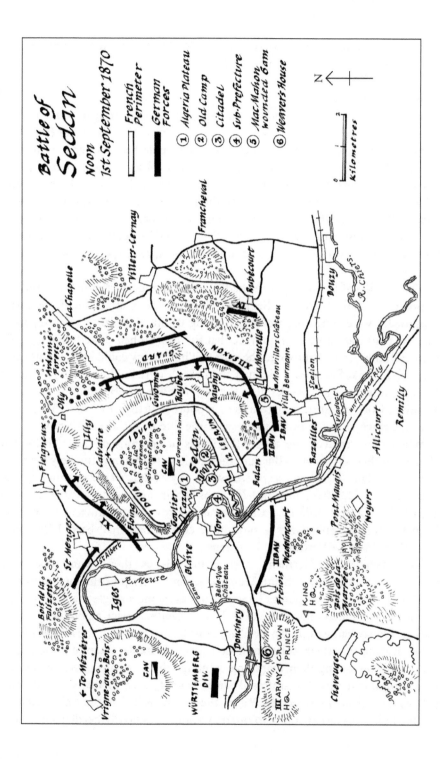

Battle of
Sedan

Noon
1st September 1870

French
Perimeter
German
Forces

① Algeria Plateau
② Old Camp
③ Citadel
④ Sub-Prefecture
⑤ Mac-Mahon
  wounded 6am
⑥ Weaver's House

N

0   2
kilometres

near Villers-Cernay, Prince August had for some while been able to see that a second front had opened against the French.

The Trap Closes

The German high commanders, in contrast to the French, remained at observation points where they could receive information from the front and despatch orders. Crown Prince Friedrich of Prussia had his headquarters on a hill south of Donchery, from which he could observe the progress of his left wing. The early morning fog hid the crossing of the Meuse by his V and XI Corps from the French yet, frustratingly, also prevented him from seeing what either they or the French were doing. It was only when the sun began to disperse the mist after 7 a.m. that the Prince could discern, through a tripod telescope, what was unfolding in the landscape spread spectacularly beneath him.

The mission of V and XI Corps had been to advance northwards beyond the Meuse to reach the road from Sedan to Mézières and to attack the French who supposedly were retreating westwards along it, but Prussian cavalry reported that the road was clear, with no trace that the French had passed that way. To their east, the Crown Prince and the staff of Third Army could hear, but not see, heavy fighting at Bazeilles. Evidently the French were holding their position at Sedan or attempting to break out to the east, or even into Belgium. Either way, V and XI Corps must turn eastwards to support Fourth Army. At 7.30 a.m. the Crown Prince gave the order that sealed the fate of the French army.

When they received the order, the heads of columns of those corps had already reached Vrigne-aux-Bois and the Mézières road. Unfortunately for post-war French fantasies of an escape westwards, by Moltke's later testimony[32] the Germans had 52,000 infantry and 249 guns within striking distance of the road even before Ducrot ordered a withdrawal to Illy – quite sufficient to bar any French retreat as effectively as outnumbered Germans had barred Bazaine's road from Metz to Verdun on 16 August.

Nevertheless, the Germans were vulnerable as they swung eastwards towards Saint-Albert and Saint-Menges, around the top of the long loop that the Meuse makes at this point. They had to pass along a single road overlooked by the steep wooded hills of the Bois de la Falizette, a place made for ambush. Earlier, Douay had withdrawn two battalions he had posted at the mouth of this defile, fearing that their isolation made them vulnerable. Despite some delays and confusion among their marching columns, the Germans passed along the road unopposed save for scattered shots from French civilians and cavalry patrols around Saint-Albert. By 9 a.m. the Germans had seized Saint-Menges against light opposition, and two infantry companies boldly headed south into

Floing, where they skirmished in the streets before ensconcing themselves in houses where they could hold out until help arrived.

The Germans took risks in running their artillery forward close behind light skirmish lines of cavalry and infantry. At first only three batteries of XI Corps opened fire from high ground south-east of Saint-Menges against eight French batteries posted east of Floing, and took punishment. By 10 a.m., however, the Germans had seventy-two guns in action in this sector, and after another half hour had established clear superiority, with more guns and their infantry supports continually arriving. Already Blumenthal could assure the anxious Crown Prince that 'This evening will end with the hoisting of the white flag.'[33]

While the Germans were making their bold flanking march around the loop of the Meuse and fanning out from Saint-Menges, Douay's 7 Corps remained passively on the ridge above Floing, facing north-west. Douay had learned of MacMahon's wounding, but if Ducrot sent him an order to withdraw it never arrived. Logically, Ducrot's regrouping plan should have required 7 Corps to move first. It was perhaps as well it did not, for it might have been struck by the Germans while in motion.

At about 10.30 a.m. Wimpffen wrote assuring Douay that he was facing only a demonstration, and urged him to send whatever troops he could spare to help Lebrun. Then Wimpffen arrived in person, and Douay rode with him along his line to show him how matters really stood. The accuracy of German shell-fire, Wimpffen admitted, was such as 'I would have been the first to admire in other circumstances.' Douay hoped to maintain his position provided that his vulnerable right, at the northern apex of the French line, could be supported. Wimpffen promised to send ample troops from 1 and 5 Corps to bolster that point and rode off, exhorting Douay to 'Cheer up now! We must have a victory!'[34]

In some places Douay's men had the shelter of light field entrenchments, and at first held firm under bombardment. Only in one infantry unit was there brief panic when two French batteries withdrew 50 metres, but once these guns resumed firing the men steadied. As the Germans extended their gun-line southwards some well-screened *mitrailleuses* inflicted considerable losses on their crews. Meanwhile, as the Germans were deploying north-eastwards the French cavalry thought it saw its chance.

General Jean Margueritte was marked by his superiors as a potential future leader of all French cavalry. His regiments of Chasseurs d'Afrique, in their distinctive sky-blue jackets and tall caps, had sailed from Algeria in the first week of August. On the 12th Margueritte had demonstrated his and their fight-ing spirit by surrounding a party of German dragoons who had boldly crossed the Moselle at Pont-à-Mousson south of Metz. In the ensuing fight the visor of his cap was cleft by an enemy sabre, but the Germans lost eight killed and twenty-seven captured. Thereafter his brigade had been detailed to escort the Emperor to Châlons, and Margueritte was appointed to command the Light Division of the new army's cavalry reserve. Campaigning in the rain and mud of northern France had brought the Chasseurs little opportunity to shine, and no doubt, like Louis de Narcy, they pined for 'our beautiful African skies where one so easily forgets all that is sad and painful'.[35] Today they stood in rear of the right wing of Douay's 7 Corps at the Calvaire d'Illy. Soon after 10 a.m., Margueritte ordered the Marquis de Gallifet, commanding his 1st Brigade, to charge westwards against the German left which was advancing towards the village of Illy, then to attack their guns east of Saint-Menges.

Gallifet, whose counter-guerrilla operations in Mexico had earned him a reputation for ruthlessness, lined up his three regiments of Chasseurs one behind the other and started forward. The German infantry, commanded at this point by Major Count Schlieffen, saw the charge coming and made ready. They opened fire at 50 metres, causing the leading French regiment to veer off to left and right, only to come under fire from riflemen concealed in brushwood and then to be plastered with artillery shells. Having lost ninety-seven men, the regiment returned to its starting point. The two behind it fared no better. A little later Margueritte saw the guns of V Corps appearing north of those of XI Corps, but their infantry supports arrived so quickly that he abandoned plans for another charge.

Too late also was an isolated French infantry counter-attack at Floing, after the Germans had occupied it in force. The attack, a determined initiative led by Colonel Formy de La Blanchetée, remained unsupported. For an hour there was a see-saw fight in the village and cemetery until the Germans brought up reinforcements and finally ejected the French. As this combat was dying down, at about 12.30 p.m., the Germans suffered their highest ranking casualty of the day. As he directed operations from a park north of Floing General von Gersdorff, commanding XI Corps, was mortally wounded by a bullet in the chest.

By that time German rifle companies pushing north-eastwards had moved beyond Fleigneux, capturing a French wagon-train and some guns, and had pressed on through woods that were already full of French soldiers heading for Belgium. It was at about noon, near the hamlet of Olly, that infantrymen of Third Army made contact with a squadron of Hussars of the Guard from Fourth Army. The German left had joined hands with the right. The French were surrounded.

The Ring of Fire

The circle of steel guns now forged around the French was a more immediate and deadly peril than the infantry cordon. Even before the junction of Third and Fourth Armies, the converging fire of their guns from east and west was grinding down the French capacity to resist. French units found themselves shelled from front and rear, with no safe refuge. Fugitives from 1 Corps running into the Bois de la Garenne from the east ran into men from 7 Corps running the other way. Even when shells claimed relatively few victims or buried themselves in the soft earth, 'they had an enormous psychological influence'.[36]

The northern sector of the French position in particular became so shellswept that cavalry could not stay there. Margueritte managed to hold most of his units together and pulled them back into the wood, one of his brigadiers being cut in half by a shell during the withdrawal. The divisional cavalry of 1 Corps (Michel) and 5 Corps (Brahaut), after vainly seeking safety, made their separate ways northwards through the woods before the German pincers closed. Michel passed through Olly before the Germans arrived, and after dipping across the Belgian frontier reached Charleville and eventually Versailles. Brahaut was not so fortunate, being captured in an encounter with the Germans which dispersed many of his men. Most of 12 Corps' cavalry found its way barred by Prussian infantry and returned to the Bois de la Garenne, save for one regiment which found its way north. Probably a third of French cavalry had left the field before the envelopment was complete, either to fight another day (about 3,000 troopers) or to be disarmed and interned in Belgium. In all, between 8,000 and 10,000 'completely demoralized' French troops of all arms reached Mézières by woods roads during the day.[37]

On the roads to the frontier there was chaos and terror. Dr Sarazin, who had become separated from Ducrot after halting to tend an artillery officer with a smashed thigh, found them 'jammed with carriages, caissons, wagons, fugitives and riders' together with local people: 'These poor folk were dragging their weeping children along with them and were carrying off, on carts or wheelbarrows, everything they had been able to throw together in haste.' Panic spread as German cavalry attacked, riding down or sabring all who did not scatter. Escaping into brushwood, Sarazin reflected, 'What is a man once he has lost his courage! On this road, within my sight, there were at least two or three hundred infantrymen armed with Chassepots and supplied with cartridges' who might easily have defended themselves, but 'Our men, who would have fought bravely in other circumstances, fired not a single shot against the horsemen who were sabring them! How strange!' Further on, he encountered a 'wild cavalcade' of French cavalrymen from different units heading for Belgium in 'wild disorder', trailed by wounded and riderless horses. Behind them the roll of gunfire was unceasing.[38]

Between noon and 2 p.m., French infantry and artillery strove to defend the plateau at the Calvaire d'Illy. Ducrot sought out Wimpffen and, after claiming credit as a prophet, told him, 'You must hurry and send reinforcements if you want to keep hold of that position.' 'You take care of that,' replied Wimpffen, 'gather all the troops you can ... while I look after 12 Corps.'[39] Ducrot gave orders to send men and guns towards the Calvaire, but they were driven back by the weight of fire. When General Douay came to inspect his right at 12.30 p.m. he was horrified to discover that the plateau had been evacuated by 1 Corps.

During the morning Douay had sent away all the troops he could spare in response to Wimpffen's repeated requests to aid Lebrun. The brigade from 5 Corps designated to anchor his right had been despatched, and he had pulled his strongest division, Dumont's, out of line to follow it. Yet one of Dumont's brigades, Bordas's, largely disintegrated under shellfire as it emerged from the southern boundary of the Bois de la Garenne, and fled back under the trees. The other brigade, that of Bittard des Portes, was moved back and forth within the woods more than half a dozen times in obedience to successive orders and counter-orders from Dumont, Douay and Wimpffen, all the time suffering serious losses. So many men straggled as a result that the brigade had dwindled to the strength of two battalions before it was ordered into action.

Douay and his generals performed prodigies trying to rally fugitives from Dumont's Division and other units in the woods and to funnel them towards the crest of the Calvaire, using the cover of a thick hedge to shield them from German observation. Under the direction of General Doutrelaine, Douay's Chief Engineer, the infantry tried to cling on to the crest. Three of Dumont's batteries supported them and for a short while prevented the Germans from debouching from the village of Illy in the valley below, but Prussian guns soon zeroed in on them. Within half an hour they had lost over thirty men, sixty horses and three ammunition caissons. Douay sent up two batteries from the reserve to replace them. The first lasted only a few minutes before two guns were dismounted, one caisson was destroyed and sixteen men and twenty-seven horses were out of action. It was forced to abandon the position and two guns. Douay ordered the second battery to withdraw. It was all too typical of the fate of French gunners who fought against ever lengthening odds until either their guns were wrecked or their ammunition gave out. In Douay's Corps alone, forty artillery caissons were hit by enemy fire during the day, each explosion leaving a shambles of human and horse flesh. French reports groped to describe the 'rain', 'hail', 'hurricane' or 'avalanche' of enemy shells falling on and all around them. French fire was audibly slackening.

At about 2 p.m. the improvised defence of the Calvaire collapsed as German shelling drove the last defenders back into the Bois de la Garenne. Soon German infantry appeared at the Calvaire and pressed on into the woods, only to be driven out by a French counter-attack. The prisoners the Germans had taken during their foray were so dazed that they made no attempt to escape. A fire-fight developed along the northern edge of the Bois de la Garenne.

In the southern sector of the battlefield too German pressure was building. During the morning Hartmann's II Bavarian Corps had come up from Raucourt. Crown Prince Friedrich ordered one of its divisions to cross the Meuse to support Tann's men west of Bazeilles. From 11 a.m. it became embroiled in an obstinate struggle with French troops in the chateau park outside Balan. The other division of II Bavarian faced Sedan from the south, occupying the villages of Frénois and Wadelincourt, sending patrols into the Iges peninsula, and trading shots with the garrison of Sedan. On 30 August the French had closed a weir, causing the Meuse to inundate the meadows south of the town, 'so that Sedan seemed to be placed in a lake, its ancient bastions and battlements, spires and steeples, reflected in the placid waters', reminding William Howard Russell of one of Turner's views of Venice.[40] With the approaches to the town thus restricted, the real work in this sector was for the divisional and corps artillery, which opened fire from the hills to the south from 9 a.m. Finding their range with deliberation, the Bavarian gunners directed only part of their fire against the rampart guns of Sedan, which replied steadily. They also aimed at Douay's men, visible on the hills beyond, and at Lebrun's troops around Balan. The French were being tormented from all sides.

Behind the Bavarian guns, on the La Marfée heights, stood King Wilhelm and his entourage, including princes from the German states, foreign dignitaries, staff men and newspaper correspondents. From here they had a grandstand view under a hot sun. 'It was a battle panorama such as nobody will ever see again,' thought one of Moltke's officers, and Moritz Busch likened the noise to 'half-a-dozen thunderstorms'.[41] The day was now so clear that through his glass Russell could see people in the streets of Sedan, and beyond the town dark masses of advancing Prussian infantry, sunlight playing on their bayonets and the spikes of their helmets, puffs of bluish-white smoke continually spurting from hundreds of cannon, and vast clouds of black smoke rising above the trees from the direction of Bazeilles. Russell noticed that Wilhelm spoke little save for an occasional word to Moltke or Roon, but pulled his moustache frequently. Bismarck, in his white cuirassier's uniform and cap, stood slightly apart, smoking cigars a great deal and chatting with the stocky little Yankee general Phil Sheridan, erstwhile scourge of the Confederates and latterly of the

Red Indians. Sheridan's policy in the Shenandoah Valley in 1864 of leaving his enemies 'nothing but their eyes to weep with' chimed with Bismarck's increasingly splenetic view of the French.[42] Moltke gave no orders. His gaze alternated between his telescope and his map as he stood musing, his right hand pressed to his face.[43]

Under the eyes of these august spectators a crisis unfolded between 1 and 2 p.m. on the hills north-west of Sedan. On their left Douay's men were holding on doggedly to the slopes above Floing, but XI Corps was now fully deployed against them. Using dead ground, a brigade worked around the French left flank, between Floing and the Meuse. If it reached the heights above Gaulier, it could roll up the French line from the south. As it advanced, the Germans pushed forward from Floing. Liébert's division, defending this sector, made a supreme effort to throw back assaults on its front and flank. Struggling with steep terrain, the Germans gave ground to these counter-attacks in places, but soon came on again, supported by their own guns and those of the Bavarians across the Meuse, which together smothered the French positions with shell. At about 2 p.m., as the French were losing the Calvaire d'Illy to the north, intermingled German units by common impulse started pushing up the hillside above Floing and gained a foothold on the crest of the hills to its south. Desperate measures were required if the French were to stop them.

The Cavalry Charges

General Ducrot's orderly found General Margueritte in a ravine north of the La Garenne Farm and explained his orders to him. 'You know that what you're asking of me is a serious matter?' Margueritte queried, and asked for his instructions to be repeated before leading his division towards the ridge above Floing.[44] Ducrot came in person and ordered him to charge westwards down-hill to breach the German lines, then to turn right against their flank. Ducrot then went back to bring up some of his infantry to follow the cavalry.

Margueritte went forward to reconnoitre the terrain while his regiments deployed behind the crest. He sent back word that they should prepare to charge squadron by squadron in an effort to break through. It was near 2 p.m. and the air was full of bullets. As Margueritte rode back up the ridge one passed through his cheeks, breaking his jaw and partially severing his tongue. His orderlies got him back on his horse and over the crest, where his men beheld a frightful sight. A stream of blood pouring down his beard and uniform, the general gestured with his arm towards the enemy. There were cries of 'Forward!' from the nearest squadrons, which were growing restive under galling fire and were restrained from starting immediately only with difficulty.

Margueritte's successor, General Gallifet, was issuing orders for the charge when an impatient Ducrot rode up, insisting that the situation was increasingly critical.

So the bugles sounded, and off went Margueritte's 1,800 men: three regiments of Chasseurs d'Afrique (including the 4th, which had charged superbly to disengage the British Light Brigade at Balaklava sixteen years earlier), one of Chasseurs de France and one of hussars. They were joined by some squadrons of lancers and cuirassiers. As the division poured over the crest and thundered down the slope, nobody suspected that this was the last time an old-style cavalry charge would be seen on a Western European battlefield. The barrage of fire that greeted them from front and flank was withering, and was not the only hazard. The ground was steep and uneven, pitted with sudden depressions, and to the left above Gaulier there were hidden quarries. Many a horse and rider died of a broken neck. Nor did German infantrymen give way. Taking cover where they could in ditches or behind hedges, they worked the bolts of their needle guns. Where there was no cover they formed knots to defend themselves. Their volleys continued 'like the rattling of a Catherine wheel', inflicting devastating losses on the French within minutes and covering the hillside with heaps of dying white and grey horses and their masters.[45] Although most survivors veered to right or left, some pressed their charges home. The German official account conceded that 'a comparatively large number' of German riflemen received slash or stab wounds.[46] In a mêlée that extended from Cazal to north of Floing amid smoke and wild confusion, a few horsemen forced their way through the first German line. Some penetrated the streets of Floing, some sabred German gunners in a battery to its south, while some even got in among German convoys near Saint-Albert. Such exceptional local successes were short-lived, however, for German support troops soon shot down or captured those who had got through. The remainder retreated back up the hill to reform in the Bois de la Garenne, causing 'considerable disorder' among Douay's remaining infantry as they galloped through them.[47]

Ducrot meanwhile had brought up his only available infantry brigade, Gandil's, and demanded another charge to clear a way for it. Gallifet objected that the ground was unsuitable, so Ducrot directed him more to the northwest. This took the cavalry obliquely across the front of French infantry who, mistaking them for enemies, opened fire on them until Ducrot rode over to intervene. Gallifet and his men attacked with an élan and courage that won the respect of their enemies but which could not prevail against modern artillery and rifles steadily handled. The cavalry action was over in half an hour. The charge was brilliant, Bismarck conceded, but flouted the principles of war: against unbroken troops it was 'folly, but a heroic folly'.[48] Margueritte's troopers paid dearly for their ride into immortality. At daybreak the division had been 2,408 strong; next morning 1,327 answered roll call.[49]

As for Gandil's infantry, Ducrot's efforts to instil in them his own 'ardour and rage' proved vain. They had been bombarded and moved hither and thither all morning, and after brief exposure to heavy fire they retreated and disbanded.[50]

The cavalry charge later became a patriotic legend, treasured as an affirmation of chivalric virtues in the face of hopeless odds, and boosted by an aristocratic officer corps which projected itself as guardian of those virtues. The discipline and bravery of Margueritte's Division redeemed a humiliating defeat, and their feat was therefore precious to the honour of the post-war army. General Ducrot had more reason than most to emphasize the willingness of the cavalry to sacrifice themselves and their supposed insouciance in the face of death. Ten years after the battle he published words not included in his earlier accounts, but which became essential to the legend. Ducrot quoted himself as saying, on ordering the second charge, 'One more effort, my dear general ... If all is lost, let it be for the honour of our arms!', to which Gallifet replied, 'As many times as you like, general ... So long as there is one of us left!'[51]

From his vantage point, King Wilhelm expressed admiration for the charge.[52] No German witness recorded his words, though Ducrot wrote that Crown Prince Friedrich subsequently told him that they were 'Oh! The brave fellows!' The Crown Prince had not been with his father at the time, though may have heard it from him afterwards. Of his conversation with Ducrot on 3 September Friedrich wrote only that he was 'grateful for the tribute I paid to French bravery'.[53] Whether the exact words were Wilhelm's, Friedrich's or Ducrot's, 'Les Braves Gens' was fittingly carved on the Cavalry Memorial, dedicated in 1910, which stands atop the ridge as centrepiece of the military cemetery. Equally merited was the compliment Friedrich paid his own men for resisting the French cavalry onslaught. He and his staff watched the charge with bated breath, and when it failed there was 'a prolonged buzz of satisfaction'. 'That, indeed, was well done,' declared Friedrich.[54]

Once the French cavalry had been driven off, XI Corps resumed its advance up the ridge, their 'Hurrahs!' resounding above the firing.[55] Much of 7 Corps was soon in disorderly retreat on Sedan, bearing Ducrot and Gallifet along with them. Liébert's Division covered them by a fighting retreat in reasonable order. The Germans suffered significant casualties as they consolidated their hold on the ridge, took Cazal, and closed in on the western fringes of the Bois de la Garenne, where many of Douay's men had taken refuge. By 4 p.m. the Germans were approaching the walls of Sedan from the north-west, but were held in check by the fortress guns.

The French Collapse

For all the compliments paid to it, the cavalry charge had proved futile and sounded the death-knell for massed horsemen in warfare. Artillery now dominated the battlefield, and the Germans were employing it as never before. On 18 August at Saint-Privat the Guard advanced in closed ranks against devastating rifle fire and had been shot down in droves. At Sedan they intended to avoid such losses by thorough artillery preparation. Prince Hohenlohe, commanding the Guard artillery, anticipated grid bombardment by detailing his ninety guns to target particular sections of the Bois de la Garenne. This methodical pulverization of French positions commenced at about 2 p.m. 'At this phase of the battle,' wrote Hohenlohe, '... our superiority over the enemy was so overwhelming that we [i.e. the artillery] suffered no loss at all. The batteries fired as if at practice.'[56] They drew a crowd of spectators from Guards officers in the reserve line, among them a 22-year-old adjutant, Paul von Hindenburg.

The effects of the fire were visible and audible. Quérimont, a farm in a clearing in the wood serving as a dressing station, was set ablaze. The wood became a confused ant-heap of French troops as units lost cohesion while, Hohenlohe testified, 'the fearful cries of the victims of our shells reached as far as where we stood.'[57] On the receiving end, Louis de Narcy described how 'Cannon boomed everywhere. The earth was ploughed up, trees splintered. From clearings in the woods we could make out clouds of fire and smoke in an arc all around us ... The most formidable cannonade that had ever been fell upon the semi-circular line that we held around Sedan. Never had such a quantity of iron been fired. From 1 p.m. to 4 p.m. more than 600 cannon thundered without respite against our positions from all points of the horizon.'[58] The most telling statistics about the Battle of Sedan are that during the day the Germans used 606 guns to fire 33,134 rounds into a shrinking area of a few square kilometres.[59] Well might the German official history state, 'The fate of the battle was already to a certain extent decided by this deployment en masse of German artillery, even without the further advance of the infantry.'[60]

Expecting death at any moment, Narcy and the dozen men with him headed, like so many others, towards the illusory shelter of Sedan, its slate roofs reflecting the afternoon sun: 'for the walls of a town are an irresistible attraction for troops who are giving way.'[61] From his position south–east of town General Lebrun witnessed the descent of an avalanche of men, horses and wagons from the Bois de la Garenne, 'running as if crazed towards the defences of Sedan, seeking to enter the fortress'.[62] He sent orders to raise the drawbridge to prevent men from taking refuge within the citadel, but nothing could keep them out.

There was no escaping the shells under the walls of the fortress. With great difficulty, Ducrot pushed his way through the crowds of wounded men and fugitives as shells continued to fall, and entered the citadel through the postern gate. He tried to organize soldiers to man the walls, but neither pleas nor threats could sway these demoralized men. As soon as he was out of sight they disappeared. In the town, 'the spectacle was indescribable. Its streets, squares and gates were jammed with wagons, carts, cannon, and all the equipment and debris of a routed army. Bands of soldiers without rifles or packs flocked in continuously, flinging themselves down in houses and churches. There was a crush at the town gates. Several poor men were trampled to death. Through this mob rode horsemen and caissons at breakneck speed, carving a path through these panicking masses.' There were surly cries of 'We're betrayed!' and 'We've been sold by traitors and cowards!'[63]

Watching the disintegration of the French army from across the Givonne, Hindenburg remarked to his companions, 'Napoleon too is stewing in that cauldron.' They laughed in disbelief. A talkative merchant in Carignan had told Hindenburg that the Emperor was with the army, but most German officers considered this an idle rumour.[64] The question of 'what, granting the Emperor Napoleon really and truly fell into our hands, was to be done with such a prisoner,' was debated by the King and his advisers, 'but hardly more than as a joke, an incredible possibility'.[65] Bismarck assured Sheridan, 'The old fox is too cunning to be caught in such a trap; he has doubtless slipped off to Paris.'[66]

Napoleon had returned to Sedan at about 11.30 a.m., when it was already thronged with thousands of fugitives. The sound of shells passing overhead reminded one of his aides of a terrible wind whistling through a ship's rigging during a storm. Shattered tiles and masonry were falling into the streets, and one shell burst just in front of the Emperor.[67] Suffering greatly from his long ride, Napoleon entered the Sub-Prefecture. There, at about 2 p.m., he received a note from Wimpffen written at 1.15, announcing that he intended to break out to the east, 'rather than be taken prisoner in the fortress of Sedan. Let Your Majesty come and place himself amid his troops, who will consider it an honour to open a passage for him.'[68]

If Napoleon had been passively seeking death on the battlefield, the mood had passed. He and his advisers recognized that the battle was lost; that Wimpffen's proposed breakout was impracticable and could only lead to useless sacrifice of life. Napoleon added that 'he could not allow himself to be taken.'[69] By his order, the white flag was raised over the citadel towards 3 p.m. The task fell to Arthur de Lauriston, who sobbed, 'Me! Me! The grandson of a Marshal of France!'[70] Amid the smoke from fires burning in the town and gun-smoke, few at any distance noticed the flag.

One by one Napoleon's generals arrived: Margueritte was carried in, able to communicate only with a pencil. (He would die at a chateau in Belgium on 6 September.) Ducrot arrived, and noted that the Emperor's usually impassive face betrayed deep melancholy. We may perhaps discount the speech that Ducrot put in his mouth, confessing that he should have paid more heed to the general's pre-war warnings about Prussia. Napoleon rejected any notion of escaping by night and insisted, as shells fell in the courtyard and garden of the Sub-Prefecture, that a ceasefire was 'absolutely necessary'. Ducrot refused his request to sign a ceasefire order to the army, pointing out that this was Wimpffen's role. However, as Wimpffen's whereabouts were unknown, they agreed that the army's chief of staff should sign. When this message reached General Faure he angrily refused, adding that he had just had the white flag taken down.[71]

Lebrun was more helpful, advising Napoleon that it was insufficient merely to raise a white flag: a formal request for an armistice must be sent to the enemy commander-in-chief. Lebrun too refused to act as a principal in seeking a ceasefire, but volunteered the services of his own chief of staff, provided that Wimpffen consented. Lebrun wrote out a request to the Germans for an armistice for Wimpffen to sign and set off to find him. Assuming that Lebrun himself was the Emperor's envoy, the imperial staff had a cavalryman with a white serviette tied to his lance follow behind him.

Death Throes

By 1 p.m. Wimpffen had abandoned his hopes of the army holding out until nightfall and perhaps escaping under cover of darkness, but he remained intent on breaking out towards Carignan.[72] His order to Douay to cover the army's rear reached that general just as his line was breaking, and Douay responded that it was as much as he could do to manage an orderly retreat. Ducrot had reached Sedan when he received Wimpffen's summons to come and help. His first reaction was that he had tried everything, but it was impossible: 'I can do no more.' Then he called on the generals around him for a last effort, but they replied that it was useless, their troops had melted away. It was then that Ducrot entered the citadel.[73]

Wimpffen waited impatiently and in vain for Napoleon to join him. He gathered up five or six thousand men at the Old Camp outside Sedan, including some Marines and Abbatucci's brigade from 5 Corps, and directed them against the Bavarians around Balan. The fighting in that village and its surrounding parkland, orchards and gardens had swayed back and forth during the middle of the day as one side or the other brought up reinforcements. By 2.30 p.m. the Bavarians controlled the village but were unable to break out of it.

The new French charge pushed them back through the village until they held only a few houses on its southern fringe. The fighting was as intense as in Bazeilles, and similarly lethal for civilians. A 75-year-old Napoleonic veteran brought down several Germans with accurate fire until he was hit. At least three other men were killed by the Germans for doing the same thing. Five Balan residents were killed by random fire, but seven were massacred apparently for being in the wrong place at the wrong time, including Madame Matagne, who was 'grossly outraged' before being clubbed to death. In all, eighteen civilians died. The village priest was almost executed by the Germans after being denounced by one of his own parishioners for allegedly directing French artillery fire, and was kept prisoner for a month. On their part, French Marines shot down a group of Bavarians they surprised at an inn.[74]

Men from many French units took part in the fighting, taking orders from whatever officers happened to be present. A lieutenant recalled their wild firing. He told a Marine to take care with his aim as there were French troops in front of them. A moment later he turned back and saw that the man had accidentally blown off the top of a French corporal's head. When reproved, the Marine flung down his rifle and ran off, sobbing dementedly.[75] Outside the village, the French retook the chateau park and woods and took prisoners after a 'long and murderous fight'.[76] But, though they drove back a counter-attack, they were running low on ammunition and were pinned down by artillery fire. Their two supporting cannon were knocked out, and eventually they were forced back.

Wimpffen meanwhile headed for Sedan to rally reinforcements. En route he met the Emperor's orderly with a note requesting him to order a ceasefire and open negotiations with the enemy. Wimpffen indignantly refused, and when he encountered Lebrun was too incensed even to listen. 'No, no, I won't have a capitulation ... I want to carry on the fight,' he insisted, and one of his officers threw down the cavalryman's white flag. When Lebrun presented him with the letter for him to sign requesting an armistice, he thought Wimpffen was going to tear it to pieces.[77] Instead, Wimpffen rode into the town not, as requested, to see the Emperor, but to gather more men. Arriving about 4 p.m., he reached the Place Turenne and had his aides shout 'Bazaine is coming!' to galvanize the troops.[78] Many refused to follow him, but he succeeded in mustering about 2,000 men including National Guardsmen and civilian volunteers, plus two cannon, and marched them back to Balan.

As they marched, the perimeter held by the French was shrinking. The German operation at this juncture reminded Russell of a circle of beaters gradually closing in on their quarry, with the French at bay like 'some wounded tiger'.[79]

Having completed its deployment, the Prussian Guard advanced on the Bois de la Garenne at 3 p.m. Their artillery fire had been 'so annihilating . . . that the French were scarcely capable of any organized resistance'.[80] Nevertheless, there was sporadic resistance by clusters of French soldiers, and confusion as the Germans tried to deal with it whilst taking thousands of prisoners. Seeing groups of their comrades still firing, some Frenchmen had second thoughts about surrender and picked up their rifles again. The Germans were momentarily driven out of the Quérimont clearing, yet, as XI Corps entered the wood from north and west, the outcome was beyond doubt. Within the wood, Melchior de Vogüé remembered, small branches of the oak trees severed by firing rained upon the heads of the French and the bullets sounded 'like a swarm of bees'. A line of German infantry appeared and fired at close range: 'Their fire was extremely heavy. Our officers fell one after the other. Our sergeants made us withdraw under cover . . . There, converging shells skimmed the earth, sending up flurries of dead leaves. We felt ourselves surrounded, hunted down in this wood like rabbits. We looked for shelter to lay our wounded officers: we saw a large white wall, with a gendarme mashed to pulp by a shell against a doorpost. We went inside. This was La Garenne Farm, a dismal charnel-house where a few doctors were mopping their brows and swearing about the lack of water, scurrying between heaps of wounded who were imploring their aid. The Prussians were entering from all sides at the same time as us.'[81]

Louis de Narcy, who had returned to the wood, found himself surrounded by a 'terrified horde' of Frenchmen. Some waved white handkerchiefs, some called for the shooting to stop, others shouted 'Down with the Emperor!' and grosser insults.[82] If the moment of capture was tense, there was often a release of tension afterwards for both sides. The Bavarian Lieutenant Carl Tanera found himself fighting with Saxon units. His company surrounded seventy-five Frenchmen in a quarry so quickly that they had no chance to fire. With a circle of rifles pointing at them, they obeyed shouts to 'Lay down your arms!' Once the surrender was completed, Tanera exchanged cards with four captured officers, and he and his comrades shared a meal with them that evening.[83]

By 5 p.m. the Germans had secured the wood, and the carnage within its shattered acres deeply impressed many of them. The ghastly spectacle of masses of men slaughtered by artillery fire foreshadowed the wars of the next century. 'It was with the greatest difficulty that a man on horseback could move amongst the dead and wounded soldiers,' recalled a staff officer.[84] A veteran of Sadowa, Paul von Hindenburg, wrote simply that 'The picture of destruction I beheld . . . [in] the Bois de la Garenne surpassed all the horrors that had ever met my gaze, even on the battlefield.'[85]

The German High Command deployed units to ensure that there could be no French breakout at any point, and still had plenty of fresh troops at its disposal. The Württemberg Division had crossed the Meuse west of Sedan that morning to support XI and V Corps, and was still intact after driving westwards French skirmishers from Vinoy's forces at Mézières. Significant portions of V, IV and II Bavarian Corps and the Guard had not yet been engaged. Two small, desperate attempts to break through the German circle were crushed: one by about a hundred cuirassiers under Major d'Alincourt who rode hell for leather through German lines near Cazal until all were shot down or taken; the other by a few hundred men near Daigny led by General Wolff, one of Ducrot's division commanders, who was severely wounded in the attempt. In the wake of this foray Colonel Christopher 'Kit' Pemberton, a correspondent of the London *Times* accompanying Saxon headquarters, was shot dead as he rode towards a group of Frenchmen he thought had surrendered.

There remained Wimpffen's forlorn hope at Balan. By the time he returned to the village his 2,000 men had dwindled to 1,200 at most. Though Lebrun thought it a hopeless sacrifice of life, he joined Wimpffen for the last charge.[86] The attack went through the village at the run, picking up survivors of previous attempts. It reached the church at the southern end of Balan and captured a large house. General von der Tann had some anxious moments, but made dispositions to deal with the attempted breakthrough. Before long, a barrage of German shells was battering the church tower and making Balan untenable. Finally Wimpffen had to admit that 'nobody is following us, and there is nothing more to be done.'[87] He ordered the retreat to be sounded, and returned to Sedan at about 5.30 p.m., leaving Lebrun to manage an orderly retreat towards the town. As the French withdrew, buglers sounded the retreat repeatedly to ensure that nobody had been left behind, 'but no one appeared; there remained only the dead and the dying.'[88]

In Sedan meanwhile there was pandemonium. At 4 p.m. King Wilhelm ordered all German artillery south of the Meuse to bombard the town. As shells burst in the packed streets and squares, killing soldiers, civilians and senior generals, men crammed into cellars in search of safety. Incendiary rockets set more fires burning. The bombardment was intended to force the French to a decision, and it succeeded. Another white flag was raised, this time on the Torcy side of town, where the Germans made it out through palls of black smoke billowing from a blazing paraffin factory. Bavarian soldiers reached the town gates and opened a parley with the French within. As word spread on both sides, the guns gradually fell silent.[89]

Ceasefire

In the name of King Wilhelm, Lieutenant Colonel Paul Bronsart von Schellen-dorff of Moltke's staff appeared at the Torcy gate under a white flag to demand capitulation. He was met by General Beurmann, commander of the citadel, who led him into the town. As nobody blindfolded him, Bronsart could see for himself 'the immense disorder that reigned in the streets' and that most French troops were 'not averse to the prospect of capitulation'. Eventually he was led through a crowd of inquisitive French officers in the courtyard of the Sub-Prefecture, then upstairs and, to his surprise, into the presence of the Emperor of the French. Napoleon struggled to his feet using a stick, looking 'very ill at ease and tired'. He produced a sealed letter and arranged for one of his aides, General Reille, to return with Bronsart to deliver it personally to King Wilhelm. The little cavalcade rode up towards the La Marfée heights at about 6.30 p.m. Bronsart, the earnest Prussian deeply conscious of the historic signi-ficance of the moment, disapproved of the Frenchman's 'frivolous' attempt to ease the tension by banter. However, both Reille and Wilhelm now played their parts with dignity.

Wilhelm stood alone, with his entourage in a semicircle behind him. Reille dismounted, removed his cap and approached, handing over the envelope with its large red seal. Wilhelm opened it and read the letter enclosed:

> Monsieur My Brother,
>
> Having been unable to die amidst my troops, it only remains for me to place my sword in Your Majesty's hands.
>
> I am Your Majesty's dear brother, Napoleon

While courtesies were exchanged with Reille, who had acted as orderly to the Crown Prince during his visit to the 1867 Paris Exhibition, a reply was written:

> Monsieur My Brother,
>
> Regretting the circumstances in which we meet, I accept Your Majesty's sword, and invite you to nominate one of your officers invested with full powers to negotiate the capitulation of your army, which has fought so bravely under your orders. For my part, I have designated General Moltke for this purpose.
>
> I am Your Majesty's dear brother, Wilhelm.[90]

Reille returned to Sedan at about 7 p.m., his Crimean and Italian campaign medals reflecting the setting sun. There was much mutual congratulation among the German dignitaries before they dispersed to their quarters. Shaking hands with a British correspondent, Bismarck disclaimed any role in the military victory, but rejoiced that Bavarians, Saxons and Württembergers had taken such a large share in it: 'That they are with us and not against us, that is my doing. I don't think the French will say now that the South Germans will not fight for our common fatherland.'[91]

So ended the Battle of Sedan. The Germans had achieved their historic triumph with remarkable economy of force, having committed fewer than 150,000 troops to battle.[92] They had lost 2,320 men killed, 5,910 wounded and 702 missing, for a total of 8,932 casualties: a marginally less costly victory than Frœschwiller, for a far more decisive result. The Bavarians had suffered the heaviest losses.[93]

The scale of the French disaster was never established with precision. Eight hundred officers were killed or wounded. Based on incomplete returns, the French later calculated their losses in men killed and wounded at 10,000. The Germans estimated 3,000 French dead, 14,000 wounded and 21,000 taken prisoner during the battle. The German figure for French wounded probably included some men wounded at Beaumont and hospitalized in Sedan. Independent estimates of French wounded varied between 11,000 and 12,500. After the capitulation the Germans counted a further 83,000 prisoners, including the garrison of Sedan. They estimated those interned in Belgium at 3,000, though Belgian sources put the figure nearer 8,000. In all, over 120,000 French troops, the entire Army of Châlons, had been taken out of the war in a day, with 419 field guns (including 70 *mitrailleuses*), 139 fortress guns, over 1,000 wagons and 6,000 serviceable horses added to the booty. It was victory and defeat on a staggering scale.[94]

A long night of suffering began for the wounded, the darkness lit by burning villages. Raging fires in Bazeilles cast a reddish glow on the Meuse, in which the bodies of men and horses floated. Balan too was nearly torched, but Bavarian officers managed to stop their men setting fires and pillaging houses.[95] Yet a mood of awe and thanksgiving prevailed in German ranks. When news of the French surrender reached Karl Geyer's company 'several minutes went by before anyone could say a word or move from the spot. Each man bowed his head in silent wonder at the mighty workings of destiny.' Then there were shouts of jubilation and cheering: 'With deep thanks to God, the whole regiment joined in when ... the band struck up the hymns "Now Thank We All Our God" and "Our God is a Mighty Fortress".'[96] This scene was repeated throughout the German camps. Hopes were raised for a speedy end to the war.

French gloom would have deepened had they known that 100 kilometres to the south that day Bazaine had failed to break the German blockade of Metz.

On 29 August he had received a note from Ducrot dated the 27th warning him to be ready 'to march at the first sound of cannon'.[97] Yet Bazaine's attempted sortie on 31 August–1 September was ineptly planned and executed, and his unsupported troops fell back. With all prospect of rescue gone, the capitulation of France's first line army too was now only a matter of time. It would surrender on 29 October.

Chapter 12

Aftermath

Capitulation

Furious that the Emperor had raised the white flag without his agreement, Wimpffen sent in his resignation as commander-in-chief. After Ducrot and Douay had resolutely declined the poisoned chalice, Napoleon refused to accept the resignation, urging that Wimpffen had a duty to the army and country to try to obtain the best terms possible. Reluctantly, Wimpffen acceded and arrived at the Sub-Prefecture towards 8.30 p.m. in rancorous mood. He burst into the Emperor's presence, declaring, 'Sire, if I have lost the battle, if I have been beaten, it is because my orders were not executed, and because your generals refused to obey me.'

At this the resentment that Ducrot had harboured all day erupted. He squared up to Wimpffen, shouting, 'What are you saying? Who refused to obey you? Do you mean me? Your orders were followed all too well, alas. If we have suffered a disaster more frightful than anyone could have imagined, we owe it to your mad presumption. You alone are responsible, for if you hadn't halted the withdrawal in spite of my pleas, we would now be in safety in Mézières, or at least out of the enemy's clutches.'

'Well then,' rejoined Wimpffen, 'if I'm incompetent, the more reason that I should relinquish command.'

This further inflamed Ducrot: 'You claimed command this morning when you thought there were honour and profit in exercising it; I didn't contest it, though I could have. But now you can't refuse it. You alone must shoulder the shame of capitulation.'

Wimpffen parried: 'I took command to avoid a defeat which you would have hastened by your withdrawal ... Besides, General, I'm not here to confer with you. Please leave us.'[1] Officers present separated the two men, and Ducrot left.

Armed with full powers to negotiate, Wimpffen, accompainied by Chief of Staff General Faure and General Castelnau of Napoleon's suite, rode into enemy lines, where the discipline and efficiency of German sentinels attested to the quality of their opponent. The Frenchmen were ushered into a ground-floor room of the mayor's house in Donchery, where Moltke had his head-quarters. They were joined by Moltke, Bismarck, and a group of senior officers.

The packed room was dimly lit by candles and an old oil lamp. 'The varied uniforms, the solemn silence, the grave faces covered with perspiration and dust in the almost uncanny light, all this I shall never forget,' wrote a German officer, adding that 'the scene was made still more spectral by a ray of light ... [which] fell upon an excellent portrait of Napoleon I.'[2]

Moltke curtly demanded the French officers' credentials and shortly announced his terms: the entire French army would become prisoners of war, with all its arms and equipment. Officers would be allowed to keep their side-arms in recognition of their courage. Considering these terms harsh, Wimpffen tried several gambits to soften them. Could not his army march out with its flags and arms and go to Algeria or some agreed part of France, on oath to take no further part in the war? Moltke refused. Would he not grant more honourable terms out of professional consideration for a fellow general who had just arrived from Africa to be faced with a disaster not of his own making? Moltke was unmoved. Wimpffen then threatened that if better conditions were not offered, his army would fight on. Moltke lectured him on the hopeless military position of the French army, showing an intimidating knowledge of its condition and prospects.

Changing ground, Wimpffen urged that generous terms would be gratefully appreciated by the French and lead to better future relations, whereas harsh ones risked 'igniting an interminable war' between the two countries.

Bismarck dismissed Wimpffen's argument as specious. What faith could be placed in the gratitude of a country which had changed governments so frequently in the last eighty years? It would be folly for Germany, Bismarck insisted, to trust in the goodwill of an 'excessively envious, jealous and proud people', which had declared war on her umpteen times in the past two centuries. France thought she had a monopoly on military glory, and had not forgiven the victory of Sadowa. What security had Germany that France would not seek revenge for Sedan within five or ten years? Bismarck painted the Germans by contrast as a quiet people who desired no conquests, but only to live in peace. (A French officer present was put in mind of a crafty pickpocket who, after robbing someone, is the first to cry 'Stop, thief!') 'Now,' continued Bismarck, 'enough is enough. France must be punished for her pride, aggression and ambition.' Germany must have territory and fortresses.

Wimpffen objected that France had changed since 1815, and was now devoted to peaceful industry and the fraternity of nations, but Bismarck was in full spate: French popular love of glory, whipped up by journalists, had conspired with dynastic interest to provoke war, and moderate opinion had acquiesced. No doubt there would soon be a government in Paris which respected nothing and which would refuse to accept any capitulation agreement. Germany could not take the risk of allowing the French army its liberty.

Castelnau pleaded that the Emperor had surrendered his sword in the hope of obtaining honourable terms for the army. Bismarck wished to know whether the sword was that of France or merely Napoleon's own. 'Solely that of the Emperor,' Castelnau replied. Moltke jubilantly declared that in that case his conditions were unchanged. Wimpffen rose, announcing his intention to renew the battle. Moltke rejoined that he would reopen fire at 4 a.m. precisely. It was Bismarck who urged the uselessness of further bloodshed. At his behest, Moltke conceded Wimpffen a few hours to consult and respond before the recommencement of hostilities at 9 a.m.[3]

Wimpffen returned to Sedan after midnight and reported to the Emperor, who undertook to ride out early to make a personal appeal to King Wilhelm to moderate the terms. At 6 a.m. on 2 September Bismarck was awoken at Donchery by General Reille, who called up from the street that the Emperor wished to speak with him. Hastily pulling on his uniform, Bismarck rode down the poplar-lined road to Frénois, where he encountered Napoleon's carriage. The Emperor seemed reluctant to go into Donchery to talk, selecting instead a modest house nearby, the home of a weaver named Fournaise.

Neither man got satisfaction from the ensuing interview, first inside the stuffy house, then on chairs in front of it. Napoleon sought better terms for his army, even its internment in Belgium, but Bismarck repeatedly blocked him, declaring that this was a solely military matter. Moltke appeared, and shortly rode off to warn the king, who readily agreed that he should not meet Napoleon until after the capitulation had been signed. Meanwhile, when Bismarck tried to explore peace terms, Napoleon maintained that he was a prisoner with no power to negotiate, and referred him to the government in Paris. Bismarck left before 9 a.m., leaving Napoleon to pace up and down a potato patch smoking cigarettes as a crowd of officers and reporters looked on.[4]

In Sedan, Wimpffen put the German terms to a formal council of war of his generals. Only two junior men, Bellemare and Pellé, argued for fighting on, but withdrew their objections when the army's plight was spelled out to them. With little ammunition or food and in utter disorder, the French had the bleak option of surrender or being massacred by artillery in the streets of Sedan. Capitulation was unanimously accepted, and as Wimpffen wrote up his notes one of Moltke's officers arrived to demand an immediate answer, or firing would be resumed. Understanding that his attempts to stall until after an interview between the sovereigns were bootless, Wimpffen rode out to the Château de Bellevue, a mock-gothic mansion near Frénois owned by a manufacturer, Louis Amour (brother of the mayor of Donchery), which the Germans had selected as a suitable venue. Napoleon had been escorted there by Bismarck and a German honour guard, and he had to confess to Wimpffen that he had been unable to see the king.

The military capitulation was signed by Wimpffen and Moltke at about 11 a.m. By its terms the French army became prisoners of war. All its weapons and equipment, together with the garrison and citadel of Sedan, were surrendered. Wimpffen negotiated one concession that later earned him a censure from a Court of Inquiry. French officers who signed an undertaking to take no further part in the war would be allowed to return home. This was contrary to French military law, which forbade officers to separate their fate from that of their men, and illustrated the class divide that had so undermined morale in the French army. Of 2,866 French officers captured, some 500 – nearly one in six – took advantage of this clause. They alone were permitted by the Germans to retain their sidearms, unlike those who remained prisoners.[5]

Wilhelm waited on the hills above until all was concluded, meanwhile expressing his thanks to those around him, since 'these great successes will indeed cement more strongly the union with the Princes of the North German Confederation and my other allies.'[6] He went to meet Napoleon at the chateau at 2 p.m., having rejected hard-line advice to inflict a ceremonial submission on him, though such a humiliation would have been popular with many in Germany.

Despite his age, Wilhelm's tall, imposing figure towered above the ashen-cheeked and tearful Napoleon. Wilhelm shook hands with him with the words, 'Sire, I am very sorry to see you again in such painful circumstances,'[7] then took him by the arm and led him to a room where they talked privately. Wilhelm offered the castle of Wilhelmshöhe near Cassel for Napoleon's internment, which he gratefully accepted. Napoleon complimented him on the performance of his army, admitting that 'in my artillery I feel myself personally conquered,'[8] and lamented the indiscipline of his own troops. Evidently he imagined that the whole German army was present, and was visibly shaken when told that Friedrich Karl with seven army corps was still blockading Metz.

In his talk with Bismarck, Napoleon had stressed that he personally had not wanted the war, but had been forced into it by public opinion, and he again played the innocent bystander in his interview with Wilhelm. Napoleon habitually distanced himself from unpleasant developments, and conveniently forgot that he had endorsed Gramont's declaration on 6 July and strengthened the demand for guarantees on the 12th. It had been within his power to prevent both, and he would have used a victorious war to strengthen his position. Wilhelm willingly ascribed blame to the Liberal ministry, but pointedly observed that it had led public opinion.[9]

When they emerged, Napoleon spoke graciously to the Crown Prince and Bismarck. The red kepis and trousers, gold braid and white kid gloves of the Emperor and his companions and the gold livery of his attendants contrasted strikingly with the drab, campaign-soiled uniforms of the Prussian military. After a farewell that moved both monarchs deeply, Wilhelm set off on a triumphal tour of his troops, and was cheered to the echo far into the evening.

Death, Wounds and Imprisonment

In the days following the battle, surgeons had few breaks between operations, and when they did venture outside they found little to relieve their spirits. 'The natural beauty of the country serves only to throw out into blacker, more fearful relief, the horrible desolation of the battlefield,' wrote one.[10] The Germans organized burial parties quickly, not least to spare their men demoralizing sights, but the work took time. Male citizens of Sedan were requisitioned to help from 6 September.[11] Meanwhile, the dead lay in the open: 'Their features in some instances were contorted and dreadful to behold – some with portions of their skulls and faces blown away, whilst what was left of their features remained unchanged; others with their chests torn open and bowels protruding; others, again, mangled and dismembered.'[12] Feet, legs and heads sometimes lay far from the bodies to which they belonged, and limbs had been blown into trees. William Howard Russell stopped at random to contemplate the body of a lancer, who bore 'a small blue wound in his chest which let out his life', and examined his papers which, by their suddenly poignant personal and family details, testified silently but eloquently to thousands of individual tragedies.

This corpse, like others, had been plundered. Russell saw a man using the cover of a Red Cross armband to fill an enormous bag with watches, purses, gold and silver taken from the dead and dying.[13] The battlefield was littered with debris: weapons of all sorts, knapsacks, caps, helmets, belts, plumes, shakos, spurs, boots, brushes, letters, sheet-music, whips and bridles, which all in all 'would furnish an immense bazaar'. On the outskirts of Sedan gardens and cemeteries were in ruins. Many horses lay writhing in agony from wounds or trapped beneath upturned wagons, 'until either a friendly revolver or death from exhaustion put an end to their torment'.[14] Many unceremonious interments of men and horses were in graves that were too shallow, giving rise to a nauseating stench that hung over Sedan for weeks.[15]

Care of the wounded was better organized than at Waterloo a generation earlier, thanks to the railways and improved medical services. The Hanoverian Dr Georg Stromeyer, the German Surgeon General, established a large, well-ventilated and clean hospital at Floing. Belgium and Luxembourg gave effective aid. Under the direction of Dr Merchie, the Belgian hospital service treated 1,800

French and 1,150 Germans. Although the Germans only belatedly informed the Belgian government, during September and October they evacuated 6,500 wounded from the battles of Beaumont and Sedan by rail to Aachen across Belgian territory.[16]

Flawed organization made French efforts less effective. During August the French Society for Aid to the Wounded used the donations that poured in to equip eighteen large 'Ambulances', that is, mobile field hospitals staffed by civilian volunteers, and despatched them from Paris to the front. But the lavish supplies they carried were sometimes ill-considered. Ambulance No. 5, for instance, carried copious cucumber pomade but little chloroform, and its surgeons had to beg a carpentry saw to perform amputations. The ambulances were overstaffed with largely unvetted and untrained crews: too often hospital orderlies were pilferers looking for opportunities. Moreover, when the volunteer ambulances reached the front the army sometimes proved hostile or indifferent, and they were left to fend for themselves. Nevertheless, Ambulance No. 5 treated six hundred patients during the campaign.[17]

One of the best run ambulances was the Anglo-American, headed by Dr Marion Sims, who like several of his American colleagues was a veteran of the Confederate medical service. Based at the Asfeld Barracks at Sedan, they treated two thousand patients. The war had also provided the stimulus for the formation of the British Red Cross, which organized relief and sent trained nurses to Sedan.

Impressive as were these international efforts to relieve suffering and save life, they could not transcend the limits of the medical science of the day. Skilled civilian surgeons tried to save limbs using the best 'conservative' techniques known, but William MacCormac, for one, regretted having yielded so often to the temptation of trying to save seriously damaged limbs.[18] Where immediate amputation might have saved a man, it was too late once infection set in. Subsequent amputations were rarely successful, and doctors found patients who had been doing well succumbing. Even when antiseptic dressings were applied, they were of little value once the surgeon's probing fingers or instruments, or fragments of cloth driven into the wound, had introduced infection.

Disease began to spread. Even the Germans found that typhus and dysentery were wreaking havoc among patients who had not been evacuated.[19] In the Anglo-American Ambulance, staff and patients began falling sick. One cause, the half-decomposed body of a Zouave who had fallen into the well, was removed; but still patients died by the dozen daily from fever, secondary haemorrhage, dysentery and hospital gangrene. Charles Ryan, a young Irish surgeon, lamented that for all their efforts, their hospital had become 'a centre of the plague, and threatened to be a death-trap' to all admitted. Often comfort was the best treatment that could be offered. When a wounded Chasseur officer asked plaintively, 'Tell me, Doctor, is it possible that Christ suffered as much as I am suffering now?' Ryan could only console him with the thought that 'Your pain is as nothing to his.'[20]

In Sedan on 2 September the French army prepared for imprisonment: 'Everything and everybody looked utterly wretched and miserable. At each corner were the bloody skeletons and entrails of horses, from which every scrap of flesh had been cut, but bread was not to be had for love or money.'[21] Men lay in the street or cooked horsemeat. Most smashed and flung down their weapons and burned their flags rather than surrender them. Discipline was at a low ebb: 'the common soldiers felt and expressed the heartiest contempt for their officers.'[22] General Lebrun struck across the face with his cane a man who was loudly denouncing generals. A cavalry colonel was put under arrest for his outburst during his brigadier's farewell speech: 'You want to say goodbye to us? Do we know you? Since we've been under your command you haven't once come to see your regiments. You never enquired about their needs. You never did anything for them.'[23]

Yet there was also relief at being out of danger, particularly among French troops who had crossed the frontier and were on their way to internment at Beverloo Camp in Belgium. A despondent Dr Sarazin was shocked to see them laughing and joking, seemingly completely carefree. No doubt cheerfulness was a strength in a soldier, but this struck him as 'a little premature'.[24]

On 3 September the French army was marched from Sedan through Torcy to Glaire, the only entrance to the Iges peninsula, which had been designated as a giant holding pen. Bounded by the Meuse on three sides and by the canal to its south, the camp was easy for the Germans to guard. The few prisoners who attempted to escape by swimming the polluted waters of the Meuse were shot. Many of the French arrived drunk, having been too generously plied with wine and spirits by the people of Sedan. With few tents for shelter, few cooking utensils and little firewood or fresh water, the exhausted prisoners had to sleep in torrential rain and cold mud. The desolate, sodden, stinking Iges peninsula was remembered by survivors as 'Camp Misery'. Rations were at first quite inadequate. Men scrambled for what was available, or cut hunks off rotten horse carcasses that lay about. Groups of horses that had been turned loose frantically chewed tree bark or each other's manes, and became a hazard at night as they stampeded, trampling sleepers. Gangs of marauders preyed on the village of Iges, the only habitation, or on fellow soldiers. Dysentery became rife among thousands of men suffering from exposure.[25]

Food got through to the prisoners all too slowly and was badly distributed. The Germans were caught unawares by the numbers they had to cope with and the railways were overburdened with the needs of their own troops. After General Lebrun and others made representations on behalf of their men, the situation began to improve, and General Bernhardi, the German commandant, made efforts to get supplies in. Over the next fortnight, as prisoners were loaded onto trains for Germany in batches of 2,000, the situation eased until Camp Misery was empty. French officers, distributed between several German cities, enjoyed relative liberty of movement after signing an oath not to escape. Their men were kept occupied with manual work in camps, or were hired out to local employers.[26] A few weeks later, another 173,000 prisoners arrived from Metz. Thus by November virtually all the survivors of the army France had put on her frontier at the beginning of August – over a quarter of a million men – were in captivity. Over 17,200 Frenchmen died there of wounds or disease during an exceptionally hard winter.[27] Repatriation began in March 1871 following the armistice, and was completed after the signing of peace between France and Germany in May.

Departures

Napoleon III's departure from the Château de Bellevue on 3 September resembled a funeral cortège. Escorted by a troop of Prussian Black Hussars, the imperial convoy trundled through Donchery under dark skies as the heavens opened and thunder rolled. Bystanders caught a glimpse of Napoleon wistfully twisting the end of his waxed moustache. Bismarck and Moltke watched from a window, and it was Moltke who said, 'There is a dynasty on its way out.'[28]

Napoleon skirted the battlefield to the north, passing through Saint-Menges and Fleigneux, evidently wishing to avoid contact with his own troops. When he passed within sight of prisoners there were occasional shaken fists, cries of treason, and a shout of 'You sold us to save your baggage!'[29] For many, however, his departure was a matter of 'icy and disdainful indifference'.[30] At La Chapelle he sent money to the wounded, then crossed into Belgium, leaving France forever.

He had already wired Eugénie that he had been defeated and captured, and in a letter confided, 'it is impossible for me to tell you what I have suffered and am suffering. We have conducted a campaign contrary to all military principles and common sense. It was bound to lead to catastrophe; it is complete. I would rather have died than witness such a disastrous capitulation, and yet in the circumstances it was the only way of avoiding a slaughter.'[31]

When the Empress received news of the disaster on the afternoon of the 3rd she refused to believe it. Her features distorted with anger, she loosed a hysterical tirade in front of her terrified attendants: 'No, the Emperor hasn't capitulated! A Napoleon doesn't capitulate. He's dead! . . . Do you hear me: I tell you he's dead and they want to hide it from me! ... Why didn't he get himself killed? Why isn't he buried under the walls of Sedan? ... Didn't he think that he was dishonouring himself? What name will he leave his son?'[32]

Next day, 4 September, a beautiful Sunday in Paris, crowds formed calling for a Republic and chanting 'Down with the Empire!' As they threatened to break into the Tuileries, Eugénie fled to England with the help of her American dentist. The mob had already invaded the Legislature, where Gambetta declared the Empire deposed. He and Jules Favre led the jubilant crowds to the Hôtel de Ville, where the Republic was proclaimed. General Trochu, who had made no move to defend an Empress who mistrusted him, became President of a new Government of National Defence. The revolution in Paris was bloodless. A regime that had lived on prestige could not survive its catastrophic loss. One republican took satisfaction in the irony that the survival of the Emperor ensured the death of the Empire.[33]

In March 1871, at the end of his captivity, Napoleon rejoined Eugénie in exile in England. He was planning a return to French politics when in January 1873 he died following an operation for removal of the large bladder-stone that had tormented him. His last coherent words were 'We weren't cowards at Sedan, were we?'[34] Hopes for a revival of Bonapartism rested on the Prince Imperial until he was killed in 1879 seeking a military reputation as a British army officer in South Africa. Thus the Bonaparte dynasty was felled by Krupp's steel guns and despatched by Zulu assegais.

On 2 September Wimpffen addressed a farewell proclamation to the army that scarcely knew him, saluting it for fighting 'to the last cartridge'.[35] Two days later he abandoned it, having sought special permission from Moltke to spend his internment with relatives in Stuttgart. His corps commanders had a stricter sense of duty and remained with their men in the Iges peninsula. In Ducrot's case this was not for long. Like other officers, he was trusted to make his own way across country to Pont-à-Mousson and to surrender himself for embarkation to Germany. Officers taking this route found themselves abused and reviled for their failure by peasants in Lorraine.[36] When Ducrot reached Pont-à-Mousson he hid a set of peasant's clothes in the mayor's house before duly surrendering himself to the German authorities. While waiting under guard on the station to embark he and his staff were insulted by French troops.[37] Amidst the crowds, Ducrot slipped through the station buffet, retrieved his disguise, and made his way to Paris, where he would command an army.

Lebrun considered that his word of honour did not allow him to take such opportunities to escape, and like Douay he went into captivity. Among the prisoners too was General de Failly, who would never hold another military command. Popular feeling against him remained so strong that the police feared disturbances at his funeral in 1892. Marshal MacMahon recuperated slowly from his wound at Pouru-aux-Bois, but once well enough insisted on going into captivity. He left for Wiesbaden in late November, distancing himself from the intrigues of the imperial court and avoiding all polemics about the battle.

The most momentous departure from the disease-stricken town of Sedan in the first week of September 1870 was that of the German army. Orders for an advance on Paris via Rheims were issued on the 3rd. Bismarck initially had reservations. He would have preferred to make peace with the imperial regime on the basis of French cession of Alsace and Lorraine and payment of a large indemnity.[38] But Moltke saw no sense in allowing the enemy a breathing space: he intended to retain the initiative and to force a military decision. Besides, the war had started in Paris, and Paris must be punished. In the spirit of Protestant crusaders against the modern Babylon, the Germans advanced on the French capital, chalking 'On to Paris' on doors and fences as they marched. As one of Moltke's officers wrote, 'most of us believed that we had now only to push on rapidly to Paris and there dictate peace.'[39] The prospect of a victory parade down the Champs-Élysées beckoned.

The news of Sedan had caused rejoicing throughout Germany and astonishment in Europe. Final French submission and the consummation of German unity appeared imminent. Yet both were to prove more elusive than anyone expected in the heady days following the victory, as a sequel to this volume will tell.

Recrimination and Memory in France

No French leader wished to be held responsible for a disaster of the magnitude of Sedan, and the arguments begun on the day of the battle were developed afterwards with great bitterness. From captivity, Wimpffen inspired or ghost-wrote newspaper articles and anonymous pamphlet attacks on Napoleon, MacMahon and Ducrot. His withering indictment of MacMahon's competence in his 1871 book about the battle shocked fellow officers. He also argued that Ducrot's attempted withdrawal, and subsequent failure to support him in a breakout to the south-east, had robbed him of the chance for victory, and that Napoleon had shown cowardice in not coming to lead his offensive: 'Whilst I, the commanding general, was on the battlefield, believing that my lieutenants were there too and ready to execute my orders, they were with the Emperor in Sedan deciding to capitulate!'[40]

General Ducrot proved an equally ferocious paper warrior. Since his youth in Algeria he had displayed a facility for embellishing his own exploits, and he was stung into responding to 'this wretch de Wimpffen'.[41] In his own 1871 account of Sedan, Ducrot figures as a commander of Napoleonic prescience and decision who might have saved the army by an early retreat to Mézières had it not been for Wimpffen's purblind obstinacy in halting it, and he belittled Wimpffen's offensive at Balan.

If Wimpffen's insistence on the chances of a breakout to the south-east rested heavily on wishful thinking, so did Ducrot's championship of a break-out westwards. Underestimating German strength in that direction, he argued that it would have been possible to brush them aside and open the road to Mézières.[42] In reality, the hazards of a withdrawal under heavy attack pointed out by Lebrun and Ducrot's chief of staff were weightier than Ducrot admitted, and the road west was barred by 8 a.m. One critic wondered acidly which would most astonish history, 'the prodigious nerve of General Ducrot or the wonderful naivety of a portion of his contemporaries, listening all agape to his grotesque justification of his plan of retreat!'[43] Competent military analysts subsequently concluded that Ducrot's orders would at best have led to a vulnerable pile-up of French troops around Illy, or at worst to a rout. The chance for his plan to work had already passed by the time he took command.[44]

From exile, Napoleon defended himself against Wimpffen's charges through articles and pamphlets written by his aides, which emphasized his suffering during the campaign and his humanity. They portrayed him as a martyr, pushed into war against his will, betrayed by the Chamber which had thwarted his military reforms and by indiscipline stirred by republicans in the army. Napoleon took responsibility for raising the white flag, but maintained that it had been done after consultation with senior generals, whereas his corps commanders all stated that it was flying before they spoke with him.

These controversies shaped the writing of the history of Sedan from the French side. Yet supporting documentation amassed by the protagonists illustrated that there was little agreement on the timing or sequence of events or the exact words spoken during the mayhem of battle. Post-war arguments over responsibilities also had political overtones. Napoleon's dynastic motives were obvious. Ducrot, whose book on Sedan ended with a paean to 'Honour and Country ... Work and Discipline'[45] notoriously became a man of the ultra-Catholic Right, earmarked by the Legitimist pretender to the French throne, the Count de Chambord, to lead a coup d'état if circumstances required.[46] The Protestant Wimpffen, by contrast, became a staunch republican, whose criticisms of Napoleon resonated with all those inclined to blame defeat on a 'corrupt' authoritarian regime. Thus the claim of both generals to be the man who had almost saved France on 1 September 1870 merged personal vanity into the political struggle of the 1870s over the country's future.

In 1872 a Court of Inquiry into the capitulation of Sedan deplored the consequences of the successive changes in the French high command. Noting that Wimpffen either 'was unable, or did not know how, to make himself obeyed completely', it blamed his faulty strategic conception for aggravating his army's plight. Conceding that Ducrot's plan was improvised and would have been difficult to execute, it judged it rational to the extent that it might have allowed more of the army to escape into Belgium, so avoiding the shame of capitulation.[47] Wimpffen left the army soon afterwards.

In July 1873 occupying German troops marched out of Sedan, and in September evacuated French territory altogether. That autumn the military failures of the war were publicly dissected at the court martial of Marshal Bazaine. The inquiry scrutinized Bazaine's curious passivity at Metz, including his communications with MacMahon. In finding Bazaine guilty of failing to do all that duty and honour required to avoid capitulation, the court felt that he had 'waited for support from Marshal MacMahon's army that, on the contrary, he should have provided to it'.[48] MacMahon, now French President, let it be known that he would not execute his former colleague, and the death sentence was commuted to twenty years' imprisonment. The contrast between the situations of the two men was striking. Bazaine, the scapegoat for failure, was generally reviled. MacMahon had been no more successful, but was still widely trusted as a chivalrous man who had tried his best against daunting odds. His wound had saved him from signing a capitulation, and so helped preserve his reputation. In 1878 he opened a new Paris Exhibition which symbolized French recovery from the war.

All the controversies over the Battle of Sedan itself had by then come to a head. In August 1874 Paul de Cassagnac, the fanatically Bonapartist editor of *Le Pays* who had fought as a Zouave at Sedan, published articles accusing Wimpffen of incompetence, of betraying of the Emperor, and of bearing the main responsibility for loss of the battle. Wimpffen brought a libel case, heard in Paris in February 1875, in which Ducrot, Lebrun, Douay and other generals who resented his accusations queued up to testify for Cassagnac, who was acquitted.[49]

Wimpffen's loss of the case only fuelled his rancour. During the political crisis of 1877 the Left feared that President MacMahon might follow his dismissal of the National Assembly with a military coup. Gambetta made plans for a rival republican government, with Wimpffen as War Minister. Wimpffen drew up a contingency plan which provided for MacMahon's arrest, indictment for treason and punishment 'according to the rigour of the law'.[50] But the crisis passed, disappointing Wimpffen's dreams of shooting his old rival. MacMahon resigned the presidency in 1879. Ducrot died in 1882, lamenting that he had failed to restore the monarchy. An apoplectic stroke killed Wimpffen in 1884.

Beyond the feuding of the generals, France struggled to come to terms with the memory of Sedan which, for contemporaries, remained 'after more than twenty years, still as poignant as on the day after the disaster'.[51] An initial public tendency to condemn as cowards those who had surrendered and to treat those who had fled the battlefield as heroes who had 'broken through' proved transient. That the army had been defeated only by superior numbers and the failures of Napoleon III, 'The Man of Sedan', became widely accepted as an article of faith. Popular literature and images emphasized feats of individual valour by French soldiers in the face of hopeless odds. Most popular of all was Alphonse de Neuville's *The Last Cartridges* (1873), which became the abiding French image of Sedan and the war. Although Bazeilles had been defended by blue-clad Marines, for artistic and symbolic effect the painter represented all French infantry by including men in varied uniforms. The image, widely distributed as a print, soothed and nurtured injured patriotism. There is no white flag, no scene of submission, no indiscipline or panic, only stoic resistance and courage which transfigure military defeat. Such was the picture's emotive power that stage representations of the scene remained popular into the early twentieth century. Bazeilles itself became a focus of patriotic commemoration, particularly for the Marines who had suffered nearly 2,700 casualties during the battle.

In contrast, the greatest literary evocation of Sedan was permeated by *fin de siècle* anxieties about the supposed degeneracy of the French in comparison with the Germans and the need for regeneration. Émile Zola's *La Débâcle* (1892) was based on extensive research, including interviews with veterans and inhabitants conducted during a visit to the locality in April 1891. Conservative critics took umbrage at Zola's portrayal of French mismanagement and indiscipline, accusing him of attacking the army. Nevertheless, the novel sold better than any of his others, and continues to be the best-known depiction of the battle.

Sedan became a battlefield again on 25–26 August 1914, when its surrounding villages were largely destroyed, then endured four years of harsh and ruinous German occupation. With victory in November 1918 the ghosts of 1870 seemed finally to have been laid, only to be violently resurrected in May 1940 when the invading Germans forced a passage of the Meuse at Sedan, breaking the French line. Once again heavy fighting there was the prelude to the fall of France. Defeat at Sedan presaged the death of the Third Republic, just as it had heralded its birth seventy years earlier. The town suffered great destruction during the 1940 battle, then underwent its fourth German occupation since 1815. The tide of war ebbed back in 1944. A German column retreating through Bazeilles was attacked by Allied aircraft on 29 August. After further fighting, American tanks liberated Sedan on 6 September. Thus the ill-fated town bears a tragic distinction in the history of the Franco-German conflict. On the hills above Floing the graves from 1940 greatly outnumber those of 1870, and the earlier conflict is submerged by the horrors of the world wars.

After 1945 Frenchmen and Germans sought to break the cycle of conflict, moving towards cooperation then, gradually, reconciliation. In this process the emotions once aroused by the memory of Sedan on both sides have no place. In Sedan today traces of the war of 1870 are unobtrusive. Yet visitors to the citadel may well pause to contemplate an inscription over an archway: 'Let us wipe away hatreds, but preserve the memory of events.'

Conclusion

By the victory of Sedan Germany eclipsed France as the foremost military power of Europe. At dinner at his headquarters on 3 September King Wilhelm raised a toast to his victorious army: 'You, General von Roon, have sharpened the sword; you, General von Moltke, have wielded it; you, Count Bismarck, have conducted my policy in such an able manner that, in thanking my army, I think of you three in particular.'[1]

While this trio were the architects of victory, Moltke had not directed the battle at tactical level, apparently confident that his generals knew their trade. If at Sedan the Germans closed the jaws of their trap around their enemy more completely than at Königgrätz, it was the achievement of the army commanders: of Crown Princes Friedrich of Prussia and Albert of Saxony, with their respective chiefs of staff, Blumenthal and Schlotheim, and particularly of their corps commanders, who had seized tactical opportunities on the day to seal the pocket.

High standards of professionalism among German officers, combined with good organization and an unfaltering common instinct to seek and destroy the enemy, had brought an historic reward. The Germans had made superior use of their cavalry during the campaign to observe and harass the enemy. Except at Bazeilles, they had learned from the Metz battles to spare their infantry, and the employment of open tactical formation served them well in a battle in which their artillery played the decisive role. The power of that artillery and the shock it inflicted had been the real surprise of 1870; yet the bold tactical use the Germans made of it was quite as important as the superior numbers and technical qualities of their breech-loaders. The credit for this was largely General von Hindersin's.

Yet when all is said of the marching abilities of their troops and the skill and intelligence with which they were led, the Germans were exceptionally favoured by the cumulative errors of their opponents. Disorganized and unready, the French lost the initiative in the crucial opening phase of the campaign. By poor deployment they exposed themselves to defeat in detail by an enemy superior in numbers and artillery, consistently making poor strategic decisions. In retrospect it is evident that MacMahon should have avoided fighting Third Army in Alsace until he had united his Corps with those of Failly and Douay. The defeat of Frœschwiller and the subsequent retreat led directly to the disaster of Sedan, draining the strength and confidence of the troops who would form the majority of the Army of Châlons.

Though numerically formidable, that unhappy army came to grief in just a fortnight. The blame was widely shared. Perhaps any French government would have felt political pressure to send a force to relieve Bazaine after his encirclement in Metz, just as after Sedan the new republican government would sacrifice strategic sense to the political priority of relieving Paris. But Palikao, and behind him the Empress, insisted on a plan that took little account of German strength and mobility. Their persistence in it when MacMahon faced encirclement by overwhelming numbers was insensate. Palikao's indiscretions to the press and his peremptory order to MacMahon on the evening of 27 August all but sealed the army's fate.

Bazaine too was culpable, allowing himself to be trapped in Metz, then failing either to give MacMahon clear instructions and information or to attempt a breakout in earnest while one remained feasible.

Napoleon III must bear ultimate responsibility for the ill-preparation of his army on entering a war which France declared. Contemporaries also blamed him for the military decisions which led to the trap of Sedan, but by that stage he had devolved command to MacMahon. His presence with the army was merely a nuisance. Yet Napoleon's lack of dynamic leadership had terrible consequences. A Napoleonic system without a Napoleon worthy of the name to exercise coherent political and military command invited the divided counsels that led to disaster. Admirable as was Napoleon's wish to spare his men's lives on the afternoon of the battle, he might have saved more, and possibly even his army and his Empire, by having the will to overrule the Empress and Palikao earlier. In recent years Napoleon has been viewed more sympathetically, though contemporaries would no doubt have objected that indulgent judgements are the prerogative of generations that have not known invasion.

The heaviest responsibility for the loss of the Army of Châlons rested with its commander. Marshal MacMahon's indecision, combined with supply failures and wretched weather, cost irreplaceable time. Having finally resolved on a junction with Bazaine, his procrastination and misuse of cavalry invited discovery. His resolve to cross the Meuse without fighting a battle seemed justifiable, but from 26 August onwards he sacrificed successive opportunities to fall on advance units of the German army and damage the claws that were seeking to close on him. A partial defeat might have made German commanders more cautious, while restoring the morale of his own men. Since he underestimated the numbers facing him, it is curious that he did not bring his superior numbers to bear while he had a fleeting chance.

His obedience to Palikao's order of 27 August, when his better judgement dictated withdrawal northwards, was much condemned, though even then the loss of his army was not inevitable. Failly could certainly have avoided the inexcusable surprise at Beaumont on 30 August. Had Douay marched swiftly to his aid, a more orderly withdrawal across the Meuse might have been possible. On 31 August the Germans could have been delayed by a more effective defence of the line of the Chiers and the destruction of key bridges over the Meuse, notably at Bazeilles and Donchery. MacMahon might then have got his troops to Mézières and thence by rail to Paris, where opportunities existed to damage and delay the enemy, with a safer line of retreat.

As it was, MacMahon lingered in Sedan, oblivious to his peril. His men, shaken by defeat and hungry and exhausted after a week of ill-managed and unnecessary night marches, were neither set in motion for Mézières nor placed in well-considered defensive positions. The performance of Lebrun's men at Bazeilles, and the value of even light earthworks on Douay's front, suggest that entrenchments and the fortification of all the villages along the Givonne to the east, and of Saint-Albert and Saint-Menges to the west, might have delayed the Germans, inhibiting their ability to bring a devastating cross-fire to bear. Doubtless the French would still have lost, but holding a wider perimeter until after dark might have enabled more men to escape into Belgium. In the event, the French army fought disjointedly and without cohesion in a fatally confined position. General Sheridan observed large masses of French infantry lying idle under fire.[2] Many who did fight did so with bravery and tactical skill at small unit level, but too many never got to fire a shot through faulty dispositions. Wimpffen's blinkered conduct of the battle merely pushed his army further into the wolf's mouth, though by that time victory was beyond his reach or anybody else's.

Thus Moltke won a battle that ranks as a modern Cannae – and, unlike Hannibal, he would not fail to march on the enemy's capital. Sedan made German might feared. From it, reflected a German officer, dated 'a new era in world history, in which my Fatherland will see itself raised far above other nations, and give the world a Germanic character'.[3] The victory exalted the status of the General Staff and of the military generally in German society higher than ever before.

Yet, though tactically as decisive as any general could wish, Sedan did not end the war. France had received a body blow, and could not replace the regular troops it had lost, but neither its resources nor its will to resist were yet exhausted. Even in the decade following final military victory in February 1871,

Germany's pride in her triumph was troubled by insecurity, even paranoia, at the spectre of a revived France. For if the war settled the immediate issue of power in Germany's favour, it only intensified the national fears and hatreds that had given rise to war in the first place, and made military and political tension between the two countries an ever-present poison in European politics. In the spring of 1870 Bismarck had prophesied, 'We could now fight France and beat her too, but that war would give rise to five or six others; and while we can gain our ends by peaceful means it would be foolish, if not criminal, to take such a course.'[4] His words came home to roost, and he spent the rest of his long career working to keep France isolated.

Germany's post-war military planners understood that the diplomatic and military circumstances that had favoured their victory at Sedan were unlikely to recur. Yet the very scale of that victory encouraged them to contemplate an exclusively military solution to the threats they perceived to German security: a super-Sedan that would achieve the rapid destruction of the enemy's entire army and spare Germany a protracted war. Some of them dreamed of a pre-emptive strike to win a new war that they considered inevitable. Such circular thinking among the elite of Europe's strongest power was manifested in the war scare of 1875. It would prove dangerous under the unstable and arrogant Kaiser Wilhelm II, who had neither his grandfather's sense of European realities nor his professional military understanding.

As for France, Sedan and its aftermath demoted her to the second rank among European powers more completely than Waterloo had done. This was illustrated within three weeks of Sedan when Italian troops marched into Rome. The French garrison had been withdrawn in August, and Napoleon III's pretensions as arbiter of the Italian peninsula disappeared with it. And, humiliatingly, the German army immediately displaced the French as the most admired and studied armed force in the world.

For the next generation, France had to adjust herself to a German neighbour whose population and industrial growth far outstripped hers. The financial and social costs of maintaining a larger army based on universal conscription that she had been so reluctant to accept after Sadowa had to be borne in the years following Sedan. Though a noisy minority called for a war of revenge, successive French governments were more concerned with protecting the country against future invasion, and with seeking diplomatic support against renewed German aggression. Thus while the German War Academy taught its officers how to win a new Sedan, French officers studied how to avoid one. Like Prussians after Jena, they studied in the shadow of defeat, with bitter knowledge of the price France had paid in 1870 for 'the culpable forgetfulness into which we had fallen of the true principles of warfare'.[5]

Those lessons were relearnt, sometimes imperfectly. Obsessed with avoiding the passive defensive tactics that had ruined them in 1870, the French would suffer staggering losses in frontal attacks in August 1914. Yet at least they went to war that month with unified command, a professional staff, an effective mobilization plan and a superb field gun – and this time the Germans did not break through. French determination to resist and commitment to victory owed much to the impact of 1870. That determination was personified by President Raymond Poincaré, who as a boy in August 1870 had fled from Lorraine with his family before the advancing Germans, and by General Joseph Gallieni, Military Governor of Paris. It was both symbolic and entirely fitting that the defence of Paris during the Battle of the Marne which saved the capital from the advancing Germans in September 1914 was inspired by the fighting spirit of that former Marine who had fought at Bazeilles.

Appendix

Order of Battle

(k = killed; mw = mortally wounded, w = wounded)

Part One: French

Note: strengths shown are those at Châlons Camp at the commencement of the Sedan campaign.

Army Of Châlons

Commander-in-Chief: Marshal de MacMahon
Chief of Staff: General Faure
Commanding Artillery: General Forgeot

1 Corps
General Ducrot

1st Division: General Wolff (w. 1.9.70)
1st Brigade: Colonel Bréger
18th & 96th Line Regiments, 13th Rifle Battalion
2nd Brigade: General Postis du Houlbec
45th Line Regiment, 1st Zouaves

2nd Division: General Pellé
1st Brigade: General Pelletier de Montmarie (w. 1.9.70)
50th & 74th Line Regiments, 16th Rifle Battalion
2nd Brigade: General Gandil (w. 1.9.70)
78th Line, 1st Algerian Sharpshooters

3rd Division: General L'Hériller (w. 1.9.70)
1st Brigade: General Carteret-Trécourt (w. 1.9.70)
36th Line Regiment, 2nd Zouaves, 8th Rifle Battalion
2nd Brigade: General Lefebvre
48th Line Regiment, 2nd Algerian Sharpshooters

4th Division: General de Lartigue (w. 1.9.70)
1st Brigade: General Fraboulet de Kerléadec (w. 1.9.70)
56th Line Regiment, 3rd Zouaves, 1st Rifle Battalion

2nd Brigade: General Carrey de Bellemare
3rd Algerian Sharpshooters

Cavalry Division: General Michel
1st Brigade: General de Septeuil
3rd Hussars, 11th Chasseurs
2nd Brigade: General de Nansouty
2nd & 6th Lancers
3rd Brigade: Colonel Perrot
10th Dragoons, 8th Cuirassiers

Effective strength of 1 Corps: 28,185 officers and men.
(48 infantry battalions, 26 cavalry squadrons, 19 artillery batteries,[1] 6½ engineer
   companies)

5 Corps
General de Failly
(de Wimpffen from 31.8.70)

1st Division: General Goze
1st Brigade: General Saurin
11th & 46th Line Regiments, 4th Rifle Battalion
2nd Brigade: General Nicolas
61st & 86th Line Regiments

2nd Division: General L'Abadie
2nd Brigade: General de Maussion
49th & 88th Line Regiments, 14th Rifle Battalion

3rd Division: General Guyot de Lespart (mw. 1.9.70)
1st Brigade: General Abbatucci
27th & 30th Line Regiments, 19th Rifle Battalion
2nd Brigade: General de Fontanges (w. 1.9.70)
17th & 68th Line Regiments

Cavalry Division: General Brahaut
1st Brigade: General de Bernis
5th Hussars, 12th Chasseurs
2nd Brigade: General Simon de la Mortière
5th Lancers

Effective strength of 5 Corps: 21,434 officers and men.
(31 infantry battalions, 12 cavalry squadrons, 14 artillery batteries, 5 engineer
   companies)

7 Corps
General F. Douay

1st Division: General Conseil-Dumesnil
1st Brigade: General Le Normand de Bretteville (w. 30.8.70)
3rd & 21st Line Regiments, 17th Rifle Battalion
2nd Brigade: General Chagrin de Saint-Hilaire (w. 1.9.70)
47th & 99th Line Regiments

2nd Division: General Liébert
1st Brigade: General Guiomar (w. 1.9.70)
5th & 37th Line Regiments, 6th Rifle Battalion
2nd Brigade: General de la Bastide
53rd & 89th Line Regiments

3rd Division: General Dumont (w. 1.9.70)
1st Brigade: General Bordas
52nd & 72nd Line Regiments
2nd Brigade: General Bittard des Portes (w. 1.9.70)
82nd & 83rd Line Regiments

Cavalry Division: General Ameil
1st Brigade: General Cambriel
4th Hussars, 4th & 8th Lancers

Effective strength of 7 Corps: 26,375 officers and men.
(38 infantry battalions, 13 cavalry squadrons, 15 artillery batteries, 5 engineer
  companies)

12 Corps
General Lebrun (w. 1.9.70)

1st Division: General Grandchamp (w. 30.8.70)
1st Brigade: General Cambriels (w. 1.9.70)
22nd & 34th Line Regiments, 2 companies from 1st & 2nd Rifle Battalions
2nd Brigade: General de Villeneuve
58th & 79th Line Regiments

2nd Division: General Lacretelle
1st Brigade: General Morand (mw. 30.8.70)
1st & 2nd Régiments de marche, 2 Rifle companies
2nd Brigade: General Marquisan
3rd & 4th Régiments de marche

3rd Brigade: General Louvent (w. 1.9.70)
14th, 20th & 31st Line Regiments

3rd Division: General de Vassoigne
1st Brigade: General Reboul
1st & 4th Marines
2nd Brigade: General Martin des Pallières (w. 31.8.70)
2nd & 3rd Marines

1st Cavalry Division: General de Salignac-Fénelon (w. 1.9.70)
1st Brigade: General Savaresse
1st & 7th Lancers
2nd Brigade: General de Béville
5th & 6th Cuirassiers

2nd Cavalry Division: General Lichtlin
Brigade: General Leforestier de Vendeuvre
7th & 8th Chasseurs

Effective strength of 12 Corps: 38,672 officers and men.
(45 infantry battalions, 26 cavalry squadrons, 26 artillery batteries, 6 engineer
   companies)

Cavalry Reserve
1st Division: General Margueritte (mw. 1.9.70)
1st Brigade: Colonel (General from 30.8.70) de Gallifet
1st, 3rd & 4th Chasseurs d'Afrique
2nd Brigade: General Tilliard (k. 1.9.70)
1st Hussars, 6th Chasseurs

2nd Division: General de Bonnemains
1st Brigade: General Girard (k. 1.9.70)
1st & 4th Cuirassiers
2nd Brigade: General de Brauer
2nd & 3rd Cuirassiers

Total effectives of Cavalry Reserve: 5,211.
(31 squadrons, 1 battery)

Total effectives of the Army of Châlons: 119,877 officers and men.
(162 infantry battalions, 108 cavalry squadrons, 75 artillery batteries, 22½
   engineer companies)
Ration strength 21 August 1870 (including non-combatant personnel): 130,566.

Part Two: German
Note: strengths shown are for 22.8.70.

Third Army
Commander-in-Chief: Crown Prince Friedrich Wilhelm of Prussia
Chief of Staff: General von Blumenthal
Commanding Artillery: General Herkt

V Corps
General von Kirchbach

9th Division: General von Sandrart
17th Brigade: Colonel Flöckher
58th & 59th (Posen) Regiments
18th Brigade: General von Voigts-Rhetz
7th King's Grenadiers, 47th (Lower Silesian) Regiment
4th (Silesian) Dragoons, 5th Rifle Battalion
10th Division: General von Schmidt
19th Brigade: Colonel Henning auf Schönhoff
6th (West Prussian) Grenadiers, 46th (Lower Silesian) Regiment
20th Brigade: General Walther von Montbary
37th (Westphalian) Fusiliers, 50th (Lower Silesian) Regiment
14th Dragoons

Effective strength of V Corps: 18,574 infantry (25 battalions), 2,110 cavalry
(8 squadrons), 84 guns (14 batteries), 3 pioneer companies.

VI Corps
(Operating to west of main army on 1.9.70)
General von Tümpling

11th Division: General von Gordon
21st brigade: General von Malachowski
10th (Silesian) Grenadiers, 18th (Posen) Regiment
22nd Brigade: General von Eckartsberg
38th (Silesian) Fusiliers, 51st (Lower Silesian) Regiment
8th (Silesian) Dragoons, 6th (Silesian) Rifle Battalion

12th Division: General von Hoffmann
23rd Brigade: General Gündell
22nd & 62nd (Lower Silesian) Regiments
24th Brigade: General von Fabeck

23rd & 63rd (Lower Silesian) Regiments
15th (Silesian) Dragoons

Effective strength of VI Corps: 23,953 infantry (25 battalions), 1,278 cavalry
(8 squadrons), 84 guns (14 batteries), 3 pioneer companies.

XI Corps
General von Gersdorff (k. 1.9.70)

21st Division: General von Schachtmeyer
41st Brigade: Colonel Grolmann (w. 1.9.70)
80th (Hessian) Fusiliers, 87th (Nassau) Regiment
42nd Brigade: General von Thile
82nd (Hessian) Regiment, 88th (Nassau) Regiment
11th (Hessian) Rifle Battalion, 14th (Hessian) Hussars

22nd Division: General von Schkopp
43rd Brigade: Colonel von Kontzki
32nd & 95th (Thuringian) Regiments
44th Brigade: Colonel von Bieberstein
83rd (Hessian) Regiment, 94th (Thuringian) Regiment
13th (Hessian) Hussars

Effective strength of XI Corps: 20,638 infantry (25 battalions), 1,239 cavalry
(8 squadrons), 83 guns (14 batteries), 3 pioneer companies.

I Bavarian Corps
General von der Tann

1st Division: General von Stephan
1st Brigade: General Dietl
Lifeguard Regiment, 1st King's Own Regiment, 2nd Rifle Battalion
2nd Brigade: General von Orff
2nd (Crown Prince's) Regiment, 11th Regiment, 4th Rifle Battalion
9th Rifle Battalion, 3rd Light Horse

2nd Division: General Schumacher
3rd Brigade: Colonel Heyl
3rd (Prince Karl) Regiment, 12th Regiment, 1st Rifle Battalion
4th Brigade: General von der Tann
10th (Prince Ludwig) Regiment, 13th Regiment, 7th Rifle Battalion
4th Light Horse

Cuirassier Brigade: General von Tausch
1st (Prince Karl) Cuirassiers, 2nd (Prince Adalbert) Cuirassiers, 6th Light Horse

Effective strength of I Bavarian Corps: 20,817 infantry (25 battalions), 2,369 cavalry (20 squadrons), 96 guns (16 batteries), 3 pioneer companies.

II Bavarian Corps
General von Hartmann

3rd Division: General von Walther
5th Brigade: General von Schleich
6th & 7th Regiments, 8th Rifle Battalion
6th Brigade: Colonel von Wissell
14th & 15th Regiments, 3rd Rifle Battalion
1st Light Horse

4th Division: General von Bothmer
7th Brigade:[2] General von Thiereck
5th & 9th Regiments, 6th Rifle Battalion
8th Brigade: General Maillinger
3rd Battalions of 1st, 5th, 11th, & 14th Regiments, 1st Battalion of 7th Regiment, 5th Rifle Battalion
10th Rifle Battalion, 2nd Light Horse[3]

Lancer Brigade: General von Mulzer
1st & 2nd Lancers, 5th Light Horse

Effective strength of II Bavarian Corps: 20,783 infantry (25 battalions), 3,985 cavalry (20 squadrons), 96 guns (16 batteries), 3 pioneer companies.

Württemberg Division
General von Obernitz

1st Brigade: General von Reitzenstein
1st (Queen Olga) Regiment, 7th Regiment, 2nd Rifle Battalion
2nd Brigade: General von Starkloff
2nd Regiment, 5th (King Karl) Regiment, 3rd Rifle Battalion
3rd Brigade: General von Hügel
3rd & 8th Regiments, 1st Rifle Battalion
Cavalry Brigade: General von Scheler
1st, 3rd & 4th Cavalry Regiments

Effective strength of Württemberg Division: 13,322 infantry (15 battalions), 1,527 cavalry (10 squadrons), 58 guns (9 batteries), 2 pioneer companies.

Baden Division
(Besieging Strasbourg on 1.9.70)
General von Beyer

2nd Cavalry Division
General Stolberg-Wernigerode
3rd Brigade: General von Colomb
1st (Silesian) Cuirassiers, 2nd (Silesian) Lancers
4th Brigade: General von Barnekow
1st & 5th Hussars
5th Brigade: General von Baumbach
4th & 6th Hussars

Effective strength of 2nd Cavalry Division: 3,624 cavalry (24 squadrons),
  8 infantry, 12 guns (2 batteries).

4th Cavalry Division
Prince Albrecht of Prussia
8th Brigade: General von Hontheim
5th (West Prussian) Lancers, 10th (Posen) Lancers
9th Brigade: General von Bernhardi
1st (West Prussian) Lancers, 6th (Thuringian) Lancers
10th Brigade: General von Krosigk
2nd Hussars, 5th (Rhenish) Dragoons

Effective strength of 4th Cavalry Division: 3,435 cavalry (24 squadrons),
  12 guns (2 batteries).

Totals for Third Army: 118,095 infantry (140 battalions), 19,567 cavalry
  (122 squadrons), 525 guns (87 batteries).

Fourth Army (Army of the Meuse)
Commander-in-Chief: Crown Prince Albert of Saxony
Chief of Staff: General von Schlotheim

Guard Corps
Prince August of Württemberg

1st Division: General von Pape
1st Brigade: General von Kessel

1st & 3rd Foot Guards
2nd Brigade: General von Medem
2nd & 4th Foot Guards, Fusilier Guards
Guard Rifle Battalion, Guard Hussars

2nd Division: General von Budritzki
3rd Brigade: Colonel von Linsingen
1st & 3rd Grenadier Guards
4th Brigade: General von Berger
2nd & 4th Grenadier Guards
Guard Sharpshooters Battalion, 2nd Guard Lancers

Cavalry Division: General von der Goltz
1st Brigade: General von Brandenburg
Life Guard Regiment, Guard Cuirassiers Regiment
2nd Brigade: Prince Albert of Prussia
1st & 3rd Guard Lancers
3rd Brigade: General von Brandenburg
1st & 2nd Guard Dragoons

Effective strength of Guard Corps: 20,027 infantry (29 battalions), 4,215
   cavalry (32 squadrons), 90 guns (15 batteries), 3 pioneer companies.

IV Corps
General Gustav von Alvensleben

7th Division: General von Schwarzhoff
13th Brigade: General von Borries (w. 30.8.70)
26th & 66th (Magdeburg) Regiments
14th Brigade: General von Zychlinski
27th (Magdeburg) Regiment, 93rd (Anhalt) Regiment
4th (Magdeburg) Rifle Battalion, 7th (Westphalian) Dragoons

8th Division: General von Schöler
15th Brigade: General von Kessler
31st & 71st (Thuringian) Regiments
16th Brigade: Colonel von Scheffler
86th (Schleswig-Holstein) Fusiliers, 96th (Thuringian) Regiment
12th (Thuringian) Hussars

Effective total of IV Corps: 24,916 infantry (25 battalions), 2,157 cavalry
   (8 squadrons), 84 guns (14 batteries).

XII (Saxon) Corps
Prince George of Saxony

23rd Division: General von Montbé
45th Brigade: Colonel Garten
100th & 101st Grenadiers, 108th Fusiliers
46th Brigade: Colonel von Seydlitz
102nd & 103rd Regiments
1st Cavalry Regiment

24th Division: General von Holderberg
47th Brigade: Colonel von Elterlein
104th & 105th Regiments, 12th Rifle Battalion
48th Brigade: General von Schulz (w. 1.9.70)
106th & 107th Regiments, 13th Rifle Battalion
2nd Cavalry Regiment

12th Cavalry Division: General zur Lippe
23rd Brigade: General Krug von Nidda
Guard Cavalry Regiment, 17th Lancers
24th Brigade: General Senfft von Pilsach
3rd Cavalry Regiment, 18th Lancers

Effective total of XII Corps: 25,085 infantry (29 battalions), 3,570 cavalry
(24 squadrons), 96 guns (16 batteries), 3 pioneer companies.

5th Cavalry Division
General von Rheinbaben

11th Brigade: General von Barby
4th (Westphalian) Cuirassiers, 13th (Hanoverian) Lancers
19th (Oldenburg) Dragoons
12th Brigade: General von Bredow
7th (Magdeburg) Cuirassiers, 16th (Altmark) Lancers
13th (Schleswig-Holstein) Dragoons
13th Brigade: General von Redern
10th (Magdeburg) Hussars, 11th (Westphalian) Hussars
17th (Brunswick) Hussars

Effective total of 5th Cavalry Division: 4,147 cavalry (36 squadrons), 12 guns
(2 batteries).

6th Cavalry Division
Duke Wilhelm of Mecklenburg-Schwerin

14th Brigade: Colonel von Schmidt
6th (Brandenburg) Cuirassiers, 3rd (Brandenburg) Lancers
15th Brigade: Colonel von Alvensleben
15th (Schleswig-Holstein) Lancers, 16th (Schleswig-Holstein) Hussars

Effective total of 6th Cavalry Division: 2,158 cavalry (16 squadrons), 6 guns (1 battery).

Totals for Fourth Army: 70,028 infantry (83 battalions), 16,247 cavalry (116 squadrons), 288 guns (48 batteries).

Grand Total for Third and Fourth Armies: 188,123 infantry (223 battalions), 35,814 cavalry (238 squadrons), 813 guns (135 batteries).

Detached besieging Toul: 4,200 infantry, 450 cavalry, 12 guns.

German troops engaged at Sedan: 128,246 infantry (186 battalions), 20,110 cavalry (177 squadrons).

Notes

Preface

1. Emperor to Empress, 3 September 1870, 'Lettres à l'Impératrice Eugénie (1870–1871)', *Revue des Deux Mondes*, 1 September 1930, p. 7.

Chapter 1

1. Chenu, *De la mortalité*, p. 325.
2. Emperor to Marshal Randon, 26 May 1859, Randon, vol. 2, p. 11.

Chapter 2

1. Bismarck, *Die Gesammelten Werke* (hereafter *GW*), vol. 10, no. 94, p. 140.
2. Pflanze, p. 237 and fn.
3. Bismarck to Manteuffel, 26 April 1856, *GW*, vol. 2, no. 152, p. 142.
4. Bismarck to Gustav von Alvensleben, 5 May 1859, *GW*, vol. 14 (1), no. 724, p. 517.
5. Quoted in La Gorce, vol. 4, p. 630.
6. Ibid., pp. 601–2.
7. Du Barail, vol. 3, p. 64.
8. La Gorce, vol. 5, p. 12.

Chapter 3

1. Randon, vol. 2, p. 145.
2. Quoted in Case, p. 216.
3. Pierre Magne to Napoleon, 20 July 1866, [France] Ministère des Affaires Étrangères, *Les Origines diplomatiques de la Guerre de 1870–1871* (hereafter *OD*), vol. XI, no. 3064, pp. 123–5.
4. Cowley to Clarendon, 3 July 1866, quoted in Pottinger, p. 155.
5. La Valette Circular, *OD*, vol. XII, no. 3598, pp. 301–6.
6. Franz von Roggenbach, quoted by Lerman, p. 129.
7. Goncourt, vol. 2, p. 26, entry for 2 July 1866.
8. Benedetti to Drouyn de Lhuys, 8 August 1866, *OD*, vol. XII, no. 3377, p. 24.
9. Meding, pp. 44–5.
10. La Gorce, vol. 5, p. 206.
11. Du Barail, vol. 3, p. 108.
12. La Gorce, vol. 5, p. 331.
13. Véron, vol. 1, pp. 72–3.
14. Chuquet, p. 2.

15. *Moltke's Military Correspondence*, p. 34, no. 20.
16. Stoffel, *Rapports*, pp. 302, 338.
17. Caro, p. 95.
18. Gordon, p. 20.
19. Du Camp, *La Croix Rouge de France*, pp. 103–5.
20. La Gorce, vol. 6, p. 130.
21. Napoleon to Niel, 19 February 1869, *OD*, vol. XXIII, no. 7249, pp. 280–1.
22. Lerman, p. 138.
23. Carr, *Origins*, p. 171.
24. Bismarck to Werthern, 26 February 1869, *GW*, vol. 6B, no. 1327, p. 2.

Chapter 4

1. Antonmattei, p. 69.
2. Williams, *Henri Rochefort*, p. 52.
3. La Gorce, vol. 6, p. 118; Antonmattei, p. 73.
4. La Gorce, vol. 5, p. 516; vol. 6, p. 177.
5. Vitzhum to Beust, 7 October 1869, Oncken, pp. 203–4.
6. Lebrun, *Souvenirs*, p. 141.
7. *Moniteur Universel*, 2 July 1870, p. 962.
8. Benedetti, p. 307.
9. Benedetti to La Valette, 31 March 1869, *OD*, vol. XXIV, no. 7363, pp. 118–20; Benedetti to Rouher, 11 May 1869, ibid., no. 7466, pp. 285–9.
10. Karl Anton to Bismarck, 25 February 1870, Bonnin, doc. 5, p. 63.
11. Bismarck to Rudolph Delbrück, 13 May 1870, *GW*, vol. 14 (2), no. 1299, p. 776.
12. King Wilhelm to Leopold, 21 June 1870, Bonnin, doc. 203, p. 198.
13. Mercier to Gramont, 3 July 1870, *OD*, vol. XXVIII, no. 8243, pp. 23–7.
14. Karl Anton to Bismarck, 25 February 1870, Bonnin, doc. 5, p. 64.
15. Bismarck, *Reflections and Reminiscences*, vol. 2, pp. 86–7.
16. Bismarck to Foreign Office, 3 October 1868, *GW*, vol. 6A, no. 1186, p. 412.
17. Versen's diary entry for 19 June 1870, Bonnin, p. 278.
18. Bismarck to Reuss, 22 March 1868, *GW*, vol. 6A, no. 1108, p. 321.
19. Oubril to Gorchakov, February 12/24 1869, in Chester W. Clark, pp. 197–9.
20. Bismarck to Reuss, 9 March 1869, *GW*, vol. 6B, no. 1334, p. 11.
21. Busch, *Bismarck: Some Secret Pages from His History*, vol. 1, p. 8.
22. *Le Pays*, 21 July 1870, quoted in Dupuy, p. 43.
23. *The Times*, 8 July 1870.
24. Gladstone to Granville, 8 July 1870, quoted in Millman, p. 183.
25. Lyons to Granville, 5 July 1870, quoted in Steefel, p. 121.
26. Baron Werther, quoted in Lord, p. 40.
27. Gramont to Benedetti, 10 July 1870, *OD*, vol. XXVIII, no. 8378, p. 190.
28. Lyons to Clarendon, 30 January 1870, quoted in Steefel, p. 227.
29. *Moniteur Universel*, 8 July 1870, p. 998.
30. Quoted in Lehautcourt, *La Candidature Hohenzollern*, p. 250.

31. Metternich to Beust, 8 July 1870, quoted in Salomon, p. 241.
32. Gramont to Benedetti, 7 July 1870, *OD*, vol. XXVIII, no. 8298, pp. 90–1.
33. Quoted in Steefel, p. 120.
34. Lehautcourt, *La Candidature Hohenzollern*, pp. 375–6.
35. Text in Steefel, p. 187; on Bismarck's stoking of the press, Busch, *Bismarck: Some Secret Pages from His History*, vol. 1, pp. 35–48.
36. Bismarck, *Reflections and Reminiscences*, vol. 2, p. 100.
37. Garets, p. 187; Metternich to Beust, 8 July 1870, quoted in Salomon, p. 215.
38. At this time 15 August (Napoleon I's birthday) rather than 14 July was the national holiday.
39. Ollivier, *Histoire et philosophie d'une guerre*, pp. 170–1.
40. *Moniteur Universel*, 17 July 1870, pp. 1067–71.
41. M. Dréolle in [France] Assemblée Nationale, *Enquête parlementaire: Dépositions*, vol. 1, p. 230.
42. Allinson, p. 6.
43. Quoted in Rousset, vol. 1, p. 31.
44. Oubril to Westmann, July 17/29 1870, in Chester W. Clark, p. 208.
45. Rousset, vol. 1, p. 419.
46. Cobban, vol. 3, p. 234.
47. Ollivier, *Histoire et philosophie d'une guerre*, p. 166.
48. Beust to Metternich, 11 July 1870, *OD*, vol. XXVIII, pp. 229–30.
49. *The Times*, 16 and 18 July 1870.

Chapter 5

1. Allinson, pp. 8, 10.
2. Ibid., p. 9.
3. Moltke, *The Franco-German War*, p. 8.
4. Darimon, *Notes*, p. 73.
5. Reuss, *Siège de Strasbourg*, p. 32.
6. Piton, p. 10.
7. Lehautcourt, *Histoire de la Guerre de 1870–1871* (hereafter *HG*), vol. 2, p. 135.
8. Reproduced in Fay, pp. 325–7.
9. [France], Commission chargée de réunir, classer et publier les papiers saisis aux Tuileries, *Papiers et Correspondance de la famille impériale*, pp. 437–51.
10. Text in Rousset, vol. 1, pp. 137–8.
11. Yves-Charles Quentel and François Aubriot, quoted in Lecaillon, pp. 38–40.
12. Filon, p. 99.

Chapter 6

1. Beaunis, pp. 10–11.
2. Sarazin, p. 11.
3. MacMahon, *Souvenirs inédits*, quoted in Picard, *1870: La Perte de l'Alsace*, pp. 125–7.

4. Ducrot, *Vie militaire*, vol. 2, p. 321.

5. Ibid., pp. 333–6; Du Barail, vol. 3, p. 135.

6. Ducrot, *Vie militaire*, vol. 2, p. 330.

7. Revue d'Histoire, *La Guerre de 1870–71* (hereafter *Guerre*), vol. 2: *Les Opérations en Alsace et sur la Sarre: Journées des 3, 4, et 5 août*, p. 10, n. 1.

8. Ibid., p. 44, n. 1.

9. Picard, *1870: La Perte de l'Alsace*, p. 193.

10. Allinson, p. 28; Lonlay, *Français et Allemands: Niederbronn-Sedan*, p. 34.

11. Narcy, p. 54.

12. Lehautcourt, *HG*, vol. 3, p. 85.

13. Klein, p. 111.

14. Ducrot, *Vie militaire*, vol. 2, pp. 374–5.

15. Lehautcourt, *HG*, vol. 3, p. 329.

16. Allinson, p. 31.

17. German General Staff (hereafter GGS), vol. 1, p. 159.

18. Saint-Genest, p. 44.

19. Lieutenant Colonel Lardeur, 8th Cuirassiers, quoted in Massa, p. 299.

20. Lehautcourt, *HG*, vol. 3, Annexe 7.

21. GGS, vol. 1, Appendix XII.

22. Saint-Genest, p. 46.

23. Quoted in Lecaillon, pp. 60–3.

24. Narcy, pp. 81–4.

25. Sarazin, pp. 13–14.

26. Ibid., p. 36.

27. Ibid., pp. 42–3.

28. *Guerre*, vol. 7: *Bataille de Frœschwiller: documents annexés*, p. 13.

29. Klein, pp. 174–8; Sabatier and Stroh, pp. 140–8.

30. Delmas, pp. 57, 95.

31. Klein, p. 314.

32. Delmas, p. 97.

33. Sarazin, pp. 54–5.

34. Beaunis, p. 290.

35. Delmas, p. 62.

36. [Officier du 1er Corps], *De Freschwiller* [sic] *à Sedan*, p. 26.

37. Journal of Commandant Jean Alfred David, 45th Line Regiment, in Fay, p. 367.

38. Lehautcourt, *HG*, vol. 6, p. 10.

39. Narcy, pp. 104–5.

40. [Officier du 1er Corps], *De Freschwiller à Sedan*, p. 37.

41. David, in Fay, p. 370.

42. Narcy, p. 106.

43. Allinson, p. 43.

44. David, in Fay, p. 369.

45. [Officier du 1er Corps], *De Freschwiller à Sedan*, pp. 42–3.

46. Jacqmin, p. 137.
47. [Officier du 1er Corps], *De Freschwiller à Sedan*, p. 30.
48. Bibesco, p. 29.
49. Ibid., p. 34.

Chapter 7

1. Goncourt, vol. 2, pp. 265–6.
2. Quoted in La Gorce, vol. 7, p. 5.
3. Goncourt, vol. 2, p. 266.
4. Darimon, *Notes*, p. 171.
5. La Gorce, vol. 7, pp. 23, 24.
6. Richard Metternich to Mensdorff, 26 July 1866, quoted in Barker, p. 153.
7. Lebrun, *Souvenirs*, pp. 280–1.
8. Quoted in Girard, *Napoléon III*, p. 479.
9. Bazaine, p. 71; Baumont, *Bazaine*, p. 113.
10. Andlau, p. 66.
11. Trochu, vol. 1, pp. 110–11.
12. General Schmitz in [France] Assemblée Nationale, *Enquête parlementaire: Dépositions*, vol. 2, p. 278.
13. Trochu, vol. 1, p. 122.
14. Ibid., pp. 143–5.
15. War Minister to Emperor, 10.27 p.m., 17 August, [France], Commission . . ., *Papiers et Correspondance*, vol. 1, p. 426.
16. Emperor to War Minister, 7.55 a.m., 18 August, *Guerre: Armée de Châlons* (hereafter *AdC*): *documents annexés*, I, p. 38.
17. Bazaine to MacMahon, 12 noon, 18 August, ibid., p. 39.
18. MacMahon to War Minister, 19 August, [France], Commission . . ., *Papiers et Correspondance*, vol. 1, p. 427; MacMahon in [France] Assemblée Nationale, *Enquête parlementaire: Dépositions*, vol. 1, p. 30.
19. Bazaine to Emperor, 8.20 p.m., 18 August, *Guerre: Metz*, III: *documents annexés*, pp. 85–6; Lehautcourt, *HG*, vol. 6, p. 122.
20. Lehautcourt, *HG*, vol. 2, p. 162.
21. GGS, vol. 1, Appendices XV and XXI; vol. 2, Appendix XXIV.
22. Lehautcourt, *HG*, vol. 4, Annexe 9; vol. 5, Annexes 1 and 4.
23. Hoenig, pp. 63, 168.
24. Sarcey, p. 16.
25. Bitteau, pp. 47–50.
26. Claretie, *Histoire de la Révolution*, p. 154.

Chapter 8

1. Bonnal, p. 462.
2. Narcy, p. 161.
3. Lebrun, *Bazeilles-Sedan*, p. 11.

4. *Guerre: AdC*, I, pp. 4–10: *documents annexés*, I, pp. 118–19; Bastard, *Sanglants Combats*, p. 8.
5. Narcy, pp. 157–8.
6. David, in Fay, p. 373; Narcy, p. 158.
7. Stoffel, *Dépêche*, pp. 19–20.
8. Colonel de Ponchalon, quoted in Lehautcourt, *HG*, vol. 6, p. 172.
9. MacMahon to Palikao, 4.45 p.m., 20 August, [France], Commission . . ., *Papiers et Correspondance*, vol. 1, p. 428.
10. Lehautcourt, *La Candidature Hohenzollern*, pp. 595–6.
11. Trochu, vol. 1, p. 125.
12. Rouher in [France] Assemblée Nationale, *Enquête parlementaire: Dépositions*, vol. 1, p. 239.
13. Bazaine to Emperor, 19 August, [France], Commission . . ., *Papiers et Correspondance*, vol. 1, pp. 46–7.
14. MacMahon to Bazaine, 10.45 a.m., 22 August, *Guerre: AdC: documents annexés*, I, p. 136.
15. War Minister to Emperor, 1.05 p.m., 22 August, [France], Commission . . ., *Papiers et Correspondance*, vol. 1, p. 47.
16. Stoffel, *Dépêche*, p. 67.
17. Caro, p. 99.
18. Sarazin, pp. 80–1.
19. Second Lieutenant Louis Lebeau, 68th Infantry, quoted in Lecaillon, p. 183.
20. Bibesco, p. 57.
21. Stoffel, *Dépêche*, pp. 83–4.
22. MacMahon to War Minister, 8.30 p.m., 27 August, *Guerre: AdC: documents annexés*, I, p. 278.
23. Thoumas, *Paris, Tours, Bordeaux*, pp. 29–31.
24. War Minister to Emperor, 11 p.m., 27 August, *Guerre: AdC: documents annexés*, I, pp. 278–9.
25. MacMahon, *Souvenirs inédits*, ibid., p. 279.
26. General Broye, 28 February 1904, quoted in Picard, *Sedan*, vol. 1, p. 161; Massa, p. 308.
27. MacMahon in [France] Assemblée Nationale, *Enquête parlementaire: Dépositions*, vol. 1, p. 33.
28. Palikao to MacMahon, 1.30 p.m., 28 August, *Guerre: AdC*, II, p. 199.
29. *Moniteur Universel*, 25 August 1870, p. 1241.
30. Bibesco, p. 80.

Chapter 9

1. Bismarck to Bernstorff, 21 August, *GW*, vol. 6B, no. 1755, p. 455; Busch, *Bismarck in the Franco-German War*, vol. 1, pp. 40–2, 69–72.
2. Text in Rousset, vol. 1, p. 423.
3. Sorel, vol. 1, pp. 206–10.

4. Reuss, *Histoire de Strasbourg*, pp. 413–14.
5. Quoted in Pflanze, vol. 1, p. 478.
6. GGS, vol. 2, Appendix XXXI.
7. Lonlay, *Français et Allemands: Niederbronn-Sedan*, pp. 294–5.
8. Allinson, p. 75: entry for 28 August.
9. Busch, *Bismarck in the Franco-German War*, vol. 1, p. 59; GGS, vol. 2, pp. 200–01; Lehautcourt, *HG*, vol. 6, pp. 228–30.
10. Busch, *Bismarck in the Franco-German War*, vol. 1, p. 61.
11. Sorel, vol. 1, p. 261n.
12. Busch, *Bismarck in the Franco-German War*, vol. 1, p. 59.
13. Text in Rousset, vol. 2, p. 54.
14. Roon, vol. 3, p. 196.
15. Bronsart, p. 49: entry for 24 August.
16. Moltke, *The Franco-German War*, pp. 70–1.
17. Verdy, p. 113.
18. Ibid., p. 111.
19. Allinson, p. 73: entry for 26 August.
20. Hohenlohe, *Letters on Strategy*, vol. 2, p. 208.
21. Russell, pp. 143–44.

Chapter 10

1. Bibesco, pp. 82–3.
2. Caro, p. 114; Sarazin, p. 93; Narcy, pp. 187–9; GGS, vol. 2, p. 222; 'Mémoire sur l'incendie de Vonq (Ardennes)', in Ducrot, *Vie militaire*, vol. 2, pp. 391–9.
3. Caro, pp. 117–18.
4. MacMahon to Failly, 28 August, Failly, p. 39.
5. Sarazin, p. 95.
6. Narcy, pp. 193–5.
7. Journal Clémeur, *Guerre: AdC: documents annexés*, II, p. 100.
8. Defourny, pp. 91–7; Canonge, p. 96.
9. Moynac, *Souvenirs d'un chirurgien d'ambulance 1870*, Bayonne, 1911, quoted in Lecaillon, pp. 190–91.
10. Bibesco, pp. 96–7, 104–5.
11. GGS, vol. 2, Appendix XL.
12. Bronsart, p. 54.
13. Defourny, p. 134.
14. Bibesco, p. 115.
15. [France], Commission . . ., *Papiers et Correspondance*, vol. 1, p. 436.
16. Ducrot, *Journée*, p. 10; Pajol; Castelnau, pp. 518–19; Massa, pp. 311–12; Ryan, pp. 33–4.
17. MacMahon, *Souvenirs inédits, Guerre: AdC: documents annexés*, I, p. 115; Darimon, *Notes*, p. 259.
18. Unsent letter from Eugénie to Captain Charles Duperré, Filon, p. 134.

19. Empress to Emperor, 7.05 a.m., 31 August, *Guerre: AdC: documents annexés*, II, p. 280.
20. Yriarte, pp. 19–20, 28–9.
21. [Officier du 1er Corps], *De Freschwiller à Sedan*, p. 59, entry for 23 August.
22. Massa, pp. 275–9, 304.
23. Monod, p. 22n.
24. Castelnau, p. 520; Rousset, vol. 2, pp. 296–7.
25. Wimpffen (1871), pp. 3, 10; Broglie, pp. 127, 153–4.
26. Wimpffen (1871), p. 124.
27. MacMahon to War Minister, 1.15 a.m., 31 August, [France], Commission . . ., *Papiers et Correspondance*, vol. 1, p. 431.
28. Ducrot, *Journée*, p. 14.
29. Douay's statement to the Court of Enquiry quoted in *Guerre: AdC*, II, p. 236; Bibesco, p. 124.
30. Lebrun, *Bazeilles-Sedan*, p. 74; Yriarte, p. 28.
31. Vinoy, p. 36.
32. MacMahon in [France] Assemblée Nationale, *Enquête parlementaire: Dépositions*, vol. 1, p. 37; Army Order, 31 August, *Guerre: AdC: documents annexés*, II, p. 279.
33. Bibesco, p. 127.
34. Douay's statement to the Court of Enquiry quoted in *Guerre: AdC*, II, p. 236. Bibesco, p. 124, gives 'vous' (you) rather than 'nous' (us).
35. Bibesco, p. 132n.
36. Ducrot, *Vie militaire*, vol. 2, p. 406.
37. Sarazin, p. 115.
38. Army Order, 11 p.m., 30 August, GGS, vol. 2, Appendix XLII.
39. Bismarck to Balan, 30 August, *GW*, vol. 6B, no. 1771, p. 465.
40. Army Order, 11 p.m., 30 August, GGS, vol. 2, Appendix XLII.
41. Banning, p. 250; Order for the Army of the Meuse, 6 a.m., 31 August, GGS, vol. 2, Appendix XLII.
42. Monod, pp. 27–31, 35–6.
43. Russell, pp. 174–5.
44. Ibid., pp. 175–9.
45. Blumenthal, p. 110.
46. Moltke to Blumenthal, 7.45 p.m., 31 August, *Moltke's Military Correspondence*, no. 243, p. 125.
47. Allinson, p. 82.

Chapter 11

1. Lieutenant E. S. Buisson d'Armandy, 4th Marine Regiment, *Guerre: AdC*, III, p. 30.
2. Louis Rocheron, 1st Marine Regiment, quoted in Lecaillon, p. 220.
3. Tanera, p. 65.
4. Ibid., p. 66.

5. MacMahon in [France] Assemblée Nationale, *Enquête parlementaire: Dépositions*, vol. 1, p. 38.
6. Sarazin, p. 120.
7. Ibid., p. 121; Aragonnès d'Orcet, p. 165; Ducrot, *Journée*, p. 22.
8. Lebrun's report in *Guerre: AdC: documents annexés*, III, pp. 305–6; Ducrot, *Journée*, pp. 23–4 and Colonel Robert's account, ibid., pp. 123–4; *Guerre: AdC*, III, pp. 56–9.
9. Ducrot, *Journée*, pp. 28–9.
10. Sarazin, p. 123; Ducrot, *Journée*, p. 31.
11. Wimpffen (1871), pp. 165, 212; Lebrun's report loc. cit., and his *Bazeilles-Sedan*, pp. 111–13.
12. Sarazin, p. 119 (2nd edn).
13. Colonel Robert, quoted in *Guerre: AdC*, III, p. 55; Aragonnès d'Orcet, p. 165.
14. General Castelnau, quoted in Pajol.
15. Déroulède, pp. 189–91.
16. Reports of Generals de Vassoigne and Reboul, *Guerre: AdC: documents annexés*, III, pp. 336–9.
17. Cogniet, pp. 74–5.
18. Report of Captain Bourgey, 2 September, *Guerre: AdC: documents annexés*, III, pp. 339–41.
19. Letter of Chaplain Emmanuel Domenech, 21 July 1871, in Claretie, *Histoire de la Révolution*, pp. 223–4; Lavenue and Sériot, quoted in Lecaillon, pp. 219–21.
20. *The Times*, 15 September, p. 10; Busch, *Bismarck: Some Secret Pages from His History*, vol. 1, pp. 198–200.
21. Letter of 20 June 1871 to the Augsburg *Allgemeine Zeitung*, Helvig, p. 95; Claretie, *Histoire de la Révolution*, p. 223.
22. GGS, vol. 2, p. 316.
23. Domenech, p. 221.
24. Ryan, pp. 55–6.
25. Mayor Bellomet, *Liste des habitants de Bazeilles tués, blessés ou disparus lors des combats des 31 août et 1 septembre 1870*, 23 April 1871, in Gollnisch, pp. 19–20. Further (though occasionally inconsistent) details of victims in Fouquet, *Bazeilles*, pp. 50–5, and Bastard, *Défense de Bazeilles*, pp. 93–149, which includes survivor testimony.
26. Mayor of Bazeilles to General Lebrun in Lebrun, *Bazeilles-Sedan*, pp. 325–6; Letter of Dr Frank, *Pall Mall Gazette*, 30 September, p. 11; François-Franquet, pp. 132–3.
27. Kühnhauser, *Kriegserinnerungen*, quoted by Stoneman, p. 282.
28. Proclamation of Richard Gœlch in François-Franquet, p. 143.
29. Tanera, p. 71.
30. Narcy, p. 220.
31. Ibid., pp. 220–32.
32. Wimpffen (1887), p. 148.

33. Allinson, p. 85; Blumenthal, p. 111.
34. Wimpffen (1871), pp. 165–6; Bibesco, p. 146, and Douay's report ibid., pp. 196–7.
35. Narcy, p. 148.
36. Sarazin, p. 126.
37. Vinoy, pp. 54–6.
38. Sarazin, pp. 126–8.
39. Ducrot, *Journée*, p. 33.
40. Russell, p. 187.
41. Bronsart, p. 57; Busch, *Bismarck: Some Secret Pages from His History*, vol. 1, p. 144.
42. Busch, *Bismarck: Some Secret Pages from His History*, vol. 1, p. 171.
43. Russell, p. 191.
44. Faverot, p. 71.
45. Russell, p. 203.
46. GGS, vol. 2, p. 375.
47. Liébert's report, *Guerre: AdC: documents annexés*, III, p. 241; Douay's report, Bibesco, p. 198.
48. Bismarck quoted by Castelnau, p. 861.
49. Rozat de Mandres, p. 236.
50. Ducrot, *Journée*, p. 37.
51. Ducrot to Prince de Bauffremont, 3 April 1880, in Lebrun, *Bazeilles-Sedan*, pp. 318–20; Faverot, p. 79. Compare Ducrot, *Journée*, pp. 35, 141.
52. Schneider, p. 99; Gallifet, p. 104.
53. Ducrot, *Journée*, pp. 35–6; Allinson, p. 104.
54. Russell, p. 203.
55. Ducrot, *Journée*, p. 37.
56. Hohenlohe, *Letters on Artillery*, p. 41.
57. Ibid.
58. Narcy, p. 240.
59. Van Creveld, *Supplying War*, p. 102.
60. GGS, vol. 2, p. 370.
61. Sarazin, p. 124.
62. Lebrun, *Bazeilles-Sedan*, pp. 122–3.
63. Ducrot, *Journée*, p. 46.
64. Hindenburg, p. 41.
65. Allinson, p. 91.
66. Sheridan, vol. 2, pp. 402–3; *Pall Mall Gazette*, 5 September, p. 4.
67. Moskowa, pp. 969–70; Pajol.
68. Wimpffen (1871), p. 170.
69. Statement of Captain de Lanouvelle, *Revue historique*, 26 (1884), p. 316; Castelnau, p. 853.
70. Massa, p. 324.
71. Ducrot, *Journée*, pp. 47–50, 130.

72. Wimpffen (1871), p. 168.
73. Statement of Marquis de Laizer, *Revue historique*, 26 (1884), p. 309.
74. Fouquet, *Balan*, pp. 40, 48–54.
75. Lieutenant M. Grand-Didier, 34th Line Regiment, quoted in Lecaillon, p. 232.
76. Historique du 27 de Ligne, *Guerre: AdC: documents annexés*, III, p. 187.
77. Lebrun, *Bazeilles-Sedan*, pp. 135–6.
78. Statement of Count d'Ollone, *Revue historique*, 26 (1884), p. 311.
79. Russell, p. 205.
80. GGS, vol. 2, p. 387.
81. Vogüé, pp. 255–6.
82. Narcy, pp. 241–2.
83. Tanera, pp. 69–70.
84. Verdy, p. 133.
85. Hindenburg, p. 41.
86. Lebrun, *Bazeilles-Sedan*, p. 139.
87. Ibid., p. 140.
88. Lieutenant Grand-Didier, quoted in Lecaillon, p. 236.
89. Allinson, p. 91; Russell, p. 210.
90. GGS, vol. 2, Appendix XLVIII; Bronsart, pp. 58–60; Busch, *Bismarck: Some Secret Pages from His History*, vol. 1, p. 147.
91. *Pall Mall Gazette*, 5 September, p. 4.
92. *Guerre: AdC*, III, p. 361.
93. GGS, vol. 2, Appendix L.
94. GGS, vol. 2, p. 408; Lehautcourt, *HG*, vol. 6, p. 702 and Annexe 9; Martinien, p. 137; *Guerre: AdC*, III, p. 352; Banning, p. 251; François-Franquet, p. 137n.; Ryan, p. 93.
95. Fouquet, *Balan*, pp. 18–20; *Pall Mall Gazette*, 30 September, p. 11.
96. Geyer, p. 71.
97. Bazaine, pp. 167–8.

Chapter 12
1. Wimpffen (1871), p. 229; Ducrot, *Journée*, pp. 52–3.
2. Verdy, p. 136.
3. Aragonnès d'Orcet, pp. 120–54, is the fullest eyewitness account of the negotiation, and is consistent with Wimpffen (1871), pp. 239–45; Verdy, pp. 136–7, and Busch, *Bismarck in the Franco-German War*, vol. 1, pp. 105–7.
4. Bismarck's communiqué, *The Times*, 15 September 1870, p. 10; Busch, *Bismarck in the Franco-German War*, vol. 1, pp. 104–5, 107–10; Russell, pp. 260–1; Forbes, vol. 1, pp. 243–9.
5. Text of protocol in GGS, vol. 2, Appendix XLIX; officer figures in Borbstaedt, p. 651 and n.
6. Schneider, pp. 107–8.
7. Moskowa, p. 968.

8. Verdy, p. 31.
9. Allinson, pp. 98–9.
10. MacCormac, p. 67.
11. Proclamation by Mayor Philippoteaux, 5 September, in Gollnisch, pp. 19–20.
12. Ryan, p. 62.
13. Russell, pp. 219, 222, 236.
14. Ryan, pp. 48, 63.
15. *Le champ de bataille de Sedan: rapport du docteur Guillery, 21 mars 1871*, in Gollnisch, pp. 38–43.
16. Banning, pp. 251–3; GGS, vol. 6, p. 224n.
17. Lucas-Championnière, pp. 105–6; Chenu, *Service des Ambulances et des Hôpitaux*, vol. 1, pp. 127–31.
18. MacCormac, p. viii; Lucas-Championnière, pp. 157–9.
19. GGS, vol. 6, p. 22.
20. Ryan, pp. 80, 90–8.
21. MacCormac, p. 45.
22. Ryan, p. 58.
23. Lebrun, *Bazeilles-Sedan*, pp. 153–4; 170–1.
24. Sarazin, p. 136.
25. Lebrun, *Bazeilles-Sedan*, pp. 175–93; Vidal, pp. 191–250; Achard, pp. 42–76.
26. GGS, vol. 6, pp. 245–6.
27. Chenu, *Service des Ambulances et des Hôpitaux*, vol. 1, p. xxvi.
28. Bronsart, p. 65; Massa, pp. 337–40; Russell, pp. 225–7.
29. Dr Anger, *Notes de guerre*, quoted in Guériot, p. 58n.
30. Aragonnès d'Orcet, p. 156.
31. Emperor to Empress, 2 September. Text in Guériot, p. 55.
32. Filon, pp. 139–40; Paléologue, p. 213.
33. Monod, p. 33.
34. Girard, *Napoléon III*, p. 501.
35. Wimpffen (1871), pp. 252–3.
36. Lebrun, *Bazeilles-Sedan*, pp. 176, 191.
37. Faverot, p. 100.
38. Sheridan, vol. 2, pp. 408–9, 414–17.
39. Verdy, p. 143.
40. Wimpffen (1871), pp. 174–5.
41. Rouquette, p. 8; Ducrot to Lebrun, 24 June 1872, Lebrun, p. 291.
42. Ducrot, *Journée*, pp. 24–6.
43. Duquet, *Frœschwiller, Châlons, Sedan*, p. 395.
44. Lehautcourt, *HG*, vol. 6, pp. 536–7; Robert, pp. 114–15; Le Guillou, p. 384.
45. Ducrot, *Journée*, p. 73.
46. Chalvet-Nastrac, pp. 186–8, 196, 336–7, 369–71.
47. [France], *Rapport officiel du conseil d'enquête sur la capitulation de Sedan*, pp. 6–10.
48. Notes of Duc d'Aumale, cited in Baumont, *Bazaine*, p. 170.

49. Cassagnac; Offen, pp. 61–2.
50. Wimpffen (1871), pp. xlii–xlvii.
51. Rousset, vol. 2, p. 357.

Conclusion

1. Verdy, p. 147.
2. Sheridan, vol. 2, p. 402.
3. Frankenberg, p. 161.
4. Busch, *Bismarck: Some Secret Pages from His History*, vol. 1, p. 8.
5. Rousset, vol. 1, p. 243.

Appendix

1. In both armies artillery batteries normally consisted of 6 guns.
2. Detached to Toul.
3. Detached to Toul.

Bibliography

Square brackets around the author's name indicate that the work was published anonymously.

Achard, Amédée, *Récits d'un soldat*, Paris, 1947.

Adriance, Thomas J., *The Last Gaiter Button: A Study of the Mobilisation and Concentration of the French Army in the War of 1870*, Westport, Conn., 1987.

Allinson, A. R. (trans. and ed.), *The War Diary of the Emperor Frederick III*, London, 1927.

Ambert, Joachim, Baron, *Gaulois et Germains: récits militaires*, 4 vols, Paris, 1883–5.

[Andlau, Comte Joseph d'], *Metz: Campagne et Négociations*, Paris, 1872.

[Anonymous], *La Bataille de Sedan: Napoléon III, De Wimpffen, Ducrot*, Paris, 1872.

Antonmattei, Pierre, *Gambetta, héraut de la République*, Paris, 1999.

Armengaud, André, *L'Opinion publique en France et la crise nationale allemande en 1866*, Paris, 1962.

Aronson, Theo, *The Fall of the Third Napoleon*, New York, 1970.

Arragonès D'Orcet, Stanislas, *Frœschwiller, Sedan et la Commune racontés par un témoin*, Paris, 1910.

Ascoli, *A Day of Battle: Mars-la-Tour 16 August 1870*, London, 1987.

Audoin-Rouzeau, Stéphane, *1870: La France dans la Guerre*, Paris, 1989.

Autin, Jean, *L'Impératrice Eugénie: ou l'empire d'une femme*, Paris, 1990.

Badsey, Stephen, *The Franco-Prussian War* (Osprey Essential Histories), Oxford, 2003.

Banning, Émile, *Les Origines et les phases de la neutralité belge*, Brussels, 1927.

Baratier, Anatole, *L'Intendance militaire pendant La Guerre de 1870–1871*, Paris, 1871.

Barjaud, Yves, *La Garde nationale mobile (1868–1872)*, Aire-sur-l'Adour, 1970.

Barker, Nancy Nichols, *Distaff Diplomacy: The Empress Eugénie and the Foreign Policy of the Second Empire*, Austin, Tex., 1967.

Barry, Quintin, *The Franco-Prussian War*, 2 vols, Solihull, 2007.

Bartmann, Dominik (ed.), *Anton von Werner: Geschichte in Bildern*, Munich, 1993.

Bastard, Georges, *Bazeilles – Dix ans après*, Paris, 1880.

Bastard, Georges, *Armée de Châlons: Sanglants Combats*, Paris, 1892.

——, *Armée de Châlons: Un Jour de Bataille*, Paris, 1888.

——, *Armée de Châlons: Charges héroïques*, Paris, 1892.

——, *Armée de Châlons: La Défense de Bazeilles*, Paris, 1884.

Baumont, Maurice, *Bazaine: les secrets d'un maréchal (1811–1888)*, Paris, 1978.

——, *L'Échiquier de Metz: Empire ou République 1870*, Paris, 1971.

Bazaine, Achille, *Épisodes de la Guerre de 1870 et le blocus de Metz*, Madrid, 1883.

Beaunis, Henri, *Impressions de campagne (1870–1871)*, Paris, 1887.

Becker, Jean-Jacques and Audoin-Rouzeau, Stéphane, *La France, La Nation, La Guerre 1850–1920*, Paris, 1995.

Becker, Josef (ed.), *Bismarcks spanische 'Diversion' 1870 und der preußisch-deutsche Reichsgründungskrieg*, 3 vols, Munich, 2003.

Benedetti, Vincent, *Ma Mission en Prusse*, Paris, 1871.

Bibesco, Georges, *Belfort, Reims, Sedan. Le 7e corps de l'Armée du Rhin*, Paris, 1874.

Binoche, Jacques, *Histoire des relations franco-allemandes de 1789 à nos jours*, Paris, 1996.

Bismarck, Otto von, *Bismarck the Man and the Statesman: Being the Reflections and Reminiscences of Otto Prince von Bismarck* (trans. A. J. Butler), 2 vols, London, 1898.

——, *Die Gesammelten Werke*, 19 vols, Berlin, 1924–35.

Bitteau, J., *Strasbourg – L'Armée de la Loire – L'Armée de l'Est: souvenirs d'un télégraphiste*, Épinal, 1898.

Blackbourn, David, *History of Germany 1780–1918: The Long Nineteenth Century*, 2nd edition, Oxford, 2003.

Blumenthal, Albrecht von, *Journals of Field-Marshal Count von Blumenthal for 1866 and 1870–71*, London, 1903.

Boissier, Pierre, *Histoire du Comité International de la Croix-Rouge: du Solférino à Tsoushima*, Paris, 1963.

Bongrand, Raymond, *1870: Alsace-Metz-Sedan*, Strasbourg, 1970.

Bonnal, H., *Frœschwiller*, Paris, 1899.

Bonnin, Georges (ed.), *Bismarck and the Hohenzollern Candidature for the Spanish Throne: The Documents in the German Diplomatic Archives*, London, 1957.

Borbstaedt, Adolf, *The Franco-German War, to the Catastrophe of Sedan and the Fall of Strassburg*, (trans. F. Dyer), London, 1873.

Bourgerie, Raymond, *Magenta et Solferino (1859): Napoléon III et le rêve italien*, Paris, 1993.

Bourgin, Georges, *La Guerre de 1870–1871 et la Commune*, Paris, 1947.

Bressler, Fenton, *Napoleon III: A Life*, London, 1999.

Breuilly, John, *Austria, Prussia and Germany, 1806–1871*, Harlow, 2002.

——, *The Formation of the First German Nation-State, 1800–1871*, Basingstoke, 1996.

Brice, Léon Raoul Marie and Bottet, Maurice, *Le Corps de Santé Militaire en France, 1708–1882*, Paris, 1907.

Broglie, Gabriel de, *MacMahon*, Paris, 2000.

Bronsart von Schellendorf, Paul, *Geheimes Kriegstagebuch, 1870–1871*, Bonn, 1954.

Brunet-Moret, Jean, *Le Général Trochu 1815–1896*, Paris, 1955.

Bucholz, Arden, *Moltke and the German Wars, 1864–1871*, New York, 2001.

Bury, J. P. T., *Gambetta and the National Defence: A Republican Dictatorship in France*, London, 1936.

——, *Napoleon III and the Second Empire*, London, 1970.

Bury, J. P. T. and Tombs, R. P., *Thiers 1797–1877: A Political Life*, London, 1986.

Busch, Moritz, *Bismarck in the Franco-German War 1870–1871*, 2 vols, London, 1879.

——, *Bismarck: Some Secret Pages From His History*, 3 vols, London, 1898.

Canonge, Frédéric, *Trois héros: Bataille de Beaumont-en-Argonne*, Paris, 1908.

[Caro, Emmanuel], *Histoire de l'Armée de Châlons: Campagne de Sedan, par un volontaire de l'Armée du Rhin*, Brussels, 1871.

Carr, William, *A History of Germany 1815–1990* (4th edn), London, 1990.

——, *The Origins of the Wars of German Unification*, Harlow, 1991.

Cars, Jean des, *Eugénie, la dernière Impératrice*, Paris, 2000.

Case, Lynn M., *French Opinion on War and Diplomacy during the Second Empire* (reprint), New York, 1984.

Cassagnac, Paul Granier de, *La Journée de Sedan devant la Cour d'Assises de la Seine . . . publié par Le Gaulois*, Paris, 1875.

Castelnau, Henri Pierre, 'Sedan et Wilhelmshöhe', *La Revue de Paris* (1929) 1 October, pp. 499–521; 15 October, pp. 851–74; 1 November, pp. 167–203.

Castelot, André, *Napoléon III: l'aube des temps modernes*, Paris, 1999.

Challener, Richard D., *The French Theory of the Nation in Arms 1866–1939*, New York, 1965.

Chalmin, Pierre, *L'Officier français de 1815 à 1870*, Paris, 1957.

Chalus, Adhémar de, *Wissembourg – Fræschwiller – Retraite sur Châlons*, Besançon, 1882.

Chalvet-Nastrac, Vicomte de, *Les Projets de restauration monarchique et le Général Ducrot, député et commandant du 8 Corps d'armée, d'après ses mémoires et sa correspondance*, Paris, 1909.

Chanal, Michel, *La Guerre de 70*, Paris, 1972.

Chenu, Jean-Charles, *Aperçu historique, statistique et clinique sur le Service des Ambulances et des Hôpitaux de la Société Française de Secours aux Bléssés des Armées de Terre et de Mer pendant La Guerre de 1870–1871*, 2 vols, Paris, 1874.

——, *De la mortalité dans l'armée, et des moyens d'économiser la vie humaine; extraits des statistiques médico-chirurgicales des campagnes de Crimée en 1854–1856 et d'Italie en 1859*, Paris, 1870.

Chuquet, Arthur, *La Guerre 1870–71*, Paris, 1895.

Cilleuls, J. des, *Le Service de Santé Militaire de ses origines à nos jours*, Paris, 1961.

Claretie, Jules, *La France envahie (juillet à septembre 1870); Forbach et Sedan, impressions et souvenirs de guerre*, Paris, 1871.

——, *Histoire de la Révolution de 1870–71*, Paris, 1872.

Clark, Chester W., 'Bismarck, Russia, and the Origins of the War of 1870', *Journal of Modern History*, 14 (1942), pp. 195–208.

Clark, Christopher, *Iron Kingdom: The Rise and Downfall of Prussia, 1600–1947*, London, 2006.

Cobban, Alfred, *A History of Modern France*, 3 vols, Harmondsworth, 1965.

Cogniet, Jean, *Bazeilles, 31 août–1er septembre 1870*, Paris, 1993.

Comité d'Histoire du Service de Santé, *Histoire de la Médecine aux Armées*, 3 vols, Paris–Limoges, 1984.

Congar, Pierre, Lecaillon, Jean, and Rousseau, Jacques, *Sedan et le pays sedanais: vingt siècles d'histoire*, Paris, 1969.

Contamine, Henry, *La Revanche 1871–1914*, Paris, 1957.

Corbin, Alain, *The Village of Cannibals: Rage and Murder in France, 1870*, Cambridge, 1992.

Cox, Gary P., *The Halt in the Mud: French Strategic Planning from Waterloo to Sedan*, Boulder, 1994.

Craig, Gordon A., *The Battle of Königgrätz*, London, 1965.

——, *The Politics of the Prussian Army 1640–1945* (2nd edn), New York, 1964.

Crane, Edward A. (MD), *The Memoirs of Dr. Thomas W. Evans: Recollections of the Second French Empire*, 2 vols, London, 1905.

Creveld, Martin van, *Command in War*, Cambridge, Mass., 1985.

——, *Supplying War: Logistics from Wallenstein to Patton*, Cambridge, 1977.

Daily News, *The Daily News Correspondence of the War Between Germany and France 1870–1*, London, 1871.

Dansette, Adrien, *Du 2 décembre au 4 septembre*, Paris, 1972.

Darimon, Alfred, *Histoire d'un jour: la journée du 12 juillet 1870*, Paris, 1888.

——, *Notes pour servir à l'histoire de la Guerre de 1870*, Paris, 1888.

Defourny, Pierre Guillaume, *L'Armée de MacMahon et la bataille de Beaumont* (2nd edn), Brussels, 1872.

Defrasne, Col., 'L'Armée française au lendemain de Sadowa', *Revue Historique de l'Armée* (1968), no. 2, pp. 121–36.

Delmas, Émile, *De Frœschwiller à Paris: notes prises sur les champs de bataille*, Paris, 1871.

Delpérier, Louis, *La Garde Impériale de Napoléon III*, Nantes, 2000.

Déroulède, Paul, *1870: Feuilles de route*, Paris, 1907.

Digeon, Claude, *La Crise allemande de la pensée française*, Paris, 1959.

Domenech, Emmanuel, *Histoire de la campagne de 1870–1871 et de la deuxième ambulance dite de la Presse française*, Lyon, 1871.

Du Barail, François Charles, *Mes Souvenirs*, 3 vols, Paris, 1894–96.

Du Bois, Albert, 'La Belgique pendant la Guerre Franco-Allemande, 1870–1871', *Revue de Belgique* (1892), no. 12 (December), pp. 366–85.

Du Camp, Maxime, *La Croix Rouge de France: Société de Secours aux Blessés Militaires de Terre et de Mer*, Paris, 1889.

——, *Souvenirs d'un demi-siècle*, 2 vols, Paris, 1949.

[Du Casse, Albert], Un Officier supérieur, *Le Général de Wimpffen: réponse au Général Ducrot*, Paris, 1871.

[——], 'La Bataille de Sedan', *Revue historique*, 26 (1884), pp. 303–17.

Ducrot, A., *Guerre des frontières: Wissembourg – réponse du Général Ducrot à l'État-Major allemand* (2nd edn), Paris, 1873.

——, *La Journée de Sedan*, Paris, 1871.

——, *La Vie militaire du Général Ducrot d'après sa correspondance (1839–1871). Publiée par ses enfants*, 2 vols, Paris, 1895.

Ducrot, Joseph, *L'Évasion du Général Ducrot: 11 septembre 1870*, Fécamp, 1913.

Dunant, Henry, *Mémoires* (ed. Bernard Gagnebin), Lausanne, 1971.

Dunant, J. Henry, *A Memory of Solferino* (English edition), London, 1947.

Dupuy, Aimé, *1870–1871: La Guerre, La Commune et la Presse*, Paris, 1959.

Duquet, Alfred, *Frœschwiller, Châlons, Sedan*, Paris, 1895.

——, *La Victoire à Sedan*, Paris, 1904.

Echard, William E., *Historical Dictionary of the French Second Empire 1852–1870*, Westport, 1985.

Elliot-Wright, Philipp, *Gravelotte–St. Privat 1870: End of the Second Empire*, London, 1993.

Engels, Friedrich, *Notes on the War: Sixty Articles reprinted from the Pall Mall Gazette*, Vienna, 1923.

Failly, Pierre Louis de, *Opérations et marches du 5e corps jusqu'au 31 août*, Brussels, 1871.

Faverot de Kerbrech, General, *Mes Souvenirs: La Guerre contre l'Allemagne (1870–1871)*, Paris, 1905.

Fay, Charles, *Journal d'un Officier de l'Armée du Rhin* (5th edn), Paris, 1889.

Félix, Gabrielle, *Le Général Ducrot*, Tours, 1896.

Feuchtwanger, Edgar, *Bismarck*, London, 2002.

Filon, Augustin, *Souvenirs sur l'Impératrice Eugénie*, Paris, 1920.

Fischbach, Gustave, *Le Siège et le bombardement de Strasbourg*, Strasbourg, 1871.

Flamarion, Dr A., *Le Livret du docteur: souvenirs de la campagne contre l'Allemagne et contre la Commune de Paris, 1870–1871*, Paris, 1872.

Foot, Michael R. D., 'The Origins of the Franco-Prussian War and the Remaking of Germany', *New Cambridge Modern History*, 10: *The Zenith of European Power 1830–1870*, Cambridge, 1960, pp. 577–602.

Forbes, Archibald, *My Experiences in the War Between France and Germany*, 2 vols, London, 1871.

Förster, Stig and Nagler, Jörg, *On the Road to Total War: The American Civil War and the German Wars of Unification, 1861–1871*, Cambridge, 1997.

Fouquet, E., *Balan pendant la Guerre de 1870*, Charleville, 1891.

——, *Bazeilles pendant la Guerre de 1870*, Balan–Sedan, 1895.

[France], *Annuaire de la marine et des colonies*, Paris, 1870.

[France], *Annuaire militaire de L'Empire français pour l'année 1870*, Paris, January 1870.

[France], Assemblée Nationale, *Enquête parlementaire sur les actes du Gouvernement de la Défense Nationale: Dépositions des Témoins*, 5 vols, Versailles, 1872–75.

[France], Commission chargée de réunir, classer et publier les papiers saisis aux Tuileries, *Papiers et Correspondance de la famille impériale*, 2 vols, Paris, 1870.

[France], *Les Derniers Télégrammes de l'Empire: Campagne de 1870*, Paris, 1871.

[France], Ministère des Affaires Étrangères, *Les Origines diplomatiques de la Guerre de 1870–1871*, 29 vols, Paris, 1910–32.

[France], *Rapport officiel du conseil d'enquête sur la capitulation de Sedan* (2nd edn), Paris, 1872.

[François-Franquet, Pierre Gabriel], *Sedan en 1870: La bataille et la capitulation par un Sedanais*, Paris, 1872.

Frankenberg, F. von, *Kriegstagebücher von 1866 und 1870/71*, Stuttgart, 1896.

Furet, François, *La Révolution*, 2 vols, Paris, 1988.

Fustel de Coulanges, ND, *L'Alsace est-elle allemande ou française? Réponse à M. Mommsen, professeur à Berlin*, Paris, 27 October 1870.

Gabriel, Richard A. and Metz, Karen S., *A History of Military Medicine*, 2 vols, New York, 1992.

Gall, Lothar, *Bismarck: Le Révolutionnaire blanc*, Paris, 1984.

Gallifet, General, 'Le dernier mot sur la charge de Sedan: Rapport du Général Gallifet', *Revue historique*, 27 (1885), pp. 100–5.

Garets, Marie Comtesse des, *Souvenirs d'une demoiselle d'honneur auprès de l'Impératrice Eugénie*, Paris, 1928.

Gavoy, Émile Alexandre, *Étude de faits de guerre: Le Service de Santé Militaire en 1870*, Paris, 1894.

Georges-Roux, François, *La Guerre de 1870*, Paris, 1966.

German General Staff, *The Franco-German War, 1870–71* (authorized translation by F. C. H. Clarke), 5 vols, London, 1874–84; (reprint) Nashville, 1995.

Geyer, Karl, *Erlebnisse eines Württembergischen Feldsoldaten im Kriege gegen Frankreich*, Munich, 1890.

Giovanangeli, Bernard (ed.), *Pourquoi réhabiliter Le Second Empire?*, Paris, 1995.

Girard, Louis, *La Garde Nationale 1814–1871*, Paris, 1964.

——, *Napoléon III*, Paris, 1986.

——, *Nouvelle Histoire de Paris: La Deuxième République et Le Second Empire 1848–1870*, Paris, 1981.

Goldschmidt, Dr D., *Autour de Strasbourg assiégé*, Strasbourg, 1912.

Gollnisch, André, *Quelques documents sur Sedan pendant la guerre et l'occupation, 1870–1873*, Sedan, 1889.

Goncourt, Edmond and Jules de, *Journal: mémoires de la vie littéraire*, Vol. 2: *1866–86*, Paris, 1989.

Gordon, Charles Alexander, *Lessons on Hygiene and Surgery from the Franco-Prussian War*, London, 1873.

Görlitz, Walter, *The German General Staff: Its History and Structure 1647–1945*, London, 1953.

Goyau, Georges, *L'Idée de patrie et l'humanitarisme ... 1866–1901*, Paris, 1902.

Gramont, Antoine Alfred Agénor, Duc de, *La France et La Prusse avant la Guerre*, Paris, 1872.

Grenu, René, *La Question belge dans la politique européenne de 1866 à 1870*, Paris, 1931.

Grouard, A., *L'Armée de Châlons: son movement vers Metz (1870)*, Paris, 1885.

Grunwald, Constantin de, *Le Duc de Gramont, gentilhomme et diplomate*, Paris, 1950.

Guedalla, Philip, *The Two Marshals: Bazaine and Pétain*, London, 1943.

Guérin, André, *La Folle Guerre de 1870*, Paris, 1970.

Guériot, Paul, *La Capitivité de Napoléon III en Allemagne (septembre 1870–mars 1871)*, Paris, 1926.

Guillemin, Henri, *Cette curieuse guerre de 70: Thiers–Trochu–Bazaine*, Paris, 1956.

Haffner, Sebastian, *The Rise and Fall of Prussia*, London, 1980.

Hahnke, W. von, *Opérations de la III Armée*, Paris, 1874.

Halévy, Ludovic, *Récits de la Guerre: l'invasion 1870–1871*, Paris, 1892.

Halperin, S. William, 'The Origins of the Franco-Prussian War Revisited: Bismarck and the Hohenzollern Candidature for the Spanish Throne', *Journal of Modern History*, 45 (1973), pp. 83–91.

Hazareesingh, Sudhir, *The Legend of Napoleon*, London, 2004.

Helvig, Hugo, *Operations of the I Bavarian Army Corps*, 2 vols, London, 1874.

Hérisson, Maurice d'Irisson, Comte d', *Journal of a Staff Officer in Paris during the events of 1870 and 1871*, London, 1885.

Hindenburg, Paul von, *Out of My Life* (trans. F. A. Holt), London, 1920.

Hoenig, Fritz, *Twenty-Four Hours of Moltke's Strategy* (trans. N. L. Walford), Woolwich, 1895.

Hohenlohe-Ingelfingen, Karl, Prinz zu, *Letters on Artillery* (trans. N. L.Walford), Woolwich, 1889.

——, *Letters on Strategy*, 2 vols, London, 1898.

Holmes, Richard, *Fatal Avenue*, London, 1992.

——, *The Road to Sedan*, London, 1984.

Hooper, George, *The Campaign of Sedan: The Downfall of the Second Empire* (reprint), Worley Publications, 1998.

Horne, Alistair, *The Fall of Paris: The Siege and the Commune 1870–71*, London, 1965.

Howard, Michael, *The Franco-Prussian War: The German Invasion of France, 1870–1871*, London, 1961.

Hughes, Daniel J. (ed.), *Moltke on the Art of War: Selected Writings*, Novato, Calif., 1993.

Hutchinson, John F., *Champions of Charity: War and the Rise of the Red Cross*, Boulder, Col., 1996.

Jacqmin, F., *Les Chemins de Fer pendant La Guerre de 1870–1871*, Paris, 1872.

Joly, Bertrand, 'La France et la revanche (1870–1914)', *Revue d'histoire moderne et contempraine*, 46/2 (1999), pp. 325–47.

Joubert, Léo, *La Bataille de Sedan: histoire de la campagne de 1870*, Paris, 1873.

Klein, C., *La Chronique de Frœschwiller: scènes vécus* (translated from the German by Arthur Delachaux), Neuchâtel, 1911.

Knight, Ian, *With His Face to the Foe: The Life and Death of Louis Napoleon, The Prince Imperial, Zululand, 1879*, Staplehurst, 2001.

Koch, H. W., *A History of Prussia*, London, 1978.

Kurtz, Harold, *The Empress Eugénie*, London, 1964.

La Chapelle, Alfred de, *Oeuvres posthumes et autographes inédits de Napoléon III*, Paris, 1873.

Lachnitt, Jean-Claude, *Le Prince impérial 'Napoléon IV'*, Paris, 1999.

La Gorce, Pierre de, *Histoire du Second Empire*, 7 vols, Paris, 1912–14.

Lannoy, Fleury de, *La Neutralité belge et la Guerre de 1870*, Brussels, 1925.

Lebrun, Barthelémy Louis Joseph, *Bazeilles– Sedan*, Paris, 1884.

——, *Souvenirs Militaires 1866–1870: Préliminaires de la Guerre – Missions en Belgique et à Vienne*, Paris, 1895.

Lecaillon, Jean-François, *Été 1870: La guerre racontée par les soldats*, Paris, 2002. (See also Narcy.)

Le Guillou, Louis, *La Campagne d'été de 1870*, Paris, 1938.

Lehautcourt, Pierre (B. Palat), *Bibliothèque de bibliographies critiques: La Guerre de 1870–1871*, Paris, 1906.

——, *Guerre de 1870–1871: Aperçu et Commentaires*, 2 vols, Paris, 1910.

——, *Histoire de la Guerre de 1870–1871*, 7 vols, Paris, 1900–8.

——, *Les Origines de la Guerre de 1870: la candidature Hohenzollern, 1868–1870*, Paris, 1912.

Lerman, Katherine Anne, *Bismarck*, London, 2004.

Levillain, Philippe and Riemenschneider, Rainer, *La Guerre de 1870/71 et ses conséquences*, Bonn, 1990.

L'Hospice, Michel, *La Guerre de 70 et la Commune en 1000 Images*, Paris, 1965.

Lonlay, Dick de, *Français et Allemands: histoire anecdotique de la guerre de 1870–71*, 6 vols, Paris, 1888–9.

Lord, Robert H., *The Origins of the War of 1870: New Documents from the German Archives*, Cambridge, Mass., 1924.

Lucas-Championnière, Just, 'Souvenirs de campagne, et notes médicales prises à la cinquième ambulance internationale pendant la guerre de 1870–1871', *Journal de Médecine et de Chirurgie Pratiques*, 42, 3rd Series (1871), pp. 102–10, 152–61, 199–203, 247–52.

McAllister, William B., 'Fighting Reformers: The Debate over the Reorganization of the French Military Medical Service, 1870–1889', *Essays in History* (University of Virginia), 35 (1993), pp. 93–109.

MacCormac, William, *Notes and Recollections of an Ambulance Surgeon: Being an account of work done under the Red Cross during the Campaign of 1870*, London, 1871.

McMillan, James F., *Napoleon III*, Harlow, 1991.

Malleson, G. B., *The Refounding of the German Empire 1848–1871* (2nd edn), London, 1904 (reprinted 1992).

Martinien, A., *Guerre de 1870–1871: État nominatif par affaires et par corps des officiers tués ou blessés dans la première parte de la campagne (Du 25 Juillet au 29 Octobre)*, Paris, 1902.

Massa, Philippe, Marquis de, *Souvenirs et impressions 1840–1871*, Paris, 1897.

Maurice, J. F. (ed.), *The Franco-German War 1870–71 by Generals and Other Officers who took part in the Campaign*, London, 1900 (translated from Julius von Pflugk-Harttung (ed.), *Krieg und Sieg 1870–71*, Berlin, 1895).

Maynard, Marie-Noëlle, *Panorama de Sedan 1880–1885*, Sedan, 1988.

Meding, Oskar, *De Sadowa à Sedan: Mémoires d'un ambassadeur secret aux Tuileries*, Paris, 1885.

Medlicott, W. N., *Bismarck and Modern Germany*, London, 1965.

Merchie, Z. Z., *Les Secours aux blessés après la bataille de Sedan*, Brussels, 1876.

Michel, Marc, *Gallieni*, Paris, 1989.

Millman, Richard, *British Foreign Policy and the Coming of the Franco-Prussian War*, Oxford, 1965.

Milner, John, *Art, War and Revolution in France 1870–1871*, Yale, 2000.

Mitchell, Allan, *Bismarck and the French Nation 1848–1890*, New York, 1971.

——, *The Great Train Race: Railways and the Franco-German Rivalry, 1815–1914*, Oxford, 2000.

Mohrt, Michel, *Les Intellectuels devant la défaite, 1870*, Paris, 1943.

Moltke, Helmuth von, *The Franco-German War of 1870–71* (introduction by Michael Howard), London, 1992.

——, *Moltke's Military Correspondence 1870–1871* (ed. Spenser Wilkinson), Aldershot, 1991.

Monod, Gabriel, *Allemands et Français. Souvenirs de Campagne: Metz – Sedan – La Loire*, Paris, 1872.

Montesquiou, Léon de, *1870: Les causes politiques du désastre*, Paris, 1915; (reprint) 1979.

Moorehead, Caroline, *Dunant's Dream: War, Switzerland, and the History of the Red Cross*, London, 1998.

Moritz, Victor, *Frœschwiller, 6 août 1870*, Strasbourg, 1970.

Moskowa, Prince de la [N. H. E. Ney], 'Quelques notes intimes sur la Guerre de 1870', *Le Correspondant*, Paris, December 1898, pp. 957–71.

Mosse, W. E., *The European Powers and the German Question 1848–1871*, Cambridge, 1958.

Napoleon III, 'Lettres à l'Impératrice Eugénie (1870–1871)', *Revue des Deux Mondes*, Paris, 1 September 1930, pp. 5–30.

[Napoleon III (attributed to)], *Des Causes qui ont amené les désastres de l'Armée française dans la Campagne de 1870*, Brussels, 1870.

Narcy, Louis de, *Journal d'un officier de Turcos*, Paris, 1902; (reprint with a foreword by J.-F. Lecaillon) Paris, 2004.

Oberhauser, Louis, *Sedan 1870: L'Émouvant récit du Caporal Louis Oberhauser*, Paris, 2006.

Offen, Karen, *Paul de Cassagnac and the Authoritarian Tradition in Nineteenth Century France*, New York, 1991.

[Officier]. *See* Du Casse, A. *and* Robert, F.

[Officier attaché à l'État-Major Général], *Des Causes qui ont amené la Capitulation de Sedan* (6th edn), Brussels, 1871.

[Officier du 1er Corps], *De Freschwiller à Sedan: Journal d'un officier du 1er corps*, Tours, 1870.

[Ollier, Edmund], *Cassell's History of the War between France and Germany, 1870–1871*, 2 vols, London, 1899.

Ollivier, Émile, *Histoire et Philosophie d'une Guerre, 1870*, Paris, 1910; reprinted Paris, 1970, with a preface by Pierre Guiral; translation by George Burnham Ives, *The Franco-Prussian War and its Hidden Causes*, New York, 1912, reprinted 1970.

Oncken, Hermann, *Napoleon III and the Rhine: The Origin of the War of 1870–1871*, New York, 1928.

Pajol, Victor, 'Lettre sur la Capitulation de Sedan', *Le Moniteur universel*, 22 July 1871, p. 678.

Palat, B., *Bibliographie générale de la Guerre de 1870–1871*, Paris, 1896.

Palat, Colonel B., *La Stratégie de Moltke en 1870*, Paris, 1907.

Paléologue, Maurice, *Les Entretiens de l'Impératrice Eugénie*, Paris, 1928.

Palikao, Général Cousin de Montauban, Comte de, *Un Ministère de la Guerre de vingt-quatre jours du 10 août au 4 septembre 1870* (2nd edn), Paris, 1871.

Pastre, J. L. Gaston, *La Tragédie de Sedan*, Paris, 1931.

Patry, Léonce, 'Le Général Ducrot d'après sa correspondence', *Revue Bleue: revue politique et littéraire*, 20 July 1895, pp. 79–84.

——, 'Sedan: une campagne de dix jours', *Revue Bleue: revue politique et littéraire*, 7 September 1895, pp. 290–6.

——, *La guerre telle qu'elle est*, Paris, 1897 (English translation: *The Reality of War*, London, 2001).

Pflanze, Otto, *Bismarck and the Development of Germany*, 3 vols, Princeton, 1990.

Picard, Ernest, *1870: La Perte de l'Alsace* (4th edn), 1907.

——, *1870: Sedan*, 2 vols, Paris, 1912.

Piton, Frédéric, *Siège de Strasbourg: journal d'un assiégé*, Paris, 1900.

Plessis, Alain, *The Rise and Fall of the Second Empire 1852–1871*, Cambridge, 1987.

Poidevin, Raymond and Bariety, Jacques, *Les Relations franco-allemandes, 1815–1975*, Paris, 1977.

Pottinger, E. Ann, *Napoleon III and the German Crisis, 1865–1866*, Cambridge, Mass., 1966.

Price, Roger, *The French Second Empire: An Anatomy of Political Power*, Cambridge, 2001.

——, *Napoleon III and the Second Empire*, London, 1997.

Randon, J. L. C. A., *Mémoires du Maréchal Randon*, 2 vols, Paris, 1875–7.

Raymond, Dora Neill, *British Policy and Opinion during the Franco-Prussian War*, New York, 1921.

Rémond, René, *La Droite en France de la première restauration à la Ve République*, 2 vols (3rd edn), Paris, 1968.

Renouvin, Pierre, *Histoire des relations internationales*, Vol. 5: *Le XIX Siècle: 1. De 1815 à 1871*, Paris, 1954.

Reshef, Ouriel, *Guerre, mythes et caricature: au berceau d'une mentalité française*, Paris, 1984.

Reuss, Rodolphe, *A. Schillinger: souvenirs pour ses amis … avec des extraits du journal de Schillinger pendant le siège de Strasbourg*, Strasbourg, 1883.

——, *Histoire de Strasbourg depuis ses origines jusqu'à nos jours*, Paris, 1922.

——, *Le Siège de Strasbourg en 1870: conférence …et chronique strasbourgeoise juillet-août 1870* (textes inédits publiés par Jean Rott etc.), Strasbourg, 1971.

Revue d'Histoire, *La Guerre de 1870–71, rédigé à la Section historique de l'État-major de l'Armée*, Paris, 1901–13.

Revue Historique Ardennaise, no. 3, Jan.–June 1970, *La Guerre de 1870 dans les Ardennes*.

Richard, Jules, *L'Armée et la guerre*, Paris, 1896.

[Robert, Frédéric], *La Campagne de 1870 jusqu'au 1er septembre; par un officier de l'Armée du Rhin*, Brussels, 1871.

Robichon, François, 'Les Dernières Cartouches par Alphonse de Neuville', *Tradition*, 109 (April 1996), pp. 11–15.

Rolland, Jules, *Portraits militaires: Le Général Ducrot*, Paris, 1871.

Roon, Albrecht, *Denkwürdigkeiten aus dem Leben des General-feldmarschalls Kriegministers Grafen von Roon*, 3 vols, Breslau, 1897.

Roth, François, *L'Allemagne de 1815 à 1918*, Paris, 2000.

——, *La Guerre de 70*, Paris, 1990.

——, *La Lorraine dans la Guerre de 1870*, Nancy, 1984.

Rothan, Gustave, *L'Affaire du Luxembourg; le prélude de la guerre de 1870*, Paris, 1882.

——, *La Politique française en 1866*, Paris, 1879.

Rouquette, Jules, *Célébrités contemporaines: Ducrot*, Paris, 1872.

Rousset, Léonce, *La seconde campagne de France: Histoire Générale de la Guerre Franco-Allemande (1870–71)*, 6 vols, Paris, 1896.

Rozat de Mandres, A. J. O., *Les Régiments de la Division Margueritte et les Charges à Sedan*, Paris, 1908.

Rundle, Henry, *With the Red Cross in the Franco-German War, A.D. 1870–1*, London, 1911.

Russell, William Howard, *My Diary during the Last Great War*, London, 1874.

Ryan, Charles E., *With an Ambulance during the Franco-German War, 1870–1871*, London, 1896.

Sabatier, Robert and Stroh, Paul, *Wissembourg, Frœschwiller 1870*, Wissembourg, 1970.

Saint-Genest [A. M. Durand de Bucheron], *La Politique d'un soldat*, Paris, 1872.

Salomon, Henry, *L'Incident Hohenzollern: l'événement, les hommes, les responsabilités*, Paris, 1932.

Sarazin, Charles, *Récits sur la dernière guerre franco-allemande*, Paris, 1887.

Sarcey, Francisque, *Le Siège de Paris: Impressions et Souvenirs*, Paris, 1871.

Schneider, Louis, *Kaiser Wilhelm: Militärische Lebensbeschreibung 1867–71*, Berlin, 1875.

Seignobos, Charles, *Le Déclin de L'Empire et l'établissement de la 3e République (1859–1875)*, Paris, 1921 (Vol. 7 of E. Lavisse, *Histoire de France Contemporaine*).

Serman, William and Bertaud, J.-P., *Nouvelle histoire militaire de la France 1789–1919*, Paris, 1998.

Service Historique de l'Armée, *Revue Historique de l'Armée*, 1 (1971) (Spécial): *Guerre de 1870–1871*, Paris, 1971. See also Revue d'Histoire.

Shann, Stephen and Delperier, Louis, *French Army 1870–71: Franco-Prussian War 1: Imperial Troops*, London, 1991.

Sheehan, James, *German History 1770–1866*, Oxford, 1989.

Sheridan, P. H., *Personal Memoirs of P. H. Sheridan*, 2 vols, New York, 1888.

Showalter, Dennis, *Railroads and Rifles, Technology and the Unification of Germany*, Hamden, Conn., 1975.

——, *The Wars of German Unification*, London, 2004.

Signouret, P. Raymond, *Souvenirs du bombardement et de la capitulation de Strasbourg 1870*, Bayonne, 1872.

Sinsoilliez, Robert, *Commandant Aubert: Les dernières cartouches, Bazeilles (1870)*, Paris, 1999.

Sirinelli, Jean-François (ed.), *Histoire des droites en France*, 3 vols, Paris, 1992.

Smith, William H. C., *Napoleon III: The Pursuit of Prestige*, London 1991.

Sorel, Albert, *Histoire diplomatique de la Guerre Franco-Allemande*, 2 vols, Paris, 1875.

Steefel, Lawrence D., *Bismarck, the Hohenzollern Candidacy, and the Origins of the Franco-German War of 1870*, Cambridge, Mass., 1962.

Stern, Fritz, *Gold and Iron: Bismarck, Bleichröder and the Building of the German Empire*, Harmondsworth, 1987.

Stoffel, Baron, *La Dépêche du 20 août 1870*, Paris, 1874.

——, *Rapports militaires écrits de Berlin 1866–1870* (4th edn), Paris, 1872.

Stone, David, *'First Reich': Inside the German Army during the War with France, 1870–71*, London, 2002.

Stoneman, Mark R., 'The Bavarian Army and French Civilians in the War of 1870–1871: A Cultural Interpretation', *War in History*, 8/3 (2001), pp. 271–93.

Swain, Valentine, A. J., 'Franco-Prussian War 1870–1871: Voluntary Aid for the Wounded and Sick', *British Medical Journal*, 3 (29 August 1970), pp. 511–14.

Sylvestre de Sacy, Jacques, *Le Maréchal de MacMahon, Duc de Magenta (1808–1893)*, Paris, 1960.

Taithe, Bertrand, *Citizenship & Wars: France in Turmoil 1870–1871*, London, 2001.

——, *Defeated Flesh: Welfare, Warfare and the Making of Modern France*, Manchester, 1999.

Tanera, Carl, Diary extracts translated by Jean Lecaillon as '1870: Les combats de Beaumont, Bazeilles et La Moncelle vus par un officier du 1er Bataillon de Chasseurs bavarois', *Revue Historique Ardennaise*, 3 (1970), pp. 57–72.

Tellkampf, Adolf, *Die Franzosen in Deutschland: Historische Bilder*, Hanover, 1860.

The Times, The Campaign of 1870–1, Republished from 'The Times', London, 1871.

Thiers, Adolphe, *Notes et Souvenirs de M. Thiers 1870–1873*, Paris, 1901.

Thiriaux, L., *La Garde Nationale Mobile de 1870*, Brussels, 1909.

Thompson, J. M., *Louis Napoleon and the Second Empire*, Oxford, 1954.

Thoumas, Charles Antoine, *Les Transformations de l'Armée française*, 2 vols, Paris, 1887.

——, *Souvenirs de la Guerre de 1870–71: Paris, Tours, Bordeaux*, Paris, 1892.

Tombs, Robert, *The War Against Paris*, Cambridge, 1981.

Tranquille, P., 'Général Ducrot (1817–1882)', *Les Contemporains*, No. 222, Paris, 10 January 1897.

Trochu, General, *Oeuvres posthumes*, 2 vols, Tours, 1896.

Tulard, Jean (ed.), *Dictionnaire du Second Empire*, Paris, 1995.

Verdy du Vernois, J. von, *With the Royal Headquarters in 1870–71*, London, 1897.

Verly, Albert, *Les Étapes douloureuses (L'Empereur, de Metz à Sedan)*, Paris, 1908.

Véron, Eugène, *La Troisième Invasion*, 2 vols, Paris, 1876–7.

Vidal, Joseph P., *Campagne de Sedan du 21 août au 1er septembre 1870 ou onze jours de campagne*, Paris, 1910.

Vinoy, Joseph, *Siège de Paris: Opérations du 13e Corps et de la Troisième Armée*, Paris, 1872.

Vogüé, Melchior de, *Devant le siècle*, Paris, 1896.

[Volontaire]. See Caro, E.

Wawro, Geoffrey, *The Austro-Prussian War: Austria's War with Prussia and Italy in 1866*, Cambridge, 1996.

——, *The Franco-Prussian War: The German Conquest of France in 1870–1871*, Cambridge, 2003.

——, *Warfare and Society in Europe, 1792–1814*, London, 2000.

Welschinger, Henri, *La Guerre de 1870: causes et responsabilités*, 2 vols, Paris, 1910.

Wetzel, David, *A Duel of Giants: Bismarck, Napoleon III, and the Origins of the Franco-Prussian War*, Madison, 2001.

Williams, Roger L., *Gaslight and Shadow: The World of Napoleon III, 1851–1870*, New York, 1957.

——, *The French Revolution of 1870–1871*, New York, 1969.

——, *Henri Rochefort, Prince of the Gutter Press*, New York, 1966.

——, *Manners and Murders in the World of Louis-Napoleon*, Seattle, 1975.

——, *The Mortal Napoleon III*, Princeton, 1971.

Willing, Paul, *L'Armée de Napoléon III (1852–1870)*, Arcueil, 1983.

——, *L'Armée de Napoleon III, 2: L'expédition du Mexique, la Guerre Franco-Allemande 1870–1871*, Arcueil, 1984.

Wimpffen, Félix de, *La Bataille de Sedan: les véritables coupables* (ed. Émile Corra) (8th edn), Paris, 1887.

——, *Sedan* (3rd edn, revised and corrected), Paris, 1871.

Woyde, Charles de, *Causes des succès et des revers dans la guerre de 1870*, 2 vols, Paris, 1900.

Yriarte, Charles, *La Retraite de Mézières effectué par le 13e Corps d'Armée aux ordres du Général Vinoy*, Paris, 1871.

Zeldin, Theodore, *Emile Ollivier and the Liberal Empire of Napoleon III*, Oxford, 1963.

Zins, Ronald, *Les Maréchaux de Napoléon III*, Lyon, 1996.

——, *Spicheren, 6 août 1870. Les Prussiens envahissent la Lorraine*, Annecy-le-Vieux, 2001.

Zola, Émile, *La Débâcle* (édition établie et annotée par Henri Mitterand. Préface de Raoul Girardet), Paris, 1984. (English translations by Leonard Tancock, Harmondsworth, 1968, and Elinor Dorday, Oxford, 2000.)

Index